T0339392

John Stott

WISDOM AND PRAYERS FROM THE PEN OF

JRWS

Pages from a

PREACHER'S
NOTEBOOK

Wisdom and Prayers
from the Pen of
John Stott

Edited with an Introduction
by Mark Meynell

LEXHAM PRESS

Lexham Press, 1313 Commercial St., Bellingham, WA 98225
LexhamPress.com

Print ISBN 9781683593898
Digital ISBN 9781683593904
Library of Congress Control Number 2020933376

Lexham Editorial: Elliot Ritzema, Allisyn Ma, Danielle Thevenaz
Cover Design: George Siler
Typesetting: Justin Marr

CONTENTS

3: WORLD AND WORLDVIEWS

INTRODUCTION

A PREACHER OF
METHODICAL GENIUS

In John Stott's time as rector of All Souls Langham Place, the church has met twice on Sunday mornings (with the same sermon repeated) and once in the evening. In his final years (as Rector Emeritus), John tended to preach only at the 11:30 service. This meant that a member of the ministry team would speak at the 9:30 service, which was often an "all-age" service (albeit based on the same passage as the 11:30 service). Speaking in that context is a very different matter from speaking to a regular adult congregation, and the results usually differed considerably. One Sunday, both John and I were assigned to speak on a passage from the Sermon on the Mount. I got rather carried away with my illustrations, one of which involved my (then) young son Joshua hiding under a table until the opportune moment in the sermon.

The fact that I cannot now remember what purpose this was supposed to serve proves the point of John's subsequent remark. As we met in the vestry during the changeover time, I cheekily suggested, "I bet you're not going to be using the illustrations I used at the all-age talk, Uncle John." He looked at me and responded without a pause, but with a clear twinkle in his eye, *I don't believe in illustrations.* He was clearly being provocative, and it was just a throwaway remark. But looking back now, I can begin to see what he was getting at. It wasn't to say that he had no use for illustrations; he did occasionally use quotations and stories (as this anthology clearly testifies). But these illustrations were always secondary to the primacy of expounding the biblical text. If they did not serve that purpose, they had no place in a sermon.

A PREACHER OF BLAZING CLARITY

Phillips Brooks (of "O Little Town of Bethlehem" fame) once suggested that preaching was "truth through personality." While this may be insufficient as a definition, it does make the point that you can tell a great deal about preachers' personalities through the way they communicate the truth. This was certainly true of John Stott. As Greg Scharf has said, one of Uncle John's most remarkable characteristics was his integrity—the consistency between his preaching, writing, and living: "His clear and thoughtful preaching flowed from a disciplined and devoted life and was captured in equally lucid writings."[1]

Many have noted the wide influence of his teaching, but so often it was precisely the crystalline clarity of what he taught that was the fountainhead of this influence. Every word, every sentence, and every paragraph would be carefully weighed or refined, so that he rarely (if ever) uttered an idle thought or contradictory point when in the pulpit. The American pastor John Piper reflected on this in a memorial tribute to him. He noted that Stott had received a complaint about his 1966 commentary in the Bible Speaks Today series, *Men Made New* (on Romans 5–8), for writing a "book like a house with no windows." In other words, it had no illustrations. But Piper counters the complaint. Stott, he insists, "turned the words of Bible sentences into windows onto glorious reality by explaining them in clear, compelling, complete, fresh, silly-free English

---

1. Greg R. Scharf, "John Stott: Homiletical Lessons from His Life, Preaching and Writing" (lecture, Wycliffe Hall, Oxford, October 15, 2012).

sentences."[2] Such was his clarity, therefore, that he did not usually require illustrations.

Some teased that his was almost clarity to a fault, in that he could be "clearer on the apostle Paul than Paul himself" (as Judge David Turner reminded us in his funeral tribute).[3] But Stott's was a clarity that was hard-won. As any teacher knows, clear communication requires deep levels of comprehension. This takes time and thought. It demands careful attention to alternative interpretations, controversies, and complexities. Stott was exemplary in his engagement with these, as even his theological critics would concede. Which is where this anthology comes in; it provides genuine insight into the workings of his mind and the discipline of his scholarship.

A JOHN STOTT "COMMONPLACE BOOK"

It probably seems strange to publish an anthology of notes, quotes, and illustrations from the files of a preacher who professed not to "believe in illustrations." But of course, while he was never one of the great storytellers or showmen, he did become a preacher who took the need to interact with prevailing trends and cultural presumptions with the utmost seriousness. To that end, quotations and examples became essential, even if he used them sparingly and carefully.

Any anthology of John Stott's notes would not be a mere collection of anecdotes and poignant stories (as has been compiled, say, from George Whitefield, Charles Spurgeon, or Donald Grey Barnhouse). That would never quite reflect the Stott style. Apart from anything else, it would probably end up as quite a slim tome. Instead, what you have before you is something more akin to a "commonplace book."

---

2. John Piper, "John Stott, the Expositor, Sent at a Crucial Point in My Life" (July 28, 2011), accessed December 9, 2017, http://www.desiringgod.org/blog/posts/john-stott-the-expositor-sent-at-a-crucial-point-in-my-life.

3. Judge David Turner QC, "Tribute," spoken at John Stott's funeral (August 8, 2011).

Many thinkers, poets, artists, travelers, and opinion formers in previous generations used commonplace books. These books were handy places for jotting down thoughts, quotations, ideas, or even sketches or questions. A single page might contain profundity, trivia, and a shopping list. Such books had no order other than the chronology suggested by successive entries.

Of course, those who knew John Stott well would hardly expect to find trivia, let alone shopping lists. And instead of using notebooks, he jotted down a whole range of thoughts on 4x6-inch index cards, which he arranged under various topical headings or biblical references. He also used these cards for his notes when preaching. Some were typed up by his ever-faithful secretary Frances Whitehead, but most were handwritten. It is astonishing how early in his ministry he started doing this; some notes date to the 1940s, soon after he first became curate at All Souls. It is yet more evidence of a man of remarkable personal discipline and method. This practice continued to sustain his teaching ministry for around sixty years.

This anthology was compiled after a small army of volunteers helped accomplish the colossal job of digitally scanning the entire collection and then transcribing a selection. They are being published now because I believe the value of these notes is threefold:

- They are fascinating, insightful, and occasionally provocative.

- They reveal a great deal about John Stott's evolving working methods.

- They model a deep and broad engagement with both Scripture and the contemporary world.

This last point in particular shows us how Stott practiced in his own ministry what he called "double listening."

STOTT'S DOUBLE LISTENING

In his 1992 book *The Contemporary Christian,* Stott most clearly articulated his appeal for "double listening," building on themes from his 1982 book *I Believe in Preaching* (published in the USA as *Between Two Worlds*). He stated that preachers must seek to understand their contemporary culture to such a degree that they can "present the gospel in such a way as to speak to modern dilemmas, fears and frustrations … equally determined not to compromise the biblical gospel in order to do so."[4]

The phrase "double listening" may initially suggest a parity between the two objects listened to, as if cultural voices were equal in authority to Scripture. Stott strenuously and consistently rejected that notion. He was not

> suggesting that we should listen to God and to our fellow human beings in the same way or with the same degree of deference. We listen to the Word with humble reverence, anxious to understand it, and resolved to believe and obey what we come to understand. We listen to the world with critical alertness, anxious to understand it too, and resolved not necessarily to believe and obey it, but to sympathize with it and to seek grace to discover how the gospel relates to it.[5]

This is important because Stott is not speaking of more postmodern inclinations toward such parity, and even the primacy of the contemporary. Thus, Greg Scharf feels the need to qualify the phrase slightly into what could be called "orthodox double listening."

Perhaps a better metaphor to recapture what Stott preached and practiced might be that of biblical spectacles. The way we see and respond to the world must be refined and focused by a biblical worldview. The problem with this, however, is that it does not capture the

---

4. John R. W. Stott, *The Contemporary Christian: Applying God's Word to Today's World* (Downers Grove, IL: InterVarsity Press, 1992), 13.

5. Stott, *Contemporary Christian*, 28.

essence of careful listening or, in this case, seeing what is going on around us.

However we might describe the practice, there is no doubt that Stott did it well—and these notes demonstrate it.

SOME FEATURES OF THE NOTES

Upon leafing through Stott's cards, several observations became clear. The first is that, long before the days of Google and Wikipedia, Stott was something of a magpie when it came to interesting information or cultural artifacts. He was effectively compiling his own almanac, a resource to consult whenever required. There are several large categories of notes on culture. For example:

- One strand of notes records mini-summaries of important political and historical events. One card lists the outcomes of all the British general elections since the 1960s, each with a few remarks about the key issues of the election. He did the same thing for all the Indian general elections too, since that was a country he visited several times and which clearly aroused his fascination.

- Other cards report statistics or poll results on particular topics or political controversies.

- There are also carefully recorded potted biographies of key historical figures (such as Florence Nightingale or Hudson Taylor, Taiwan's Chiang Kai-shek or South Africa's Steve Biko) or summaries of background information for the subjects of various talks.

- Various topics clearly concerned him: He read widely about civil rights issues in the United States and South Africa, quoting regularly from Martin Luther King Jr. But there are also surprises, such as cards on astronomy and the rules of cricket.

- Those who knew Stott well would not be surprised to find cards picking out key themes from popular films and books that he had encountered. There are many from Woody Allen and thoughts on *Close Encounters of the Third Kind* and the original *Superman* movie. He even quotes from *The Simpsons*, though I do not think this suggests he was a regular viewer!

- Because of his global ministry opportunities, Stott inevitably encountered a vast range of people, from the totally unknown to the renowned or even notorious. Occasionally, he kept notes of some of these interactions, so the cards contain conversational snippets from Billy Graham (a long-standing friend) and the late president of Tanzania, Julius Nyerere.

Stott's careful listening was not restricted to the wider culture. He made real efforts to generously engage with and to seek to understand those within the broadest spectrum of Christian theology.

- If a major debate was raging in the British church or in global evangelicalism, it invariably found its way into Stott's notes. He would read the relevant works and write down what he thought. For example, various cards deal with the debate around Bishop John Robinson's 1963 book *Honest to God*—he records many quotations or page references from advocates and opponents alike, as well as summaries of Robinson's key arguments. Likewise, there are summary cards on the key ideas from John Hick's 1977 book *The Myth of God Incarnate*, as well as of liberation theology (which was very influential in Latin America beginning in the 1950s and 1960s).

- In his thorough preparation for his groundbreaking book *Issues Facing Christians Today*, he read very widely indeed. Various cards list personal bibliographies for each of the chapters in that book.

The cards also record stories and illustrations of the more classic kind—including the odd opening joke (which he occasionally termed a "warm-up"). However, the notes suggest he did this less and less over time. It is obvious that despite the regular twinkle in his eye and humorous self-deprecation that featured in his preaching, Stott's sermons never sacrificed clarity for levity. In addition to the quotations and stories, which make up the bulk of this anthology, there are also a number of prayers that he wrote for specific occasions. Stott's notes numbered in the thousands, and this anthology reproduces a small percentage of them. In selecting the entries, I have attempted to capture the breadth and depth of the full archive. Many have been omitted on the simple grounds of being too parochial (for instance, to All Souls or to the Anglican Diocese of London), too dated (such as some of the poll results), or too obscure (such as many of the ornithological details like species' wingspans and migratory habits). I have also omitted many of the entries that frequently appear in other anthologies (such as famous quotations from C. S. Lewis's *Mere Christianity* or G. K. Chesterton's *Orthodoxy*). A wider selection of these notes originally appeared in a digital-only form as *The Preacher's Notebook: The Collected Quotes, Illustrations, and Prayers of John Stott* (Bellingham, WA: Lexham Press, 2018). The difference between that collection and this one is that here most of the notes that consisted entirely of quotations of other sources have been removed, so that this collection focuses more narrowly on Stott's own words.

The editorial work has been light, but it has not been possible to leave the notes entirely untouched. With regard to the topical arrangement, while Stott did have a well-established system for labeling his index cards, repetition inevitably grew over time—as far as I can tell, neither he nor Frances Whitehead ever went back to review or order the files. So I have streamlined things by merging synonymous or overlapping subjects. Only a few of the note cards contained titles, so most of the ones here have been added; likewise, the themes have been added to make it easier for readers to find what they are looking for. On occasion, punctuation has been altered and abbreviations spelled out to make the notes more readable. Where words have been added, this is indicated through the use of square brackets. However, the text of these notes (as well as the source citations) is substantially original.

WHAT WE CAN LEARN
FROM THESE NOTES

Because of Stott's wide engagement with a variety of subjects, I should first insert here a word of caution regarding what we *cannot* learn. People on the social media site Twitter regularly point out that their retweets of others should not be taken as endorsement or agreement. These notes need a similar disclaimer. Drawn from Stott's private files, they were a personal resource that was never intended to be presented without qualification or context. So it would be foolish to imagine that any conclusions, theological or otherwise, can be drawn from what is included in them. With that said, I think we can take away three things about John Stott from these notes.

HIS EARLY-FORMED HABITS
THAT LASTED A LIFETIME

The rigors of Stott's personal discipline are evident on every card. From the start, he dated and noted every venue where he used an illustration or talk outline, thus preventing awkward repetition. We can see that some of the study disciplines, which stood him in such good stead throughout his ministry, were in place right from the start in the 1940s. This practice lasted well into the first decade of the new millennium. This makes for a fascinating study in itself, since it is possible to trace the broadening of his opportunities over the years. To begin with, he was regularly speaking at small Christian meetings in the boarding schools that were served by the Iwerne camps at Clayesmore School. He even kept the outlines for one or two of his camp talks. While training for ministry at Ridley Hall in Cambridge, he would speak at events held by college Christian unions (which were part of the CICCU). Once he reached London and started his curacy, these quickly broadened. It was not long before he was speaking in places like Arsenal Football Club (in the 1950s), then eventually all over the world and with prestigious opportunities such as the Chapels Royal, National Prayer Breakfast, and the BBC World Service.

It would be fascinating to compare the sermon notes in the archive with the sermons he delivered (the majority of which are freely available in the All Souls online library), and then in turn to compare this with the relevant chapter in his Bible Speaks Today commentaries. A cursory glance suggests that the changes are fairly minimal, which means that a large portion of what ended up in published form had been shaped and considered in his mind before he preached the original sermons.

HIS INTERESTS AND HUNGER FOR LEARNING

In the early days, Stott's primary sources for illustrations and quotations tended to be key figures in evangelical history, such as the Reformers, Puritans, or preachers in the Great Awakening. J. C. Ryle, Charles Spurgeon, and Charles Simeon were clear favorites, often accompanied by Anglican divines like Bishops John Pearson of Chester (seventeenth century) and Handley Moule of Durham and Archbishop William Temple (both early twentieth century).

But within a decade or so of the beginning of his ministry, his horizons stretched significantly. We find extensive notes about Gandhi, Martin Luther King Jr., and Samuel Escobar (to name just three from overseas). It is clear from these notes that even though his theological moorings never wavered far (but went deeper), his cultural moorings certainly loosened. Another indication of this, in addition to many majority world sources and topics, is his engagement with theologians like Lesslie Newbigin.

This is evidence of a profoundly curious mind, always eager to plumb depths and hungry to learn new things. This was never driven by a fruitless yearning for novelty, but a compassionate mind in service to his Creator. It marked a constant desire to overcome the inevitable parochialism of Englishmen of his class and generation, living as they did in the twilight of Britain's empire. As he himself said, "Life is a pilgrimage of learning, a voyage of discovery, in which our mistaken views are corrected, our distorted notions adjusted, our shallow opinions deepened and some of our vast ignorances diminished."[6]

Greg Scharf puts it like this:

Fundamentally the human trait that underlies this [passion for learning] is humility; he did not overestimate what he knew; he was eager to learn. He was teachable, and willing to confess the embarrassing occasions when some of this learning took place. For instance, he recounts how having in a sermon made some spiritually helpful but chemically inaccurate claims concerning how table salt (NaCl) loses its saltiness, someone who knew better had to gently set him straight. He not only learned some chemistry, he learned the importance of knowing what he was talking about.[7]

HIS GENEROSITY EVEN IN CONTROVERSY

In a different context, historian John Kilner outlines the challenge of what Stott called "double listening," both in terms of discovering what the Bible teaches and listening to the prevailing winds of the culture.

There is a tremendous reluctance to go the second intellectual mile. Many people exhaust themselves developing explicitly biblical positions on issues. They stop short of taking the next step of developing arguments for those positions in language the society is willing to consider. Others, anticipating

---

6. John R. W. Stott, *Christian Mission in the Modern World*, updated and expanded ed. (Downers Grove, IL: InterVarsity Press, 2015), 10.

7. Scharf, "Lessons from His Life."

the difficult challenge of developing socially persuasive arguments, simply skip the first step of formulating an explicitly biblical account. The first group is not likely to engage with society with their thoroughly biblical concerns. The second group is not likely to have thoroughly biblical concerns with which to engage society.[8]

There is no question that John Stott went the second intellectual mile. This is indicated by his extensive notes on debates that were highly controversial while they raged. In fact, it is possible to trace the big questions of the 1960s and 1970s through his notes. There are frequent engagements with Marxism and Communism (and its relationship with South American liberation theology); he read papers written by members of the Far Right (the National Front, as it was then called) and was greatly preoccupied by the issues of civil rights. While many of the specific concerns of these debates might have now shifted, they are still important today for illustrating the church's challenge in engaging with the problems of human society.

The remarkable thing is that these notes provide further evidence of Stott's generosity of spirit to those with whom he disagreed, sometimes radically. He was determined to do justice to opponents' views, which sometimes caused him real intellectual turmoil when he wrestled with complex problems. Moreover, he would not let disputes in one area prevent him from being willing to learn from a person in another area. This can be seen in his frequent quotations from and allusions to Dr. Martyn Lloyd-Jones, even after their very public disagreement in 1966.

The huge work of transcription would have been impossible without a small experiment in crowdsourcing at All Souls. The following individuals very kindly gave their time and effort to type up the scans of the handwritten cards (while all those that were originally typed were

---

8. John Kilner, "Culture War Casualties," *Christianity Today* (March 6, 1995), 26.

done by Frances Whitehead): Cheryl Carter, Lily Fok, Jenny George, Mei Ling Routley, and Leah Low.

I hope that this anthology will provide a rich mine for preachers in the future. I also believe it will lay down a challenge for all who preach and teach to take seriously the need for rigor and method in our own cultural engagement.

—Mark Meynell
Director (Europe & Caribbean),
Langham Preaching, Langham Partnership
London and Maidenhead

1

GOD AND GOSPEL

BIBLE

APOSTOLIC AUTHORITY IN THE CHURCH

Themes: Scripture

The church has always recognized the unique authority of [the] apostles of Jesus. He chose, appointed, and authorized them to teach in his name.

- Ignatius (AD 110): "I do not issue you with commands like Peter and Paul. For I am not an apostle, but a condemned man."

- Tertullian (third century): "It is forbidden for Christians to introduce anything on their own authority or to accept something which a person introduced by his own authority. The apostles of the Lord are our authority."

- Martin Luther: "Jesus has submitted the whole world to the apostles, who are the only people who can enlighten it. ... And the people of the world, kings, princes, lords, educated men, wise men, must sit down while the apostles stand up, listen while the apostles speak."

C. S. LEWIS ON HOW TO ENJOY ART AND NATURE

Themes: Scripture; Submission

When C. S. Lewis as a boy was under "the Great Knock," his private tutor in Great Bookham, Surrey, he used to love exploring the countryside on afternoons and Sundays. With regard to the appreciation of art and nature, he writes: "Total surrender is the first step towards the fruition of either. Shut your mouth; open your eyes and ears. Take in what is there and give no thought to what might have been there or what is somewhere else."[1]

CHURCH FATHERS ON INSPIRATION

Themes: Scripture

- Origen wrote that [the] Holy Spirit was [a] coworker with the evangelists in the composition of the Gospel, and that therefore lapse of memory, error, or falsehood was impossible to them (on Matthew 16:12 and John 16:18).

- Irenaeus claims for Christians clear knowledge that "the Scriptures are perfect, seeing that they are spoken by God's word and his Spirit" (*Adv. Haer.* ii.28).

- Polycarp considered [the] Scriptures the very voice of the Most High and pronounced "whosoever perverts these oracles of the Lord" the firstborn of Satan (*Ep. ad Phil.* vii).

- Augustine "firmly believes that none of their authors has erred in anything, in writing" (*Ep. ad. Hier.* Lxxxii.3).[2]

---

1. C. S. Lewis, *Surprised by Joy* (Geoffrey Bles, 1955), 139.
2. B. B. Warfield, *Inspiration and Authority of the Bible*, ed. Samuel G. Craig (Presbyterian & Reformed, 1948), 108.

FARRAR'S HISTORY OF BIBLICAL INTERPRETATION

Themes: Scripture

F. W. Farrar's 1885 Bampton Lectures were printed in 1886 by Macmillan as the *History of Interpretation*. He calls it a history of "exegesis" ("the explanation of the immediate and primary sense of the sacred writings," p. vii) and describes his task as "melancholy" (p. 8) because of the centuries of untenable exegesis.

He then unfolds seven main "systems":

1. Rabbinic (457 BC–AD 498): 1,000 years according to Hillel's seven rules

2. Alexandrian (from Aristobulus around 180 BC to Philo's death)

3. Patristic (from Clement of Rome to and through the Dark Ages)

4. Scholastic (from Abelard [died 1142] to the Reformation)

5. The Reformers (16th century)

6. The Post-Reformation Epoch (Protestant Scholasticism, mid-16th–mid-18th century)

7. Modern (last two hundred years): rise of biblical criticism[3]

---

3. F. W. Farrar, *History of Interpretation* (Baker, 1961).

KILLING ANIMALS CONDEMNED?

Themes: Killing; Law; Scripture

After a "Thought for the Day" broadcast on Radio 4 in January 1974, a lady wrote to me from Brighton to give her diagnosis of the state of the world: "greed for money, power, and worst of all cruelty to God's creatures the animals. ... The matter which I have mostly in mind is the unhealthy and unnatural diet which man has chosen ... i.e., the flesh of murdered animals! The Bible repeats so many times, 'THOU SHALT NOT KILL.' "

PAUL APPEALING, PEALE APPALLING

Themes: Scripture

Adlai Stevenson was a lawyer who became governor of Illinois and gained a reputation for probity—in [the] '50s he was twice Democratic presidential candidate versus Eisenhower. He said, "I find Paul appealing and Peale appalling" [referring to Norman Vincent Peale, author of *The Power of Positive Thinking*].

PROGRESSIVE REVELATION IN GENESIS

Themes: God; Scripture

El Elyon = God Most High (Gen 14:19)
El Roi = God who sees (Gen 16:13)
El Shaddai = God Almighty (Gen 17:1)
Jehovah Jireh = the Provider (Gen 22:14)

THE PROPHETS AS GOD'S MESSENGERS

Themes: Scripture

[The] background to [the] mission of the Twelve was [the] call and commission of prophets in [the] Old Testament as Yahweh's "messengers." [According to the] James F. Ross essay "The Prophet as Yahweh's Messenger," a "messenger speech" had four characteristics:

1. An introductory formula ("thus says Y")

2. A standard conclusion ("says Y")

3. Frequent use of *salah* ("send")

4. A commissioning narrative ("go and say")

Ancient Near Eastern parallels:

1. In Mari and Ras Shamra texts, prophets were messengers of a god (see *TDNT* VI p. 810 re: Nabi in [the] Old Testament).

2. "Thus says" is a royal decree formula introducing [an] edict of [a] king to subjects. Cf. Isaiah 36–37, "Thus says [the] great king, king of Assyria. ... thus says Yahweh, God of Israel"; cf. Isaiah 37:3 of Hezekiah; 1 Kings 20:2ff. of Ben-Hadad.[4]

---

4. James F. Ross, "The Prophet as Yahweh's Messenger," in *Israel's Prophetic Heritage*, ed. B. W. Anderson (SCM, 1962), 98–107.

Background to mission of the Twelve
was call & commission of prophets
in O.T as Yahweh's 'messengers'.

* Acc. to James F. Ross 'The Prophet
as Y's Messenger' in Israel's Prophetic
Heritage ed. B.W. Anderson (SCM 1962
pp 98-107) a 'messenger speech' had
4 characteristics :-

    1. An intro' formula ('thus says Y')
    2. A standard concl" ('says Y')
    3. Frequent use of šālaḥ (send)
    4. A commissioning narrative ('Go & say')

ANE Parallels

(·) In Mari & Ras Shamra texts prophets
were sometimes messengers of a god
(see TDNT vi p. 810 re. Nabi in O T)

(²) ['Thus says' =
   A royal decree formula
   introducing edict of king to subjects

cf Is. 36 -37 'Thus says gt Y, K'of Assyria
... Thus says Yahweh, Gr. of Israel
cf Is 37² of Hezekiah too. & IKgs. 20²ff
              of Benhadad

SOME SCHOLARS TAKE PLEASURE IN FINDING DISCREPANCIES

Themes: Scripture

Oscar Cullmann complained in his *The Christology of the New Testament* that various scholars had reacted negatively to his thesis that Jesus' baptism anticipated and foreshadowed his death, simply because they are suspicious "of any thesis which harmonizes the different elements of the New Testament." He had "a desire for synthesis," they say. Well, Oscar Cullmann rejects "false attempts at harmonization," but some New Testament scholars take "an almost sadistic pleasure" in finding discrepancies![5]

THREE STAGES BEHIND THE TEXT

Themes: Scripture

The need to be aware of three stages behind the canonical text:

1. Event (the original eyewitness's understanding)
2. Tradition (the needs or *Sitz im Leben* of the early church)
3. Redaction (the biblical author's shaping of his material)

So what we have in the gospel has gone through the interpreting mind of the eyewitnesses, the Christian communities, and the evangelists.

---

5. Oscar Cullmann, *The Christology of the New Testament* (English translation SCM, 1969), 68.

VATICAN II, ATHENAGORAS, AND GREGORY THE GREAT ON INSPIRATION

Themes: Scripture

- The Vatican Council regarding [the] Scriptures: "The Church regards them as sacred and canonical, not because having been framed solely by human labour they have afterwards been approved by her authority, not again for the reason that they contain the revelation without error, but because having been written by the inspiration of the Holy Spirit they have God as their author, and as such have been given to the Church" (p. 34).

- A Vatican Council decree states that the Scriptures "have God as their author" (*Deum habent auctorem*), and adds in the previous sentence the phrase "by dictation of the Holy Spirit" (*Spiritu Sancto dictante*), quoted from the Council of Trent.

- Athenagoras, about AD 170, described the prophets as speaking in ecstasy, with the Holy Spirit speaking through them like a flute player playing on a flute (*Legatio pro Christianis* 9); and Pseudo-Justin says the same in *Cohortatio ad Graecos* 8.

- Gregory the Great describes the writers as the pen (*calamus*) of the Holy Spirit, so that it is ridiculous to inquire into the authorship of the Epistles; for "since we hold the Holy Spirit to be the author, we do nothing else if we inquire into the authorship than to inquire, when we read a letter, about the pen with which it was written" (pp. 56–57).[6]

---

6. Gabriel Hebert, *Fundamentalism and the Church of God* (SCM, 1957).

WORDS AS CONTAINERS OF MEANING

Themes: Scripture

In a review of Harold Pinter and his new play *No Man's Land*, Michael Billington mentioned "a famous word-loving comic" (not named) "who had recently explained his craft" to him by saying: "The word is a container of meaning and if you can open the box, take the meaning out and put another meaning in, it is quite a clever little trick."

Billington adds that Pinter uses this trick "all the time."

But what may be legitimate for a comedian is illegitimate in an expositor![7]

WORDS MEAN WHAT WE WISH THEM TO MEAN

Themes: Scripture

"Modernity" has deeply affected most academic fields: "In literature, a whole generation of deconstructionists has emerged within the universities who, despite their calling to be custodians of the nation's language, now make their living by denying that words have any meaning at all. Words mean only whatever we wish them to mean."[8]

CHRIST

A. J. AYER: CHRISTIANITY IS THE WORST

Themes: Atonement; Jesus: Death; Sin

A. J. Ayer, Oxford philosopher and author [of] *Language, Truth, and Logic,* an exposition of so-called logical positivism, later Sir Alfred Ayer, who died in 1989, was scathing in his references to Christianity,

---

7. Michael Billington, *Guardian Weekly* (July 5, 1975).
8. David F. Wells, *No Place for Truth* (Eerdmans, 1993), 65.

especially the cross. "Of all the religions of historical importance, there is good reason to regard Christianity as the worst." Why? Because it rests on "the allied doctrines of original sin, and vicarious atonement, which are intellectually contemptible and morally outrageous."[9]

THE GAME OF THE KING

Themes: Jesus: Passion

At the Ecce Homo Basilica in Jerusalem two basement flagstones still "bear the marks of an ancient pastime. This was the Game of the King, which was common in all Roman camps and barracks." A large capital beta (first letter of *Basileus*) covered several flagstones. A crown marked the head and a sword the foot. A convicted criminal would be jostled until he stood on either. If the sword, he'd be executed; if the crown, he'd be mocked as if a king. "This crude horseplay" was the background of what took place. He was chosen for the pantomime of the Game of the King (p. 25).

The Jews cried out, "If you release this man, you are not Caesar's friend" (John 19:12). *Amicus Caesaris* "was the one title which a provincial governor would most covet." And Pilate, "well aware of the cold, cruel, suspicious character of the ruling Caesar" (Tiberius), could not risk being declared no friend of Caesar's (p. 31).[10]

---

9. *The Guardian*, August 30, 1979.

10. Marcus Loane, *The Glory of the Cross and Resurrection* (New Creation, 1995).

JESUS OUR DIVINE BROTHER

Themes: Guilt; Jesus: Death; Jesus: Humanity; Jesus: Passion; Suffering

Jürgen Moltmann tells how as a young man in 1945 in a POW camp in Belgium, he felt utterly abandoned and hopeless. His country had collapsed, and his own life appeared to be in ruins. But through reading the Psalms and the Passion story, he felt that the Godforsaken Jesus, "our divine brother," understood. "I summoned up the courage to live, at a point when one would perhaps willingly have put an end to it all. This early companionship with Jesus, the brother in suffering and the liberator from guilt, has never left me since. The Christ for me is the crucified Jesus."

God through the crucified Jesus becomes the God and father of the forsaken, through whom hope for change and for ultimate renewal is kindled.[11]

NOT SCALES, BUT THE CROSS

Themes: Forgiveness; Good Works; Jesus: Death; Justice; Justification

Crossing Waterloo Bridge and looking northeast, one has a fine view of the city skyline, and in particular of those two domed buildings, the Old Bailey (the central criminal court) and St. Paul's Cathedral (the mother church). At the pinnacle of each dome is mounted a significant symbol. At the top of the Old Bailey stands the classical god of justice—blindfolded (for impartiality), wielding the sword of justice in her right hand, and holding a pair of scales (for the sifting of evidence) in the left. At the top of St. Paul's, however, is a great golden cross.

Many people think Christianity is a religion of the scales. They imagine that every time they sin, God flicks it into one pan, while

---

11. Jürgen Moltmann, *Jesus Christ for Today's World* (SCM, 1994).

every time they do a good deed, he flicks it into the other. And they are hoping against hope that the scales may just tip down in their favor.

But no, Christianity is not a religion of scales, but of the cross. For if the scales stand for *our* unfinished works, the cross stands for the *finished work of Christ*. It tells us Christ died for our sins once for all, that we are forgiven. It invites us to come to Christ saying, "Nothing in my hand I bring."

ONLY ONE GOSPEL, PRESENTED IN VARIOUS WAYS

Themes: Gospel

There is *only one gospel,* and Paul called down [the] curse of God on anyone (himself included) who presented "a different [gospel]." Yet [the] apostles presented it in a wide variety of ways—

- *Sacrificial* ([the] shedding and sprinkling of Christ's blood)

- *Messianic* ([the] breaking in of God's promised rule, and so of [a] new age)

- *Mystic* (receiving and enjoying eternal life, [the] life of [the] age)

- *Legal* (Judge pronouncing unrighteous righteous)

- *Personal* (Father reconciling wayward children)

- *Salvific* (heavenly liberator coming to rescue his oppressed people [in a] new exodus)

- *Cosmic* (universal lord claiming universal dominion over [the] powers)

And those seven are only a selection!

PAUL PREACHED CHRIST CRUCIFIED

Themes: Jesus: Death

Prebendary F. S. Webster (rector of All Souls 1900–1920) in a published sermon: "Paul preached Christ crucified, the hope of sinners, the joy of saints, the strength of sufferers, the study of angels, the glory of heaven, the wonder of eternity."[12]

THE PRAYER OF A JEWISH DOCTOR

Themes: Conversion; Jesus: Divinity; Prayer

Dr. Kaufman of Wimpole Street, a Jewish general practitioner, told me in 1955 that he had prayed: "O God, I want to know if Christianity is true. I want to know if Christ is what they say he is, or not. Show me. I want to know if he is the greatest fraud ever perpetrated or if he is what he said. I am a descendant of those stiff-necked people who crucified him. But I wasn't there. I want to be given a chance to accept him or reject him. Give me a chance."

THE SCANDAL OF ORIGINAL SIN AND THE CROSS

Themes: Jesus: Death; Sin

Joy [JRWS's sister] wrote to me after Billy Graham had preached at a televised service in All Souls on September 2, 1973. "He preached well (in my poor opinion)—it was the same old doctrine hammered home about original sin, and redemption through Jesus Christ—but as this seems so monstrous and vindictive and unjust, I'm afraid it's like water off Joie's goose's back."

---

12. F. S. Webster, *Trusting and Triumphing* (1914), 168.

SUPERMAN AND THE GOSPEL

Themes: Gospel; Jesus; Jesus: Divinity

Superficially, there is a readily perceived analogy between Mario Puzo's screenplay *Superman* and the Christian gospel. For Superman came as a child to earth from heaven, or at least from the planet Krypton. Moreover, his father ([played by] Marlon Brando), in sending the child to earth, has more in mind than that he should escape the destruction of Krypton. He deliberately gives "my only son," he says, to serve the inhabitants of earth. And as the boy grows up, he senses a messianic vocation and uses his supernatural powers for good.

But the "good" he does is naively understood. He repairs dams and viaducts to protect innocent human beings from the evil plots of evil men, but the "good" he does has no ultimate purpose. And when the girl Lois Lane [has] her ecstatic flight with him through space [and] says she has been "with a god," he somehow doesn't seem worthy of her.

WANTING THE HYMN'S WORDS TO MEAN MORE

Themes: Commitment; Jesus: Death; Worship

William Temple led a mission to Oxford University in 1931. On its last night, the congregation "roared out" the hymn "When I Survey." Before the last verse Temple stopped the singing and said: "I want you to read over this verse before you sing it. They are tremendous words. If you mean them with all your hearts, sing them as loud as you can. If you don't mean them at all, keep silent. If you mean them even a little, and want them to mean more, sing them very softly."

There was a deep silence while every eye was fastened on the printed hymn sheet, and then—to hear Isaac Watts's words, "Were the whole realm of nature mine," whispered by the voices of two thousand young men and women, was (in the recollection of one of them) "an experience never to be erased from my memory."[13]

WANTING TO BE SURE THAT CHRIST IS DIVINE

Themes: Jesus: Divinity

Robert Pehlivanian was an Armenian student reading chemical engineering and business administration at University of Michigan. He was truly seeking Christ and said: "If I were sure that Christ was divine, I'd become a Christian and never ever give it up!" (December 13, 1956).

"WHILE I AM HERE I AM A SINNER"

Themes: Death and Dying; Forgiveness;
Jesus: Death; Redemption; Sin

When [Charles] Simeon was dying in 1836, he was fussed by the presence of a nurse, three servants, one doctor, and two curates. He said: "I wish to be alone, with my God, and to lie before him as a poor wretched, hell-deserving sinner … but I would also look to him as my all-forgiving God … don't let people come round to get up a scene."

"If I am admitted, as I hope to be, to heaven," he said a week or two later, "then if there be one that will sing louder than the rest, I think I shall be that one. But while I am here I am a sinner—a redeemed sinner; that is my style; and as such I would lie here to the last, at the foot of the cross, looking unto Jesus, and go as such into the presence of my God."[14]

---

13. F. A. Iremonger, *William Temple, Archbishop of Canterbury: His Life and Letters* (Oxford University Press, 1948), 378.

14. Hugh Evan Hopkins, *Charles Simeon of Cambridge* (Hodder and Stoughton, 1977), 211–12.

"THE WORST BLINDNESS"

Themes: Presence of God; Prayer

1. *Where are you*, Jesus?
     You're so hard to find!
Are you somewhere out there,
     Or locked in my mind?
Do you fly with the birds,
     Or walk on the ground?
Do you hang around churches?
     Where *can* you be found?

2. Do you swim with the rivers
     Or dance on the wind?
Am I blind to your presence?
     Because I have sinned?
Do you go out the back door
     When I ring the bell?
And if I can't find you,
     Will I end up in hell?

3. Do you hide in my wardrobe?
     Or under my bed?
Am I being punished
     For things I have said?
If I call out your name,
     Do you block up your ears?
If I cried for your love,
     Would you wipe off my tears?

4. If I stretched out my hand
     Would I touch your face?
Or just find my fingers
     Floating in space?
Where are you, Jesus?
     You're so hard to find.
Why can't I see you?
     Am I really that blind?[15]

---

15. Sent to JRWS by Roger Eveleigh from Wandsworth Prison (1985).

CHRISTMAS

"ALL EYES ON THE BABY"

Themes: Birth of Jesus

In December 1948 Prince Charles was baptized in Buckingham Palace. The following day the first pictures of the royal baby and heir apparent were released to the public. One of the most popular showed the royal family (parents and grandparents) gathered around the prince and gazing at him. The caption underneath was: "All eyes on the Baby."

MOUNTBATTEN WAS ONE OF US

Themes: Birth of Jesus; Jesus: Humanity

Lord Louis Mountbatten was commander in chief [of] Southeast Asia in World War II, and the last viceroy of India. In August 1979, he was killed in his yacht by an IRA bomb. On September 5, the day of his funeral in Westminster Abbey, some members of the Burma Star Association (veterans from the Burma War) were asked by a BBC reporter what they thought of him. "He was the greatest Englishman since Nelson," said one. What were the qualities of his greatness?

"He was one of us."

"He brought himself down to our level, and became one of us."

RUMORS OF JESUS' ILLEGITIMACY

Themes: Birth of Jesus

It's clear that rumors of Jesus' possible illegitimacy were being spread [in his] lifetime.

- When he declared [that] certain Jews did not [have] Abraham for their father, but [the] devil, they blurted out, "*We are* not illegitimate"—with [the] innuendo that he was (John 8:41).

- On another occasion, [people asked,] "Is not this [the] son of Mary?" [That's] a rude question in a patriarchal society (Mark 6:3).

WHAT MADE THE WORLD READY FOR CHRIST

Themes: Birth of Jesus

What made the world ready for Christ:

1. Rome had united the world from the Euphrates to the Atlantic in one state.

2. The whole earth was enjoying the Pax Romana.

3. The empire was crisscrossed with Roman roads, making travel safe and easy.

4. The Greek language had become universal. Rome conquered Greece, but then Greek culture conquered Rome.

5. There was a widespread inarticulate moral and spiritual hunger: Socrates sighed for a teacher from heaven. Pliny prayed for a strong deliverer. Aurelius reached out for someone beyond. The old gods of Rome no longer satisfied the people.

CREATION

THE BEAUTY OF THE HUMAN HAND

Themes: Beauty; Creation

Dr. Paul Brand, formerly of Christian hospital Vellore, pioneer reconstructive hand surgeon, once led a research project to try to develop an alternative pain system for people insensitive to pain. "Our team worked specifically with the pain system of the human hand. What engineering perfection we find there! I could fill a room with volumes of surgical textbooks that describe operations people have devised for the injured hand. ... But I don't know of a single operation anyone has devised that has succeeded in improving a normal hand. It's beautiful.

"The more I delve into the natural laws—the atom, the universe, the solid elements, molecules, the sun—and even more the interplay of all the mechanisms required to sustain life, I am astounded. The whole creation could collapse like a pack of cards if just one of those factors were removed. To build a thing like our universe had to require planning and thought, and that, I believe, is the strongest argument for the presence of God in creation."[16]

BIRD MIGRATION IN ISRAEL

Themes: Creation

The Palestinian corridor is one of the best places in the world for migrating raptors. They need thermal currents, which form over desert and mountain, but not over the sea. Between February 20 and May 17, 1977, 763,737 raptors passed over the Elat Mountains alone. On May 5–6, 1983, over 200,000 honey buzzards were seen passing

---

16. Paul Brand, interview with Philip Yancey, *Christianity Today* (December 1, 1978).

over Elat in one huge wave. On September 29, 1983, between 10:35 and 14:15, 46,579 lesser spotted eagles passed over [an] eight-kilometer wide front over Kafr Qasem. Similar numbers were reported on the following days, so that around 200,000 lesser spotted eagles passed over Israel in the fall migration.[17]

THE CHRISTIAN RESPONSE TO MEANINGLESSNESS

Themes: Creation; Depression; Presence of God; Lord's Supper

What should we do when our reality seems hostile or meaningless? The answer of many is escapism, which is a denial of reality by a flight into illusion. The Christian way is better:

1. The negative ability to switch off and forget is not escapism if it is a temporary relief leading to a return to reality.

2. The positive counterpart. Not all reality is hostile. Sport, music, birdwatching, friendship are all legitimate and balance bad reality with good. (Not drugs, which anesthetize people against growth.)

3. The most positive step of all is to relate the Absolute and Ultimate Reality (God) to our lesser realities. Creation, Incarnation, and Eucharist are all doctrines which express his commitment to the material reality of our world. The answer to escapism is Incarnation. God is here. God is with us.[18]

---

17. Yossi Leshem, "Trails in the Sky: Fall Migration of Raptors over Israel," *Israel—Land & Nature vol. 10, no. 2* (Winter 1984–1985), 70–77.

18. JRWS, reflections of the Reading Group after seeing *The Purple Rose of Cairo* (December 1985).

THE COMPLEXITY OF THE UNIVERSE

Themes: Creation

- *Human brain* has about 10,000 million cells.

- *Universe.* According to Fred Hoyle at least 1,000 trillion stars with about 100 trillion planets.

- *Light* traveling at six billion miles a year takes:

  » about 100,000 years to cross [the] Milky Way

  » about 30,000 million years to cross [the] universe

- *Smallest living organism* (the mycoplasma—the soil) is one-tenth of one-millionth of a meter broad.

THE "DECADE OF THE ENVIRONMENT"

Themes: Creation

Lester R. Brown, founder/director (1974) of Worldwatch Institute, a kind of environmental think tank, thinks [the] 1990s will be the "Decade of the Environment." "We *are* doing more things to reverse the degradation of the planet, but not enough. ... Each year the forests are getting smaller, the deserts are getting larger, the topsoil is getting thinner, the ozone layer is being depleted, the concentration of greenhouse gases in the atmosphere is rising, and the number of plant and animal species on earth is diminishing."[19]

---

19. Interview with Lester Brown in *Tomorrow: The Global Environment Magazine*, vol. 1., no. 1 (1991).

FILLED WITH AWE AT A SINGLE CELL

Themes: Creation

D. H. Patey, FRCS, Middlesex Hospital, wrote to me on October 22, 1961, after [the] Doctors' Service that our knowledge of intracellular physiology has only just begun. "I am filled with the same awe and humility when I contemplate something of what goes on in a single cell as when I contemplate the sky on a clear night. And in addition, the coordination of the complex activities of the cell in a common purpose hits the scientific part of me as the best evidence for an ultimate purpose."

HIS EYE IS ON THE SPARROW

Themes: Creation; Providence

Clare Kipps described in *Sold for a Farthing* (1953) the remarkable relationship which she established during World War II with a little foundling cock sparrow, whom she called Clarence. Writing of his approaching death at the age of twelve, at the end of the book she says: "We are assured on the Highest Authority, and in no uncertain language, that no sparrow falls without the knowledge of the Father of Love. I have confidence that mine will not be an exception."

He died on August 23, 1952, four months after the book was written. "He had lived twelve years, seven weeks and four days, and was courageous, intelligent and apparently conscious to the end. The cause of death was extreme old age."[20]

---

20. Clare Kipps, *Sold for a Farthing* (Frederick Muller, 1953), 70, 72.

A DIFFERENT KIND OF BIRD-WATCHING

Themes: Creation; Birth of Jesus

"I watched a bird on Christmas Day," Timothy Dudley-Smith wrote me on New Year's Day 1979, "and took it out of the oven when it was a delightful shade of brown and gold!"

FUEL ECONOMY IN BIRDS

Themes: Creation

Aircraft use fuel up to 36 percent of their weight; some birds only 1 percent. Since some birds contain up to 50 percent fat (fuel), they can keep flying for 50 plus hours. For example, golden plovers migrate from Alaska to Hawaii nonstop, which is 2,100 miles.

GREAT MEN WHO WERE BIRD-WATCHERS

Themes: Creation; Government

Edward Grey, later Viscount Grey of Fallodon, was foreign secretary for eleven years toward the beginning of the twentieth century. He was a keen bird-watcher, author of *The Charm of Birds* (1927). [He] was delighted to discover that President Theodore Roosevelt was also keen, and on June 9, 1910, took him on his famous bird walk in the New Forest.

Speaking to the Harvard Union on December 8, 1919, Grey said, "It seemed to me very attractive that the executive head of the most powerful country in the world should have this simple, healthy, touching desire to hear the song of birds."

Other statesmen who have been bird-watchers include Neville Chamberlain and his Parliamentary Private Secretary Alec Douglas-Home, later (briefly) prime minister. More recently two chancellors of the exchequer, Norman Lamont and Kenneth Clarke, have also been enthusiastic amateur bird-watchers.

HOW THE BLOOD PICKS UP OXYGEN

Themes: Creation

There are 300 million air sacs in each lung. Flowing by the walls of these air sacs, the blue venous blood picks up oxygen. Each hemoglobin molecule leaves the lungs bright red, carrying four hitchhiking oxygen molecules. In the capillaries of the muscles, one of four passes over to the body cells, and the blood (now blue again) returns to the lungs for more oxygen.

A LITTLE LESSON IN "ORNI-THEOLOGY"

Themes: Creation; Holidays: Thanksgiving;
Thankfulness; Prayer; Worship

Q: Do you know why pigeons are the most pagan of all birds?
A: There are twenty-six orders of birds, and twenty-five of them drink by gravity. So after each sip they raise their heads until water has trickled down. In consequence, they have [a] lovely proverb in Ghana: "Even the chicken, when it drinks, lifts its head to heaven, to thank God for the water."

[And it's] not only chickens. Twenty-five of twenty-six orders do. There's only one order which doesn't: pigeons drink by suction, not gravity. When they drink, they keep their heads down in the puddle. They never lift their heads to heaven to thank God!

Don't be like the pagan pigeons. Saying grace is a very important practice. It's only a symbol, but of a vital truth: Our Creator God has given us all things, and we must thank him for them.

LOOK AROUND YOU!

Themes: Creation; Watchfulness

The medieval St. Paul's Cathedral was destroyed by the Great Fire of 1666. [Christopher] Wren began the new one in 1675, and his son finished it in 1708. Visitors are surprised there is no memorial to him. His tomb is in the crypt near massive tombs of Lord Nelson and [the] Duke of Wellington. On it a plaque bears [the] Latin inscription, [*Si monumentum requiris, circumspice*]: "If you seek his monument, look around you."

Circumspice!

OUR AMAZING HANDS

Themes: Creation

The human hand (with its twenty-seven bones, its tendons, muscles, nerves, skin, and blood vessels) is a marvelous "piece of machinery, a bewildering array of levers, hinges and power sources," all managed from the brain's motor cortex. With our hands we feel, hold, grip, lift, shake, stroke, squeeze, press, rub, pull, push, etc. And by the tools we manipulate we greatly extend the usefulness of our hands: With them we write, draw, paint, sculpt, wash and dress, cook and clean, eat and drink, saw, plane, hammer, screw, sew, knit, build, ride a bicycle, drive a car, play musical instruments, and operate our gadgets. The hand possesses an almost limitless versatility. It's practically *tireless* too. During our lifetime, we extend and flex our finger joints around twenty-five million times. *Yet*, though our legs, feet, and arms get tired, we hardly ever complain of having tired hands. So *sensitive* is the hand that, by feel alone, a farmer can assess the texture of soil, a housewife the quality of a fabric, and a baker the water content of his dough.

So useful is the hand, that to lose it would be a greater disaster than to lose even an eye or ear. For hands can substitute for eyes by reading braille, and for ears by using sign language.[21]

THE PARABLE OF THE OWL

Themes: Creation; Wisdom

There are around 140 species [of owls], but everybody can recognize [them because their] facial discs are like saucers.

There's one particular way in which *owls are superior to humans*: not their proverbial wisdom, not [their] acute eyesight or sense of hearing, but their head is mounted on such flexible bearings [that they can] turn it 180 degrees. An owl can stand with body and feet in one direction while [its] head [is] facing [the] opposite direction.

We humans can't perform this extraordinary contortion. But what we can't do *physically* we must do *spiritually*.

In John Bunyan's allegory *Pilgrim's Progress,* there's a character called Mr. Facing-Both-Ways. He was [a] bad guy, but there's a good way [to be] like [an] owl: facing both backwards (past) and forwards (future).

SOME BIRDS HIBERNATE

Themes: Creation

Still in [the] eighteenth century many believed that birds hibernated in caves, like bears, or in hollow trees. Swallows (some thought) even copied turtles and dived into the mud at the bottom of the ponds. The truth is more extraordinary. Some goatsuckers (e.g., the poorwill) and swifts do hibernate! When their insect diet is no longer available in

---

21. J. D. Ratcliff, "I Am Joe's Right Hand," *Reader's Digest* (February 1973 and February 1982).

a cold winter, they hide in a rock crevice and lapse into a "torpidity"—in which heartbeats and breathing almost cease, and the bird lives off its stored fat for up to two or three months, until insects are there again to eat.

SPACE FACTS

Themes: Creation

Earth. A minor planet, circling our star, two-thirds [of the] way toward [the] edge of [the] Milky Way, [a] galaxy of 100 billion stars, 100,000 light-years across, 1 of 100 billions of others. Three more [were] discovered [in] 1981 (NCB), 10,000 million light-years away.

Interstellar travel. To reach [the] nearest star at [the] speed of light (186,000 miles per second) [would take] four years; our fastest man-launched vehicle so far [travels at] seven miles per second. [This would take] 80,000 years! [It would] only [be] possible by hibernation, freezing, or robots.

Interstellar communication. In 1971 NASA planned Project Cyclops, [which consisted of] 1,500 antennae (each larger than [a] football field) covering 25 plus square miles—[it was] too expensive. In 1976, SETI (Search for Extraterrestrial Intelligence) at Deep Space Network, Goldstone, California, surveying entire visible sky with sensitive Caltech equipment and antennae.

Solar System. Seven billion, 328 million miles in diameter. Earth is one of nine non-luminous bodies (planets) circling [the] sun. Nearest to [the] sun [is] Mercury, then Venus, Earth (18.5 miles per second on yearlong voyage round [the] sun), Mars, asteroids, Jupiter, Saturn, Uranus, Neptune ([the] four giants) and Pluto on [the] perimeter, plus 32 moons plus comets plus meteors.

A SPECULATIVE RECONSTRUCTION

Themes: Creation

2.5 billion years ago: Earth separated from [the] sun ([the] oldest rocks [are] around two billion years old).

Moon: Torn out of Pacific bed (whose floor is basalt like [the] middle layer of earth, not granite like [the] outer layer).

Seas: When Earth's crust cooled, rains fell without (as previously) being reconverted to steam. Centuries of rain.

Fossils: 500 million years → Cretaceous Period. 100 million years ago Archbishop James Ussher (1581–1656) calculated that man was created on Friday, October 23, 4004 BC!

THE STRANGE EXPERIENCE OF A HARVEST FESTIVAL

Themes: Creation; Holidays: Thanksgiving

To lifelong city dwellers, a harvest festival is as strange an experience as [it was] to [a] little girl who came to one for the first time. With astonished delight, she found herself sitting next to [a] pile of ripe plums. She helped herself liberally: What else were they put there for? And in her mind the church's generosity in providing plums for children was only exceeded by its thoughtfulness in sending round a plate in which she could deposit the stones!

THOSE WHO LACK FAITH LACK WONDER

Themes: Creation; Faith; Revelation

Luther had a great sense of wonder before God's creation. He said, "How amazing are the clouds sustained without pillars and the firmament of heaven upheld without columns! How fair are the birds of heaven and the lilies of the field! 'If thou couldst understand a single grain of wheat, thou wouldst die for wonder.' … But who sees all this?

Only faith and spirit. The trouble with Erasmus is that he is not stupefied with wonder at the child in the womb. He does not contemplate marriage with reverent amazement, nor praise and thank God for the marvel of a flower or the bursting of a peach stone by the swelling seed. He beholds these wonders like a cow staring at a new door.

"The deficiency of faith is made evident by a lack of wonder, for nature is a revelation only to those to whom God has already been revealed."[22]

WE ARE HIS IN THREE WAYS

Themes: Creation; Election; Redemption

[A] small boy made [a toy] yacht. One day [he] lost it out to sea. Later [he] saw it for sale secondhand in [a] shop window [and] bought it. [He said to it,] "Little yacht, you are doubly mine. I made you; I bought you back."

[In the] days before [the] Industrial Revolution and mass production, [an] artisan weaved and tailored suits, selling them to London stores. [He eventually] accumulated enough money [to] buy up his stores. Later, [he] selected one of his own suits. [It was] three times his:

1. He made it.

2. He bought it (when buying up [the] shop).

3. He chose it.

And so, by creation, redemption, and election (cf. Isaiah 43:1ff.), we belong to God [by a] threefold chain.

---

22. Roland H. Bainton, *Here I Stand: A Life of Martin Luther* (Hodder and Stoughton, 1951), 216–17.

WE HAVE UPSET THE ECOLOGICAL BALANCE OF NATURE

Themes: Creation

Guy Mountfort, in *Portrait of a Wilderness* (1958), describes the 1952, 1956, and 1957 ornithological expeditions to the Coto Doñana, in Andalusia. Setting out from the *Palacio* one day they saw countless black columns, 1' wide and 25' high, of midges arising from the scrub. The variety was one which fed on plant juices, and the columns were their mating swarms.

The same day large numbers of small red dragonflies emerged from the *marismas* and joined shrikes, flycatchers, and larger warblers in preying on the midges. The dragonflies were discovered by the bee-eaters, "which circled in graceful, swooping flight to catch these tasty morsels." And Mountfort saw a short-toed eagle stoop and dive at a bee-eater.

Later, he writes: "All nature subsists on predation. ... In the space of only a few hours had I not just witnessed four progressive stages of predation—the eagle which attacked the bee-eater, which preyed on the dragonfly, which preyed on the midge, which sucked the lifeblood of the bog plants? It was like the nursery rhyme of the house that Jack built ... only modern man contrived to upset the ecological balance of nature; man the destroyer, who now killed not for survival but for pleasure; man the despoiler, who razed forests and polluted rivers."[23]

---

23. Guy Mountfort, *Portrait of a Wilderness* (David and Charles, 1968), 146–49.

WHAT J. M. W. TURNER SEES IN A SUNSET

Themes: Beauty; Creation; Creativity

A well-known story relates that a woman watching the artist Turner painting a sunset remarked, "But Mr. Turner, I can't see that in a sunset"—to which the artist replied, "No, madam, but don't you wish that you could?"

NO ONE WILL GIVE BREAD AND BUTTER

Themes: Creation; Providence; Work

In January 1963, Mr. Khrushchev visited East Germany. He is reported as having said at the Congress of the East German Communist Party: "Neither God, nor the Kaiser, nor the devil will give you your bread and butter if you do not make it with your own hands"—an interesting trinity!

    [But he was] quite right: Bread and butter [are] human products.[24]

EASTER

"CHE LIVES"?

Themes: Eschatology: Resurrection; Jesus: Resurrection

Sartre described Che Guevara as "the most complete man of his age." In his thirty-nine years, he had been a doctor, author, political and military theorist, a guerrilla fighter, economist, banker and other things besides. He was also entirely consistent in what he said and did, and he became a legend during his lifetime, a kind of folk hero. "In every Cuban classroom now, the children chant 'we will be like Che' " (p. 70).

---

24. *Times* third leader (January 25, 1963).

"In death Che has had more influence than when he was alive. ...
He has provided the Marxists with a kind of saint, who has dedicated
his life and death to the poorest of men without help from God. The
walls of the student halls of the world are chalked with the words,
CHE LIVES" (p. 881).

[Similarly,] after the death of Archbishop Makarios of Cyprus in
August 1977 the island prepared for his burial on August 8. Some
of his followers paint-sprayed buildings with the words "Makarios
Lives!"[25]

THE HISTORICITY OF THE RESURRECTION

Themes: Jesus: Resurrection

Professor Pinchas Lapide [is an] Orthodox Jew and New Testament
scholar of irenic outlook who honors Jesus as [an] Orthodox Jew
of great piety, though he cannot accept his messiahship. Yet in *The
Resurrection of Jesus* (SPCK, 1984), he argues for [the resurrection]
forcefully. He rejects the ingenuity of modern skeptical theologians
in [their] attempts to de-historicize [the] resurrection.

THE PENKOVSKY PAPERS AND THE BODY OF JESUS

Themes: Jesus: Resurrection

[Oleg] Penkovsky was a Russian spy. His "The Penkovsky Papers"
were published in 1965. Victor Zorza in the *Manchester Guardian*
argued that they were a forgery, and that no Russian manuscript
existed. Peter Deriabin (himself formerly a Soviet intelligence officer),
who translated the Papers into English, wrote to say they were *not*
a forgery: "I know, better than anyone, that the Papers are genuine,"

---

25. Andrew Sinclair, *Che Guevara* (Fontana, 1970).

but went on to say, "I do not wish to release it (the Russian manuscript) in its original form."

Zorza replied: "Since the question of the authenticity of the 'Papers' could be settled so easily by producing the Russian original, the failure to make it available—or to give any convincing reason for this, beyond the childish 'I do not wish to'—really does seem to settle the matter."[26]

GOD

CHRISTIAN ADOPTION IN CONTRAST WITH GREEK ADOPTION

Themes: Adoption; God the Father

Writing about legal practice in ancient Greece, Professor Peter Wülfing-von Martitz (Cologne) writes: "The legal process of adoption was often combined with making a will. ... Not infrequently testamentary adoption included the duty of providing for the adopting parent. The adopted son entered at once into the rights of the parent and undertook out of the assigned income to keep the testator and his family to the end of their lives. ... Hence adoption was a way of providing for old age."

[In] contrast to this secular background, God's "adoption" of Israel was in free love with no self-interest (Exod 4:22; Hos 11:1; Josh 1:2; cf. Rom 9:4).

It is the same with believers. Eduard Schweizer (Zürich) comments, "The choice of the word (υιοθεσια) shows already that the sonship is not regarded as a natural one but as a sonship conferred by God's act."[27]

---

26. Victor Zorza, *Guardian Weekly* (December 2, 1965).

27. G. Kittel and G. Friedrich, eds., *Theological Dictionary of the New Testament*, Vol. 8 (Eerdmans, 1973), 398, 399.

Writing about legal practice in ancient Greece, Prof. Peter Wülfing von Martitz (Cologne) writes: '...the legal process of adoption was often combined with making a will ... Not infrequently testamentary adoption included the duty of providing for the adopting parent. The adopted son entered at once into the rights of the parent & undertook out of the assigned income to keep the testator & his family to the end of their lives. ... Hence adoption was a way of providing for old age...'
(Kittel VIII. p 398). In contrast to this secular background, God's 'adoption' of Israel was in free love with no self interest (Ex 4²⁹f. Hos 11¹. Is 1² & Rom. 9⁴) It is the same with believers.
Eduard Schweizer (Zürich) comments: 'The choice of the word (sc. hiotesia) shows already that the sonship is not regarded as a natural one but as a sonship conferred by God's act.' (Kittel VIII. p 399).

Adopt. 0.5

EXHAUSTING THE SUBJECT OF GOD'S ATTRIBUTES

Themes: God

An annual prize is awarded for a poem at Cambridge University which (according to the unrevised university statutes) had to be about "the nature and attributes of God until such time as, in the opinion of the Master of Clare, the subject be deemed to be exhausted."

FREUD ON WHY GOD IS CALLED "FATHER"

Themes: Family: Fathers; God the Father; Image of God

1. "Freud came to believe that God was called 'Father' because children invented him as the invisible personification of their fathers, whom they basically disliked as being cruelly authoritarian."
   They also felt guilty, and "this guilt was the basis of the formation of the conscience or 'super-ego,' a kind of internal father exuding disapproval—and it was also the origin in the individual's life of the idea of God the heavenly Father."

2. Voltaire once quipped that God had made man in his image, and that man had returned the compliment.[28]

THE GREEK GODS AS FATHERS

Themes: Family: Fathers; God the Father

The old Greek deities were sometimes called "Father." When Odysseus had returned to Ithaca, he made himself known to his aged father Laertes, who, overcome with joy and amazement, cried, "O Father Zeus! Verily ye gods are still abiding in broad Olympos."

---

28. David L. Edwards, *Religion and Change* (Hodder and Stoughton, 1970), 115.

Indeed, Olympian Zeus was called "the Father of gods and men" (p. 2), and Athena called him "King of Kings and Lord of Lords" (p. 3). But these titles are empty words, for Zeus is (in Homer at least) immoral, capricious, and far from omnipotent. He is neither all-powerful, nor all-holy, nor all-wise.[29]

THE NAMING OF TRINIDAD

Themes: Trinity

Columbus on [his] third voyage to America sighted what appeared at [a] distance to be three hilly islands arising from [the] sea. As [the] ship drew near, [he] saw they were united by strips of low-lying land. So [it was] only one island, not three. [He] named it Trinidad ([the] Spanish word for Trinity), "for," he said, "this is what the Doctrine of the Trinity means: while we are far off, we can only see the three Persons; when we draw nearer, see God as He is, then we shall find that the three persons are really one God."[30]

"NOBODY BELIEVES IN THE TRINITY NOWADAYS"

Themes: Doubt; Trinity

One of the most vivid and embarrassing memories of my schooldays is of a conversation with a visiting clergyman. I was about fifteen years old. And with the invincible assurance of teenage omniscience I said to him, "Nobody believes in the Trinity nowadays."

I'd no sooner said it than I was ashamed of it.

The fact is, I'd never thought about the Trinity. I just found it difficult to understand so I assumed it was an outmoded superstition, long since discarded by intelligent people. It is perhaps an example

---

29. W. H. D. Rouse, *The Story of Odysseus* (New American Library, 1937), 403.
30. G. R. Balleine, *Lessons from the Hymn Book,* 105–7.

of the irony of God's providence that on leaving school I went to that college of Cambridge University ... dedicated to the Holy Trinity!

STUDYING GOD THIS TERM

Themes: Education; God

A schoolgirl wrote to the Church of England Enquiry Centre: "We are doing God this term; please send me full details and pamphlets."[31]

THOMAS JEFFERSON'S JESUS

Themes: Trinity; Government, Politics and National Identity; Jesus

Thomas Jefferson was not only the chief architect of the American Declaration of Independence (1776) and the third president of [the] United States (1801–1809), but a political philosopher and a deist who attempted to reconstruct a Christianity without dogma and a Jesus without miracles: "When we shall have done away with the incomprehensible jargon of the Trinitarian arithmetic, that three are one, and one is three; when, in short, we shall have unlearned everything which has been taught since Jesus' day, and got back to the pure and simple doctrines he inculcated, we shall then be truly and worthily his disciples."

---

31. Richard Bewes, at Keswick (July 1975).

GRACE

THE DIFFICULTIES OF TRANSLATING "GRACE" INTO VARIOUS AFRICAN LANGUAGES

Themes: Grace of God

John Mpaayei, formerly secretary of Kenya Bible Society and now working on a new translation into Maasai, explained in November 1973 the difficulties of the translator. Take, for example, the crucial New Testament phrase "the grace of the Lord Jesus."

- Kikuyu: "the goodness of"

- Old Maasai (1923): "the luck"

- Another: "the gift of a cow or a sheep"

- New Maasai: "a gift that is unmerited, unsolicited, and unexpected"

GRACE'S AND LAW'S RESPONSES TO THE PRODIGAL

Themes: Grace of God; Law

"When the prodigal came home, grace met him and embraced him. Law said, 'Stone him!'—grace said, 'Embrace him!' Law said, 'Smite him!'—grace said, 'Kiss him!' Law went after him and bound him. Grace said, 'Loose him and let him go!' Law tells me how crooked I am; grace comes and makes me straight."

Grace lies at the center of the imitation of Christ.[32]

---

32. John Pollock, *Moody without Sankey* (Hodder and Stoughton, 1963), 134.

JOHN NEWTON ON INVINCIBLE GRACE

Themes: Grace of God

In one of his letters to an ordained friend he suspects of being unconverted, John Newton says he prefers to call grace "invincible" to "irresistible." For grace "is too often resisted, even by those who believe; but, because it is invincible, it triumphs over all resistance when he is pleased to bestow it" (Letter No. VII, Nov. 17, 1775).[33]

HOLY SPIRIT

CONFUSED ABOUT THE HOLY BIRD

Themes: Trinity; Holy Spirit

A Chinese enquirer: "The Father I understand, and Jesus Christ his Son. But who is this holy bird?"

DAVID OYEDEPO'S UNUSUAL PRACTICES

Themes: Holy Spirit; Power

David Oyedepo is presiding bishop of the Living Faith World Outreach Centre. His Winners' Chapel in Lagos claims 20,000 plus members. I'm thankful for his missionary zeal and social action, but [he has an] unhealthy emphasis on power. He begins *The Release of Power* (Dominion Publishing, 1996):

- "The end-time church is a church of power. It is a ruling and reigning church" (p. v).

- "Once you are saved, you become a power-loaded personality" (p. 41). So "let's step into power. ... It is our birthright" (p. 23).

---

33. John Newton, *Caridphonia: or, The Utterance of the Heart* (Stereotype, 1856), 175.

Two questions:

1. *Power for what?* Answer: For signs and wonders, for witness, to get wealth, to enjoy immunity to disease but not power for holiness.

2. *[What are the] means?* [He uses] strange materials:

    a. Elijah's *mantle* he waves and strikes

    b. *The anointing oil*, which "is the Spirit of God mysteriously put in a bottle" ([p.] 146). "No sickness can stand against it. The anointing oil is irresistible, all powerful, ever conquering, ever winning" (p. 150).

    c. "*The Word of God* is the Holy Ghost on paper. ... He lives inside the pages of the Bible" (p. 47).

    d. *The Blood of Jesus*, which appears to be Holy Communion. "There is no drink, capsule or medicine that can be compared to the flesh and blood of Jesus" (p. 161). If you partake, "you will never need to take any drug."[34]

JONATHAN EDWARDS ON HOW TO TELL IF THE SPIRIT IS BEHIND A WORK

Themes: Holy Spirit; Revival

In section II of Jonathan Edwards's *The Distinguishing Marks of a Work of the Spirit of God*, he turns from the negative to the positive. Based on 1 John 4 (which begins with the command to "test the spirits"), he argues that a work is from the Spirit of God:

---

34. David Oyedepo, *The Release of Power* (Dominion Publishing, 1996).

1. if it raises people's "esteem" of the historic Jesus as both God and man, and the only Savior (1 John 4:2f., 15; 5:1; cf. 1 Cor 12:3) (pp. 109–11)

2. if it "operates against the interests of Satan's king-dom," e.g., by convicting people of sin (1 John 4:4f.; Matt 12:25f.) (pp. 111–13)

3. if it causes "a greater regard to the Holy Scriptures" (1 John 4:6 apostles; cf. Isa 8:19f.). For the devil hates the Bible, since "every text is a dart to torment the old serpent" ([pp.] 113–14).

4. if it leads people to truth and conforms them in sound doctrine, e.g., about God, themselves, and salvation (1 John 4:6) (pp. 114–15)

5. if it "operates as a Spirit of love for God and man" (1 John 4:6f., 12f., 17ff.). This is "the highest kind of evi-dence" available (p. 117).[35]

MOODY'S EXPERIENCE OF GOD'S LOVE

Themes: God's Love; Holy Spirit

What D. L. Moody called his "baptism of the Holy Spirit" took place in New York in November 1872. He'd already given ten years to the Chicago slums and the Civil War, but then he had a conflict period, including both hostility to God's will and "great hunger in my soul … that God would fill me with his Holy Spirit." Following complete surrender came "such an experience of His love that I had to ask Him to stay His hand."[36]

---

35. Jonathan Edwards, *Jonathan Edwards on Revival* (Banner of Truth, 1965).
36. John Pollock, *The Keswick Story* (Hodder and Stoughton, 1964), 18.

R. A. TORREY'S GROWTH IN PREACHING

Themes: Church Leadership; Holy Spirit

"I entered the ministry because I was literally forced to. For years I refused to be a Christian, because I was determined that I would not be a preacher, and I feared that if I surrendered to Christ I must enter the ministry."

He gave in. "But no one could be less filled by natural temperament for the ministry than I. From early boyhood, I was extraordinarily timid and bashful." He gives examples of how shy [he] was in company, that he thought he was speaking but made no audible sound. "Think of a young fellow like that entering the ministry."

He tells how [he] first plucked up [the] courage to pray in public by learning a little piece by heart ... how in [his] early days of ministry [he] memorized sermons ... and how he suffered. Then, "the thought got possession of me that when I stood up to preach, there was Another who stood by my side ... that all I had to do was to stand back as far out of sight as possible and let Him do the work. I have no dread of preaching now; preaching is the greatest joy of my life."[37]

THE REVIVAL IN SINGAPORE

Themes: Holy Spirit; Revival

[I've been asked to] *say something* regarding the *Pentecostal experience*. It's a divisive subject, but I hope [to] speak a reconciling word.

The charismatic movement has spread rapidly in Singapore. The Anglican diocese is almost entirely charismatic. When I was in Singapore in 1987, Bishop Moses Tay invited me to address his clergy [and] to visit him in [his] home.

---

37. R. A. Torrey, *The Person and Work of the Holy Spirit* (Fleming H. Revell, 1910), 73–78.

As he kept talking about the renewal exp[erience] [and] adding he couldn't deny its reality, I asked him what in his view the *essence* of it was. He replied: "It's a new experience of the presence of God."

This immediately struck me. I'd recently read J. I. Packer's *Keep in Step [with the Spirit].* He's a non-charismatic. *His* understanding [is that renewal is] "a fresh assurance of the love of God" [and] "a new experience of [the] presence of God."

Could this not be [a] basis of mutual understanding and respect? Both sides believe in [the] work of [the] Spirit in pouring God's love into [our hearts] [and] witnessing with our spirit that we [are children of God.]

TERTULLIAN ON NEW REVELATIONS FROM THE HOLY SPIRIT

Themes: Holy Spirit; Revelation

In his treatise *[On] Monogamy,* written after he left the church and identified with the Montanists, Tertullian argued that second marriages (after the death of [the] first spouse) were forbidden by the Paraclete. He asked "whether or not it is possible that the Paraclete has revealed anything at all which is an innovation opposed to Catholic tradition." The answer he gives himself is to quote John 16:12, 13. He continues: "Thus of course, he (Jesus Christ) sufficiently indicates that the Holy Spirit will reveal such things as may be considered innovations, since they were not revealed before" (§ 2).

JUDGMENT

THE HARROW & WEALDSTONE RAIL CRASH

Themes: Death and Dying; Judgment

At 8:19 a.m. [on] October 8, 1952, at Harrow & Wealdstone station, [lay] a pile of wreckage thirty or forty feet high. Underneath [it] are one hundred dead or dying. [It was] one of [the] worst disasters in British Railway history.

Under the station clock a poster uttered its silent message: "Prepare to meet thy God."

"IF GOD MADE US, HE WILL NOT DESTROY US"

Themes: Hell; Judgment

Robert G. Ingersoll (1833–1899) was a nineteenth-century American lawyer, politician, and eloquent enemy of Christianity. In 1860 he tried (unsuccessfully) to become Democratic candidate for Congress, and later a Republican nominee for [the] presidency.

In [the] article "What Must We Do to Be Saved?" he wrote: "If God made us, he will not destroy us. Infinite wisdom never made a poor investment. Upon all the works of an infinite God a dividend must finally be declared. Why should God make failures? Why should he waste material? Why should he not correct his mistakes, instead of damning them? … The doctrine of endless punishment has covered the cheeks of this world with tears. I despise it, and I defy it."[38]

---

38. Robert G. Ingersoll, *The Works of Ingersoll*, vol. 1 (Dresden Pub. Co., 1902), 457–58.

JUSTIFICATION

BILL WALKER'S ATTEMPTS AT SELF-JUSTIFICATION

Themes: Good Works; Justification

In Bernard Shaw's comedy *Major Barbara*, Bill Walker is a Cockney whose girlfriend, Mog, has been converted and has joined the Salvation Army. Bill, infuriated and drunk, goes to the hostel to get her back. He finds his way blocked by Jenny Hill, the Salvation Army girl on duty. He first takes her by the arm, then seizes her by the hair, then strikes her with his fist in the face. With returning sobriety Bill's conscience nags him, and he decides what to do to pacify it and expiate his guilt.

"I'm goin' to Kennintahn, to spit in Todger Fairmile's (the converted wrestling and boxing champion) eye. I bashed Jenny Ill's face; and now I'll get me own face bashed and come back and shew it to 'er. E'll 'it me 'arder'n I 'it 'er. That'll make us square."

But Todger wouldn't play.

Bill: "I did wot I said I'd do. I spit in 'is eye. 'E looks up at the sky and sez, 'O that I should be fahnd worthy to be spit upon for the gospel's sake!' 'e sez; and Mog sez, 'Glory Allelloolier!'; an' then 'e called me Brother ... I and't just no show wiv 'im at all. 'Arf the street prayed; an' t'other 'arf larfed fit to split theirselves."

Jenny interjects: "I'm so sorry, Mr. Walker."

Bill turns on her furiously: "I don't want to be forgive be you, or be ennybody. Wot I did I'll pay for. I tried to get me own jawr broke to settisfaw you." So next he tries to buy his redemption by offering her a sovereign: "'Ere's the money. Take it and lets 'av no more o' your forgivin' an prayin' and your Major jawrin me. Let wot I done be done and paid for; and let there be a end of it."[39]

---

39. George Bernard Shaw, *John Bull's Other Island and Major Barbara* (Constable, 1907), 218–41.

ENGLISH REFORMERS ON JUSTIFICATION

Themes: Justification

1. *Thomas Bilney*, "the shy and gentle fellow of Trinity Hall" who was enlightened by [the] Holy Spirit in 1519 as he read Erasmus's *Novum Testamentum*, wrote in his *Adversaria*: "We all might be condemned if God willed to enter into judgment with us; but O Merciful Father, thou dost not impute as sin to us the impunity or sins of men ... if we have faith that our sins be remitted to us through our Lord Jesus Christ." Burned 1531.

2. *John Frith* (who went from Kings Cambridge to Oxford) wrote in his work on purgatory: "Thro' Adam, Adam's sin was counted our own, through Christ Christ's righteousness is reputed unto us for our own" (*Works*, p. 49). Burned 1533.

3. *William Tyndale* (from Magdalen, Oxford to Cambridge): "God justifieth us actively; that is to say, forgiveth us and reckoneth us for full righteous. And Christ's blood deserveth it, and faith in the promise receiveth it." In his prison on the Vilvorde he wrote a book on [the] theme: *Sola fides justificat apud Deum* and called this "his key to the healthy understanding of Sacred Scripture."[40]

LUTHER'S JOURNEY TOWARD JUSTIFICATION BY FAITH

Themes: Faith; Justification; Righteousness

Luther was brought up, at home and school, in the fear of God, death, judgment, and hell. So was everyone else in medieval Christendom. Because [the] smartest way to gain heaven was to become a monk, in 1505 aged twenty-one, Luther entered the Augustinian cloister at

---

40. Marcus Loane, *The Just Shall Live by Faith* (tract) (Evangelical Tracts, 1958), 4.

Erfurt. He prayed seven times a day, fasted sometimes three days on end, and adopted other extreme austerities.

Later: "I was a good monk. … If ever a monk got to heaven by his monkery, it was I" (p. 45). Even his crawling up [the] twenty-eight steps of *Scala Sancta* in Rome in 1510, on [his] hands and knees, brought him no relief. "Luther probed every resource of contemporary Catholicism for assuaging the anguish of a spirit alienated from God" (p. 54). But nothing pacified his tormented conscience until [he was] appointed professor of Bible at [the] University of Wittenberg and from 1513–1516 he studied and expounded first Psalms, then Paul's Epistle to the Romans.

From Psalm 22 Luther learned that Jesus was not only [a] terrifying judge but [a] most merciful savior. [He was] godforsaken on [the] cross because of our sins. And from Romans 1 he learned that God's "righteousness" was not his *justice punishing* sinners but his *justification, pronouncing* them righteous, and that by faith alone.[41]

"YOUR BEST IS TO GET ME"

Themes: Faith; Good Works; Justification; Sin

[In a] weaving factory, [a] new and inexperienced hand managed [to] get his machine into [a] terrible tangle. Afraid [to] tell [the] foreman, [he] tried hard [to] unravel it, but [it] only got worse. In desperation [he] fetched [the] foreman [and told him], "I did my best." [The] foreman responded, "Your best is to get *me*."

Archbishop Temple's oft-quoted words expressed this very pointedly: "All is of God; the only thing of my very own which I can contribute to my own redemption is the sin from which I need to be redeemed."

---

41. Roland H. Bainton, *Here I Stand: A Life of Martin Luther* (Hodder and Stoughton, 1951).

MIRACLES

HOW SCRIPTURE USES THE WORD "MIRACLE"

Themes: Miracles; Scripture

It is true that Scripture sometimes uses the language of "miracle" for events which are "marvelous" rather than "miraculous" (in [the] strict sense of [the] word), "wonders" which arouse human amazement rather than being supernatural acts of God which defy all human explanation. For example, God's "wonders that cannot be fathomed" and "miracles that cannot be counted" include rainfall, the exaltation of the lowly, the thwarting of the schemes of the crafty and the deliverance of the oppressed—that is, God's providential ordering of nature and history (Job 5:9ff.).

PAUL CAIN'S PROPHECIES OF THE LAST DAYS

Themes: Healing; Miracles; Prophecy; Revival

At the "Beulah" meetings at Wembley in October 1992, R. T. Kendall and Paul Cain ("Paul, you need my theology, I need your power") prophesied a "post-charismatic" era when "government and people in highest places will come on bended knee to God's people and ask for help" and "children will be sovereign vessels." "We are talking about an awakening that reaches areas, people, places that heretofore were impenetrable without the aid of the media and the PR men, and the endorsement of high profile people." (NB: At Holy Trinity Brompton in July 1990, Paul Cain prophesied that revival would be released in England in October that year.) Paul Cain says [the] last days will see armies of children parading down the streets and healing all hospital patients, also one billion converts, and many raised from dead, and cripples healed.

THREE DIVISIONS OF CHRIST'S MIRACLES

Themes: Jesus: Miracles

In his *The Divine Propagandist* (1962), Lord Beaverbrook puts Christ's miracles into three main divisions:

1. the miracles of Compassion
2. the miracles of Necessity
3. the miracles of Propaganda—intended to create faith

The first category (containing all the healing miracles) outnumbers the other two. The second has few, like [the] stilling of [the] storm. The third has some of the Johannine evidential signs.[42]

THREE SKEPTICAL QUOTES ON MIRACLES

Themes: Doubt; Miracles

"We may summarily reject all miracles, prophecies, narratives of angels and demons, and the like, as simply impossible and irreconcilable with the known and universal laws which govern the course of events."

—David F. Strauss, *The Life of Jesus,* 1836

"Miracles are things which never happen; only credulous people believe they have seen them."

—Ernest Renan, *The Life of Jesus,* 1863 (preface to 13th ed.)

"Miracles do not happen."

—Matthew Arnold, *Literature and Dogma,* 1973, p. xiii

---

42. Lord Beaverbrook, *The Divine Propagandist* (Heinemann, 1962).

SALVATION

A HINDU PHILOSOPHER'S LECTURE ON GOD

Themes: God; Salvation

One day a Hindu philosopher visited a women's school of village evangelism and asked if he might lecture [the] women on Hinduism. [He was] granted permission, and returned with two others. All sat on mats round [the] floor, and [the] Hindu pundit gave [an] interesting talk on God, ending with a transcendent Being so far away and unapproachable, and man in the depths of such abysmal ignorance and degradation, that they were left gasping for breath.

When he suddenly stopped, the women cried out, "But go on, go on, you can't stop there." "Our religion stops there," he replied.[43]

TWO STORIES OF SALVATION BY FAITH

Themes: Faith; Good Works; Salvation

1. An old Chinese woman, under conviction of sin, felt the need of getting right with God. So, thinking to earn salvation by merit, [she] began [to] dig a well with [her] bare hands, twenty-five feet deep and ten feet wide. [It gave her] no peace. [Then she] heard [the] gospel of grace [as a] free gift. When [she was] eighty years old [she] met Miss Lucy Bambridge, missionary to China, and stretching out her poor crippled fingers, she sang: "Not the labor of my hands … Nothing in my hand I bring" [from the hymn "Rock of Ages"].

2. A young man said to his father, "Father, I want to become a Christian. What must I do about it?" And his father, being a wise man, answered, "Son, there is nothing for you to do. You have only to kneel down and say 'thank you.' "[44]

43. *The London Churchman* (1950).
44. Frank Colquhoun, *The Meaning of the Cross* (Tyndale, 1958).

SECOND COMING

ASSUMING ODYSSEUS WILL NEVER COME BACK

Themes: Eschatology: Last Judgment; Eschatology: Second Coming

The men of Ithaca mourned the absence of Odysseus and feared he had died after the sack of Troy. His wife, Penelope, wept for him, and his young son, Telemachos, as he grew up longed for his return. "But," he sighed, "he is dead and gone in this miserable way, and there is no comfort for us, even if there are people in the world who say he will come back. No, the day of his return will never dawn." Many of [the] local citizens behaved in [a] disgraceful way because they thought they'd never be taken to task, until at last Odysseus did return and took vengeance upon them.[45]

BETWEEN THE LIGHTNING AND THE THUNDER

Themes: Eschatology: Last Judgment; Eschatology:
Second Coming; Faith; Hope; Kingdom of God

Karl Heim uses this metaphor: We see the lightning, and seconds afterward we hear the thunder. Yes, both refer to the same event. The interval is caused by the fact that light waves travel much faster than sound waves. We are living in such an interval. Christ has already triumphed. His kingdom is already established. With the eyes of faith the Christian sees this and acknowledges Jesus as Lord. Eventually but inevitably the thunder of judgment will sound, and every knee will bow and every tongue confess the lordship of Christ.[46]

---

45. W. H. D. Rouse, *The Story of Odysseus* (New American Library, 1937), 7.
46. T. A. Kantonen, *The Theology of Evangelism* (Muhlenberg, 1954), 70–71.

THE ELABORATE FUNERAL

Themes: Eschatology: Second Coming

Gavin Reid's book on "man, doom and God," entitled *The Elaborate Funeral* (Hodder, 1972), was criticized by some reviewers as being too doomish. But he ends with the Christian's sustaining belief in God as Lord of history: "For the truth he believes in spite of his informed pessimism is that the world will not end with a bang or with a whimper. ... It will end with the triumphant sound of a trumpet—and then all heaven will be let loose"![47]

VOTING IN LIGHT OF THE RETURN OF CHRIST

Themes: Eschatology: Second Coming; Responsibility

[William] Pitt once asked Henry Thornton why he voted against him on one occasion. Thornton replied: "I voted today so that if my Master had come again at that moment I might have been able to give an account of my stewardship."[48]

---

47. Gavin Reid, *The Elaborate Funeral* (Hodder and Stoughton, 1972), 191.
48. Michael Hennell, *John Venn and the Clapham Sect* (Lutterworth, 1958), 207.

2

CHURCH AND CHRISTIAN

ASSURANCE

ASSURANCE IS NOT PRESUMPTION

Themes: Assurance

"The doctrine of assurance ... seems to me what is missing in so much of what passes for Christianity. We do not have the confidence of the early church because we are inhibited by this wretched traditional Catholic injunction against presumption. Yet the promises are there to be claimed by faith. ... One accepts with the top of one's head but dare not rejoice. Forgiven, yes, but free from the power of sin and the fear of death? Wow! There is still a long way to go. ... I want to soak up the doctrine of assurance until it is fully mine."[1]

DYING IN CONFIDENCE AND PEACE

Themes: Assurance; Death and Dying

George Williams, in *Tales of the Mystic Way*, wrote of a dying girl who said: "I have no inward religious emotions, I see no angels, I hear no music, I have none of the death-bed transports of the story-books, I

---

1. Stuart Manson, FRCS, in a letter to JRWS (May 7, 1964).

have only the tenth [chapter] of Hebrews. I am dying in confidence and peace, upon the statements of that chapter, and I am satisfied."

She was referring especially to Hebrews 10:12, 14, 17.[2]

THE FAITH OF MICHAEL FARADAY

Themes: Assurance; Creation; Faith

[A] crowded gathering of distinguished scientists had been listening spellbound while for an hour Michael Faraday had lectured on the nature of the magnet. When he finished with his lecture by a novel and brilliant experiment, and resumed his seat, [the] house rocked with tremendous applause. [The] Prince of Wales (afterwards King Edward VII) rose to propose [a] motion of congratulation.

[This was] seconded, and carried by thunders of applause. [There was a] strange silence [as the] audience waited for Faraday's reply. But [he was] gone! [The] lecturer [had] vanished!

Only two or three friends knew where. [The] great chemist [was a] great Christian. [He was an] elder in [a] little local church, and [the] hour at which [he] finished [his] lecture [was the] hour of prayer, so under cover of cheering, [he] slipped out. [He] never missed!

[Faraday] began life (1791–1867) as [a] blacksmith, then [an] apprentice to [a] bookbinder. Gradually [he] climbed [the] ladder of fame. But [he was] never too busy or proud for God. He had made great discoveries in [the] fields of chemistry and electromagnetism, but [he] knew more. On [his] deathbed [he was asked,] "What are your speculations?"

"Speculations? I have none. I am resting in certainties. I know whom I have believed."[3]

---

2. George Williams, *Tales of the Mystic Way* (Thynne & Jarvis, 1929), 29.

3. F. W. Boreham, *A Handful of Stars: Texts That Have Moved Great Minds* (Abingdon Press, 1922), 178–80.

Crowded gathering of distinguished scientists had been listening spellbound while for an hour Michael Faraday had lectured on the nature of the magnet. When he finished his lecture by a novel & brilliant experiment, & resumed his seat, house rocked with thunderous applause. Prince of Wales (afterwards King Edward VII) rose to propose motion of congratulation. Seconded, & carried by thunders of applause. Strange silence. Audience waited for Faraday's reply. But—gone! lecturer vanished!

Only 2 or 3 friends knew where. Great chemist — great christian. Elder in little local ch., a hour at wh. finished lecture = hour of prayer., So, under cover of cheering, slipped out. Never missed!

Began life (1791–1867) as blacksmith. Then apprentice to bookbinder. Gradually climbed ladder of fame. But never too busy or proud for god. — He had made great discoveries in fields of chemistry & electromagnetism, but knew more. On deathbed "what are your speculations?" "speculations? I have none. I am resting on certainties. I know whom I have believed....."

(Handful of Stars pp 178–180)

"HOW SHALL I KNOW?"

Themes: Assurance; Death and Dying; Salvation

On [his] deathbed Bishop Joseph Butler [said] to [his] chaplain: "Though I have endeavoured to avoid sin and to please God to the utmost of my power, yet, from the unconsciousness of perpetual infirmities I am still afraid to die."

Chaplain: "My Lord, you have forgotten that Jesus Christ is a Saviour."

Bishop: "True. But how shall I know that He is a Saviour for *me?*"

Chaplain: "My Lord, it is written, 'Him that cometh to me I will in no wise cast out.' "

Bishop: "True! And I am surprised that, though I have read that Scripture a thousand times over, I have never felt its virtue till this moment; and now I die happy."[4]

JEAN-PAUL SARTRE AND HOPE

Themes: Assurance; Doubt; Grief; Hope

Early in 1980 Jean-Paul Sartre: "They (world problems and a sense of personal purposelessness) tempt you incessantly, especially if you're old and can think, 'Oh, well, anyway, I shall die in five years at the most.' In fact I think ten, but it might well be five. In any case the world seems ugly, bad and without hope. There, that's the cry of despair of an old man who'll die in despair. But that's exactly what I resist, and I know I shall die in hope. But that hope needs a foundation."

Within a month he was dead, apparently without having found the foundation for which he searched.[5]

---

4. H. Watkin-Jones, *The Holy Spirit from Arminius to Wesley* (Sharp, 1929), 314.

5. Stephen Travis, *I Believe in the Second Coming of Jesus* (Hodder and Stoughton, 1982), 226–27.

LUTHER'S TERRIBLE DREAM

Themes: Assurance; Satan

Martin Luther once had a terrible dream. As he dreamed, Satan came to him with three big scrolls (old-fashioned books) under his arm. He came near and unrolled one. To Martin's horror it was closely written with sins. Satan pointed. "Did you do, say, think that?"

"Yes; any more?"

"Why yes," and [he] unrolled [the] next roll, and [the] third.

"Any more?"

"No, but isn't that enough to damn anyone? You don't really think God could forgive you all that?" And Satan leered in his face.

Martin didn't answer, but taking [a] pen wrote across each scroll, "The blood of Jesus Christ … cleanses me from all sin." And Satan vanished.

MEMORIAL TO DR. BARNARDO

Themes: Assurance; Faith

After [the] death of Dr. Barnardo, [the sculptor] Sir George Frampton, RA, erected in [the] girls' village home [in] Ilford a memorial in bronze, portraying Charity as [a] motherly figure holding her own babe to her bosom, and with [her] left arm embracing [the] motherless child of another. At the base [were] three sweet-faced little girls (modeled from children in the village at [the] time).

Just over their heads is [a] medallion portrait of [the] Doctor, and at their feet this extract from his will: "I hope to die as I have lived, in the humble but sure faith of Jesus Christ as my Saviour, my Master, and my King."[6]

---

6. A. E. Williams, *Barnardo of Stepney: The Father of Nobody's Children* (Allen & Unwin, 1953), 212.

"READ IT FOR YOURSELF!"

Themes: Assurance; Temptation

[A] Christian boy [was] sitting by [the] fireside [one] winter's evening on [the] sofa alone. [His] parents [were] out. [He felt] tempted [to] doubt Revelation 3:20. [A] voice [came] from under [the] sofa, sneering at him, "You don't really think Jesus came in, [do you]?"

[The] boy [was] upset and frightened, [so he] took out [a] New Testament and read aloud Revelation 3:20. It was a promise! He smiled, and keeping [a] finger on [his] place leaned over and put the New Testament under [the] sofa, saying, "There you are, Satan. Read it for yourself"!

CHURCH

BONHOEFFER ON CONFESSION

Themes: Confession

"'Confess your faults one to another' (James 5:16). He who is alone with his sin is utterly alone. ... The pious fellowship permits no one to be a sinner. ... So we remain alone with our sin, living in lies and hypocrisy" (p. 86). "In confession the break-through to community takes place" (p. 87).

But Bonhoeffer has a Lutheran understanding of confession—not to a priest but to any Christian brother. "Only the brother under the Cross can hear a confession" (p. 93).[7]

---

7. Dietrich Bonhoeffer, *Life Together* (SCM, 1954).

BRITISH THINKERS ON THE CATHOLIC CHURCH

Themes: Nature of the Church

- Ruskin: The most debasing and degrading of all creeds.

- Sir Walter Scott: A mean and depraving superstition.

- Gladstone: One of the worst of the religious influences of the age.

- Adam Smith: The most formidable combination that was ever formed against the reason, liberty, and happiness of mankind.

- Lord Macaulay: To stunt the growth of the human mind has been its chief object.

- Dean Alford: Rome is essentially a pagan city.

- Lecky: The bitter enemy of toleration.

- Charles Dickens: The most horrible means of political and social degradation left in the world.[8]

THE COST OF CHURCH RESTORATION WORK

Themes: Church; Law: Ten Commandments; Restoration; Revival

[It is] customary in many churches for the Lord's Prayer, Ten Commandments, and the Apostles' Creed to be painted up on [the] east wall. A village carpenter had been engaged in restoration work at the east end of the parish church. In due course the following account was received by the church council ([this was] before decimalization):

> To repairing the Lord's Prayer: 10s 0
>
> To three new commandments: 12s 0
>
> To making a completely new Creed: 17s 6

---

8. J. A. Kensit, *Churchman's Magazine* (January 1971).

"THE EPISCOPAL CHURCH IS HERE TO STAY!"

Themes: Church Fellowship and Unity

A bishop in the American Episcopal Church, expounding John 17 and waxing eloquent on the unity Christ prayed for, went so far as to prophesy that the Episcopal Church itself might one day cease to exist by merging with other churches. "Young man," said an elderly and incensed lady to him afterwards, "I would have you know that Christianity may fail, but the Episcopal Church is here to stay!"

IN ESSENTIALS UNITY; IN NONESSENTIALS LIBERTY; IN ALL THINGS CHARITY

Themes: Church Fellowship and Unity

> *In necessariis unitas*
> *In non necessariis libertas*
> *In omnibus caritas*

This was called Richard Baxter's "favourite quotation" by John T. Wilkinson in his introductory essay to *The Reformed Pastor* (1656; Epworth edition 1939, p. 31). Its origin is "Rupertus Meldenius," an anagram of Petrus Meuderlinus, which is the Latinized form of Peter Meiderlin (1582–1651), a seventeenth-century Lutheran theologian.

EXTEND THE FRANCHISE FULLY TO INCLUDE THE PAST

Themes: Nature of the Church; Wisdom

"It is too late to change Christianity," writes Harry Blamires, "because it has been handed down to us across many centuries" (p. 77). As G. K. Chesterton put it, "Tradition may be defined as an extension

of the franchise. Tradition means giving votes to the most obscure of
all classes, our ancestors."

Beware then of innovators! "If you accept the 'one man, one vote'
principle for the Christian church, the pollsters will have to do most of
their opinion sampling in heaven. ... If you extend the franchise fully,
as Chesterton would recommend, you can never put the traditional-
ists in a minority. They have a built-in majority from the past" (p. 80).[9]

GOD WANTS DOCTORS ALIVE

Themes: Church; Commitment

At [an] informal meeting for doctors I was explaining [the] work
and purpose of a church—[I was] anxious [to] see more doctors [in
church]. Lord Webb Johnson said [that] All Souls [was] a doctor's
church. [He had] attended many memorial and funeral services, and
hoped [it] always would be [a] place in which medicals [were] honored after death!

But God wants [a] body, not [a] corpse, [and] prefers you to walk
in on two feet than be carried in head first!

JESUS VS. THE CHURCH?

Themes: Nature of the Church

1. Kierkegaard: "Whereas Christ turned water into wine,
    the church has succeeded in doing something more dif-
    ferent; it has turned wine into water."

2. Scrawled on the wall of a church in Cambridge: "The
    church is dead, but Jesus lives" (1987).

3. Mick Jagger: "I think Jesus Christ was fantastic. But I
    don't like the church; it does more harm than good."

---

9. Harry Blamires, *Where Do We Stand? An Examination of the Christian's
Position in the Modern World* (SPCK, 1980).

4. [J. I. Packer:] "God wants life in his new society to be a perfect riot of affection, good-will, open-heartedness and friendship. (So what on earth are we all playing at? You tell me!)"[10]

KNEELING IN A SPORTS CAR?

Themes: Nature of the Church; Repentance

In California now [1966] there's a drive-in church—"Worship in the privacy of your own automobile." I saw that sign up once by the highway and it occurred to me that if you wished to kneel and you had a sports car, you'd have a pretty difficult job …

MORE AT HOME IN DEFENSE THAN IN ATTACK

Themes: Nature of the Church; Conflict

We evangelicals seem to be more at home in defense than in attack, in criticism than in creation, in negative reaction to the views of others than in the positive construction of our own. In his introduction to *Biblical Revelation* (Moody Press, 1971, p. 15), Clark Pinnock writes: "Sir Isaac Newton formulated a law of motion which held that a body remains at rest unless acted upon by an external force. The same could be said of evangelical theology. Only when she is goaded into it does she bestir herself to refine and improve her doctrinal formulations."[11]

---

10. J. I. Packer, *I Want to Be a Christian* (Kingsway, 1977), 116.
11. Clark Pinnock, *Biblical Revelation* (Moody, 1971), 15.

THE MULTICULTURAL NATURE OF THE CHURCH

Themes: Nature of the Church

1. Surveying the around six thousand Christians gathered from all races and nations at Vancouver for the 6th Assembly of the World Council of Churches, Margaret Mead, the distinguished American anthropologist, is said to have remarked, "You are a sociological impossibility"!

2. Our multiracial, multicultural Christian community is what Bishop Desmond Tutu calls "the rainbow people of God."

PLENTY OF PURPLE SHIRTS

Themes: Church; Clothing

At a public meeting in Perth, Western Australia, in February 1971 a questioner complained that the church was always twenty years out of date, and would it never catch up. Commenting later, Archbishop Geoffrey Sambell said he didn't think this was always true. He'd been into a shop recently to ask if by chance they had a purple shirt—to be told they had *hundreds* of them.

STEPS TO REVIVAL

Themes: Revival

> If all the sleeping folks will wake up,
> and the lukewarm folks will fire up,
> If the dishonest folks will own up,
> and the discouraged folks will cheer up,
> If the quarrelsome will make up,
> and the gossipers will shut up,
> If depressed folks will look up,
> and the cowardly will speak up,
> Then it may well be that GOD will truly bless us.[12]

---

12. Anonymous, adapted by JRWS.

TRADITION IN THE NEW TESTAMENT

Themes: Church Leadership; Education; Scripture

παραλαμβανω and παραδιδωμι are the technical words for receiving and delivering a tradition, i.e., the two stages of its transmission. The identity of the "deliverer" is usually clear. But from whom did he "receive" it?

1. From "the Lord" in 1 Corinthians 11:23: [it is] probable that the teaching goes back to the teaching of Jesus himself, with the additional thought that he, now exalted, also confirms it by his spirit (so Cullmann in *SJT* 3 1950 p. 180f.).

2. Sometimes the Twelve who were apostles before Paul … so probably 1 Corinthians 15:1ff.

3. At other times Paul seems himself to be the origin of the tradition/instruction he gives. So perhaps 2 Thessalonians 3:6ff.; 2:15; and Galatians 1. Perhaps too 1 Corinthians 11:2ff.

NB: Paul "commends" or "does not commend" the churches according to whether they stick to his teachings/traditions or not (1 Cor 11:2, 17). Cf. Galatians 1:14; Colossians 2:8; Romans 6:17.

TRAINING IN TRANSCENDENTAL MEDITATION

Themes: Church Fellowship and Unity; Cults and Non-Christian Religions

Bruce Nicholls and David Muir went in 1975 in Delhi to the inauguration of the Age of Enlightenment in Asia, announced by Maharishi Mahesh Yogi! "He now plans to push his TM in Asia, and especially in India. Armed with the 'scientifically proven' datum that if 1 percent of the population practice TM, the whole of society is affected, he plans to train one teacher of TM for every 1,000 of the population and to that end is to set up 600 teacher-training centres here in India—one for every million people. It seems he is moving into lay-training in a big way! He is perfectly serious, and has the money to back it up."[13]

THE VATICAN OR THE KREMLIN

Themes: Church; False Teaching

A correspondent wrote to Bertrand Russell in 1953 that "the defeat of dogmatic Christianity" had only led to people embracing "newer and cruder theologies." In his reply, he said that for thirty years he'd believed "that the ultimate contest will be between the Vatican and the Kremlin" and that in this contest he'd side with the Vatican. The ground for his preference was, he added, "that religions, like wine, mature with age"![14]

CHURCH FELLOWSHIP AND UNITY

COUNTERFEIT LOVE

Themes: Church Fellowship and Unity; Friendship; Love; Pride; Satan

There is such a thing as "counterfeit love," especially in groups which agree with everyone only "in those things wherein they greatly differ from all others." This "is only the working of a natural self-love, and no true benevolence any more than the union and friendship which may be among a company of pirates that are at war with all the rest of the world." By contrast, "Christian love ... is a humble love. ... Love and humility are two things the most contrary to the spirit of the devil, of anything in the world; for the character of that evil spirit, above all things, consists in pride and malice."[15]

---

13. David Muir, letter to JRWS (1975).

14. Bertrand Russell, *Dear Bertrand Russell* (George Allen and Unwin, 1969).

15. Jonathan Edwards, *On Revival* (Banner of Truth, 1965), 117–18.

DISAGREEING WITHOUT BITTERNESS

Themes: Conflict; Leadership

Max Warren succeeded Wilson Cash as general secretary of CMS. During the latter's secretariat, CMS was involved in "an unhappy theological controversy." But Cash "never allowed controversy to dirty his soul. Bilious comment he always refused to respond to with bile. This was the gentleness not of a weak man but of a very strong one. … From Dr. Cash I learned that it is possible to disagree without bitterness even about the most deeply held convictions."

Later Max Warren wrote, in connection with his involvement in the ecumenical movement, "Charles Morgan has a wise sentence which runs 'a distinction necessary to civilisation—namely, the distinction between disagreeing with an opponent versus treating his opposition as heretical.' "[16]

THE FELLOWSHIP OF THE ENGLISH REFORMERS

Themes: Church Fellowship and Unity; Friendship

1. When the Reformation began in Cambridge, its adherents met in the White Horse Inn. Bilney, Robert Barnes, George Stafford, Matthew Parker, John Rogers, Miles Coverdale, and others met night after night to study Erasmus's *Novum Testamentum*. "So oft," wrote one of the younger members (Thomas Becon) in later years "as I was in their company, me thought I was … quietly placed in the new glorious Jerusalem" (p. 10).

2. In Lent 1554 the Tower was so crowded that Cranmer, Ridley, Bradford, and Latimer were placed in a common prison. "We four" (said Latimer) "were thrust into one chamber, as men not to be accounted of, but God be

16. Max Warren, *Crowded Canvas* (Hodder & Stoughton, 1974), 116–17; Charles Morgan, *Liberties of the Mind* (Morehouse-Barlow, 1959), 24.

thanked, to our great joy and comfort! There we did together read over the New Testament with great deliberation and painful study" (p. 124).[17]

IF ALL THEOLOGIANS WERE LAID END TO END

Themes: Church Fellowship and Unity; Conflict

A lay member of [the] London Diocesan Synod (Feb 19, 1972), deploring the theological arguments which he thought were hindering Anglican/Methodist unity, said: "If all the theologians in the world were laid end to end, they wouldn't reach a conclusion."

LEADERSHIP IN A CRISIS

Themes: Church Fellowship and Unity; Leadership

In 1917 Hensley Henson was nominated to [the] See of Hereford. In January 1918 Charles Gore, Bishop of Birmingham, wrote a formal protest addressed to Archbishop Randall Davidson, published in *The Times*. In it he quoted both the bishops' reaffirmation in 1917 that "the historical facts stated in the Creeds are an essential part of the Faith of the Church" and passages from Hensley Henson's published works which denied (or appeared [to]) all miracles, including the virgin birth and resurrection, while affirming [the] incarnation.

The protest entreated [the] archbishop and "my brother bishops," in [the] event of Hensley Henson being elected to [the] See, "to refuse him consecration." Otherwise he'd resign. [It was a] first-class crisis/row.

Davidson behaved admirably. He:

1. sent for Hensley Henson and listened, and wrote to Gore, "He quite distinctly and definitely does not deny the truths of the Creed as traditionally interpreted";

---

17. Marcus Loane, *Masters of the English Reformation* (Hodder and Stoughton, 1954).

2. sent for Gore [and] assured him Hensley Henson could "repeat and accept the words of the Creed ex animo." Then wrote to Gore.

3. saw them together. Gore was convinced: Hensley Henson "believes what I thought he disbelieved, and affirms ex animo what I thought he did not affirm." With this assurance, "I beg respectfully to withdraw my protest against his consecration."

LONELINESS IS A MODERN MONSTER

Themes: Church Fellowship and Unity; Loneliness

Janet Watts in *MGW* June 9, 1973, wrote [the] article "Lonesome Road." She began: "Loneliness is a sort of a modern monster. The primitive monsters used to live under gloomy lakes and come out to attack men in the dark of night: loneliness lurks in the depths of modern man's heart and comes out in the dark night of his soul."

The assumption is it attacks "only the weak, the fat, the failing, the foolish," while others claim to be exempt. "They're lying. Nobody is immune to the monster's depredations. Loneliness is as common to us all as birth, sex, or death: but of all these taboos it is perhaps the last to go. We have all known it, but we don't like admitting it. ... Nevertheless we are all born alone, we die alone, we dream alone: most of us work alone in one way or another. Living is primarily and ultimately solitary. Loneliness is a universal monster."

There follows a series of interviews with three housewives (married), a social worker (unmarried), and Frankie Howerd (the comedian). He says: "I think that one has to expect to be lonely. Everybody's lonely to some extent, because they have their own little life encased in their head, which is never completely understood by others." Imaginative people are inclined to be more lonely than others.[18]

---

18. Janet Watts, "Lonesome Road," *Guardian Weekly* (June 6, 1973).

LOVE, HOPE, NOT YET FAITH

Themes: Church Fellowship and Unity

Billy Graham told a meeting of around six hundred ministers in London on November 25, 1970 that he had spent time not long previously with the Apostolic Delegate in London. The latter said at the beginning of their conversation that they should be clear about their position: "We are together in love and in hope, but not yet in faith."

STABILITY DEPENDS ON FELLOWSHIP AND DEPTH

Themes: Church Fellowship and Unity; Friendship; Loneliness

Out on the mountains of Switzerland the fir tree is a national symbol. The hillsides are terraced with them, row upon row. The typical English tree is the oak, and its roots are said to go down as far as the tree grows up, to support its massive, sturdy dimensions.

But how shall the tall and stately pines stand firm against winds and snows, when their roots soon hit the rock and cannot grow deeper? It is said that the roots grow outward when they cannot grow downward, and the fibers intertwine with the roots of other trees, and they hold together. So stability depends on corporate fellowship as well as personal depth.[19]

TOGETHER IN PUBLIC, DIVERGENT IN PRIVATE

Themes: Church Fellowship and Unity; Marriage

In "The Secret Sin of Septimus Brope" by Saki, Mrs. Troyle expressed dismay at [the] thought of losing her maid Florinda. "I am sure I don't know what I should do without Florinda. ... She understands my hair." (I imagine she wore a wig.) "I've long ago given up trying to

---

19. Mrs. Laurie-Walker (1950).

do anything with it myself. I regard one's hair as I regard husbands; as long as one is seen together in public, one's private divergences don't matter."

WHITEFIELD TO WESLEY ON ELECTION

Themes: Church Fellowship and Unity; Election

In 1740 George Whitefield put it to John Wesley: "Since we know not who are elect, and who are reprobate, we are to preach promiscuously to all."

On October 10, 1741, George Whitefield wrote to John Wesley: "Reverend and Dear Brother ... I find I love you as much as ever and pray God, if it be his blessed will, that we may be all united together. ... May God remove all obstacles that now prevent our union! Though I hold Particular Election, yet I offer Jesus freely to every individual soul."[20]

CHURCH LEADERSHIP

ADVICE TO LUTHER ON STICKING TO ESSENTIALS

Themes: Church Leadership; Conflict; Counseling; Wisdom

Dr. Johann von Staupitz, vicar of the Augustinian order in Wittenberg which Luther joined, was Luther's confessor in his early days as a monk (1511→). He nominated Luther to succeed him at university in the chair of the Bible, and later out of solidarity with him resigned as vicar. Yet he found Luther extreme and intemperate in his utterances. He urged him to be more "humble," whereupon Luther wrote urging him to be "proud," i.e., to come out for Christ versus the pope. Later

---

20. John Pollock, *George Whitefield and the Great Awakening* (Hodder and Stoughton, 1973), 170, 185.

Luther wrote to Staupitz hoping he wasn't offended. Staupitz replied, shortly before he died, "My love for you is unchanged, passing the love of women … but you seem to me to condemn many external things which do not affect justification. Why is the cowl a stench in your nostrils when many in it have lived holy lives? There is nothing without abuse. My dear friend, I beseech you to remember the weak. Do not denounce points of indifference which can be held in sincerity, though in matters of faith be never silent" (*Weimarer Ausgabe Briefwechsel* 726).

BISHOPS WHO DO NOT TAKE ACTION

Themes: Church Leadership; Laziness and Apathy

Bishop Gore wrote, in a letter to [George] Bell about [Randall] Davidson (July 1931) about bishops who do not take action on rulings which have been secured: "I was reminded of a saying of Dr. Jayne's (of Chester), that the bishops were like the slothful man in Proverbs who fails to roast what he took in hunting."[21]

AN EXPERIMENT IN VISITATION EVANGELISM

Themes: Church Leadership; Evangelism

In his book *The Face of My Parish*, the Rev. Tom Allan writes about an experiment in visitation evangelism. The aims of the visitation, outlined by the Rev. D. P. Thomson, evangelist of the Church of Scotland, were these:

1. To carry the greetings of the Church to every home in the parish, irrespective of congregational or denominational tie

---

21. G. K. A. Bell, *Randall Davidson: Archbishop of Canterbury* (OUP, 1952), 1158.

2. To gather as much information as possible about the family and church connection in each home

3. To bring something of the wealth and variety of the Church's literature to those who never had either the time or the opportunity to see it

4. Where no vital church connection existed (and only in such cases) to extend an invitation to the parish church, and to suggest that a follow-up visit might be made by a representative of that church

5. To make a natural witness for Christ, and do such personal work as circumstances might permit or suggest[22]

J. C. RYLE'S COMMITMENT TO HIS PRINCIPLES

Themes: Character; Church Leadership; Leadership

Having been nominated to Liverpool, Ryle addressed the Bishopric Committee at some length, telling them he was "a convinced evangelical." "You know my opinions. I am a committed man. ... I am sure you would not want me to come among you as a milk and water bishop, a colourless bishop without any opinions at all."

At the same time, he held out the right hand to all loyal churchmen. After his enthronement, he was heard to say to some friends, "I have changed my clothes, but I have not changed my coat nor my principles."[23]

---

22. Tom Allan, *The Face of My Parish* (SCM, 1958), 22.

23. Eric Russell, *That Man of Granite with the Heart of a Child: A New Biography of J. C. Ryle* (Christian Focus, 2001).

SIMEON'S INFLUENCE EXCEEDED
THAT OF A PRIMATE

Themes: Church Leadership; Leadership

"Lord Macaulay, son of Zachary Macaulay, who was a friend of
[Charles] Simeon, wrote: 'As to Simeon, if you knew what his authority and influence were, and how they extended from Cambridge to the
most remote corners of England, you would allow that his real sway
over the Church was far greater than that of any Primate' " (from a
letter to his sister).

An earnest Christian in Cambridge University until compara-
tively modern times was known in undergraduate slang as a "sim"
[= Simeonite: a follower of Charles Simeon (1759–1836), i.e., a
low-churchman or evangelical].[24]

A TEAM NEEDS DIFFERENT STRENGTHS

Themes: Church Leadership; Holy Spirit: Gifts; Leadership

D. E. Hoste, Hudson Taylor's successor as general director of the
OMF, had much to say about leadership, or the need for God's people
to recognize, develop, and exercise their gifts. A leader "recognises
that people with one particular area of gifting often lack other gifts.
We need a team of people who bring different strengths. You cannot
bore a hole with a good hammer, or drive home a nail with a saw!"

[This was] number fifteen of his thirty-six qualities of leadership.

---

24. Quoted by Donald Coggan in *Stewards of Grace* (Hodder & Stoughton,
1958), 31; also by G. R. Balleine in *A History of the Evangelical Party in the Church
of England* (Longmans, Green and Co., 1951 [1908]), 103.

CHURCH AND STATE

THE AGE OF THE CHURCH OF ENGLAND

Themes: Nature of the Church

Ecclesia Anglicana, already mentioned in Magna Carta, is as old as the English nation, and had its roots in the still older church of the British people. This is not only a matter of historical fact but the law of the land. "The accepted legal doctrine is that the Church of England is a continuous body from its earliest establishment in Saxon times."[25]

CALVIN ON CIVIL DISOBEDIENCE

Themes: Government, Politics and National Identity; Obedience and Disobedience

Book IV, chapter XX of Calvin's *Institutes* is entitled "Civil Government." After thirty-one sections in which he gives a thorough treatment of the duties of magistrates; their exercise of force; laws and law courts; and the obedience of citizens, etc., section 32 is entitled "Obedience to man must not become disobedience to God."

- "But in that obedience which we have shown to be due the authority of rulers, we are always to make this exception, indeed to observe it as primary, that such obedience is never to lead us away from obedience to him, to whose will the desires of all things ought to be subject, to whose decrees all their commands ought to yield, to whose majesty their sceptres ought to be submitted.

- "And how absurd would it be that in satisfying men you should incur the displeasure of him for whose sake you obey men themselves! The Lord, therefore, is the King

---

25. *Halsbury's Laws of England*, vol. 13, p. 34.

> of kings. ... If they command anything against him, let it go unesteemed. And here let us not be concerned about all that dignity which the magistrates possess; for no harm is done to it when it is humbled before that singular and supreme power of God."

Calvin then quotes from Daniel 6 where "the king had exceeded his limits ... and abrogated God's power." Then, after further examples, he concludes by quoting Peter: "We must obey God rather than men" (Acts 5:29).[26]

A CATHOLIC BISHOP'S CONDEMNATION OF THE RHODESIAN GOVERNMENT

Themes: Church Leadership; Government, Politics and National Identity; Justice

Mgr. Donal Lamont, Roman Catholic Bishop of Umtali, Rhodesia, was charged in August 1976 with failing to report the presence of guerillas, and inciting others to commit [the] same offense. This followed his open letter to the government condemning its racist policies and holding it responsible for escalating violence. "How can one counsel loyalty and obedience to your ordinances when to do so is tantamount to giving approval to the manifold injustices you inflict? Conscience compels me to state that your administration by its clearly racist and oppressive policies, and by its stubborn refusal to change, is largely responsible for the injustices which have provoked the present disorder."[27]

---

26. John Calvin, *Institutes of the Christian Religion* (Westminster John Knox, 1960), 4.20.32.

27. *Church of England Newspaper* (September 3, 1976).

CHURCH AND STATE IN SCOTLAND, ENGLAND, AND THE UNITED STATES

Themes: Freedom; Government

1. The Church of Scotland Act (1921), while keeping a special position for the monarch, declared forthrightly that "this church, as part of the universal church wherein the Lord Jesus Christ has appointed a government in the hands of church office-bearers, receives from him ... the right and power subject to no civil authority, to legislate, and to adjudicate finally, in all matter of doctrine, worship, government, and discipline in the church."

2. In 1913 the convocations of clergy and laity in [the] Church of England (combined as the Church Representative Council) resolved that there is in principle religious and the spiritual independence of the Church.

3. [The] American "separation of church and state" was intended to prevent any law which might give preference to one religion over another. The US Constitution's First Amendment reads: "Congress shall make no law respecting the establishment of religion." This was not, however, intended to rule out or inhibit government support of religion—though that's how [the] First Amendment has come to be interpreted.

THE ESTABLISHMENT OF THE CHURCH OF ENGLAND

Themes: Nature of the Church; Government

The "establishment" of the Church of England is symbolized and/or expressed in:

1. the Crown, the monarch being head of state or "Supreme Governor" of the Church of England;

2. Parliament's right of veto over ecclesiastical legislation;

3. [the] prime minister's role in [the] Crown Appointments Commission (1976), in appointment of bishops (twenty-four of whom sit in Lords) and archbishops (negotiated by Callaghan because bishops sit ex officio);

4. [the] presence of archbishops and twenty-four bishops in [the] House of Lords (including [a] call for Roman Catholic, Free Church, Jewish, and Muslim leaders to sit in Lords too).[28]

HISTORIC PRAYERS ON BEHALF OF GOVERNMENT

Themes: Government, Politics and National Identity; Prayer: Intercession

- In Tertullian's *Liber Apologeticus* (AD 197): "We Christians … do intercede for all the emperors that their lives may be prolonged, their government be seemed to them, that their families may be preserved in safety, their senates faithful to them, their armies have, their people honest, and that the whole empire may be at peace …" and he quotes 1 Timothy 2:2 as his reason. He goes further and says that only the continuance of Rome's empire delays "the great upheaval which hangs over the whole earth."

- Liturgy of St. Mark: "Preserve our King in peace, in virtue, and righteousness. … Subdue his enemies under him … incline him to peace towards us and towards Thy Holy Name, that in the serenity of his reign we too may lead a quiet and tranquil life in all piety and honesty." (Cf. Liturgies of St. Clement and St. Chrysostom.)

- Trinity 5: "Grant, O Lord, we beseech Thee, that the course of this world may be so peaceable, ordered by Thy governance, that Thy Church may joyfully serve

---

28. Clifford Longley, *The Times* (May 19, 1990).

Thee in all godly quietness through Jesus Christ our
Lord."

- Prayer for Church Militant also quotes from 1 Timothy
  2:2: "Almighty and everliving God, who by Thy only
  apostles hast taught us to make prayers and supplica-
  tions and to give thanks for all men ... we beseech Thee
  also to save and defend all Christian Kings ... and especially Thy servant George our King that under him we
  may be godly and quietly governed."

- A second prayer for [the] king: "... study to preserve
  Thy people committed to his charge in wealth, peace
  and godliness."

CONVERSION

AUGUSTINE'S ACCOUNT OF HIS
CONVERSION FROM *CONFESSIONS*

Themes: Conversion

Augustine was born in North Africa (Numidia = our Eastern Algeria)
[in the] mid-fourth century. Already in his teens he had become dis-
solute, even promiscuous, enslaved by passion. "Love and lust boiled
within me and swept my youthful immaturity over the precipice of
evil desire, to leave one half-drowned in a whirlpool of abominable
sins" (2:ii).

Yet [he was] dissatisfied and depressed. He also plunged into
study, and his studies took him to Carthage, then Rome, then Milan.
Yet in his mind he was torn between Christianity ([which he] rejected),
Manichaeism ([which he] embraced), and [the] secular pursuit of
philosophy, logic, mathematics, and astronomy. In this turmoil of
moral shame and intellectual confusion, "I was in utter misery" (6:vi).
Yet through his moral and mental restlessness God was pursuing,

as also through the prayers and tears of his mother Monica and the kindly teaching of Bishop Ambrose of Milan.

As with Saul of Tarsus, the climax came suddenly. Throwing himself down in the garden, weeping in great distress, he heard a child's voice repeat "take and read" (*tolle lege*). He got up and read Romans 13:13f. "Not in orgies and drunkenness, not in sexual immorality and debauchery ... but put on the Lord Jesus Christ and don't consider how to gratify the desires of your sinful nature."

"In that instant, with the very ending of the sentence it was as though a light of utter confidence shone in my heart and all the darkness of uncertainty vanished" (8:xii). Augustine attributed it entirely to God's grace: "With your calling and shouting you broke my deafness. With your flashing and shining you scattered my blindness. At your scent I drew in my breath. ... You touched me, and I am on fire for your peace" (x:38).

BEATING THE DRUM WITH JOY

Themes: Conversion; Joy

[A] Cockney drummer in [a] Salvation Army band was beating [his] drum too hard and making [a] fearful din, so that [the] bandmaster told him to quieten down a bit. [The drummer responded,] "Gawd bless you, since oi've been converted, oi'm so 'appy, 'oi cld *bust* the bloomin' drum."

THE CONVERSION OF TRAN THUYEN

Themes: Conversion

Tran Thuyen is Vietnamese, [the] son of a Confucianist father and a Buddhist mother. But to him "religion was ... nothing but superstitious mummery. Good only for ignorant, illiterate country women." [He was] sent by [his] parents to [a] French Roman Catholic secondary school at Hue, where like other boys [he was] "reciting prayers, ... crossing myself, and looking devout and angelic. But in my heart of hearts I loathed the whole thing." At [the] same time [he] became [a] fanatical nationalist, read revolutionary literature in secret, and became convinced that Christianity [was] invented by French colonialists to rob and dominate [the] Vietnamese people forever.

After World War II [he] came to France and worked in [the] Vietnamese Embassy in Paris, until in 1954 [he became] ill and had to spend two years in [a] French sanatorium. [During this time,] age-old questions began to form in [his] mind: "Where did I come from? Why am I here? Where am I going?" He restudied Confucianism and Buddhism, but [the] "thing failed to satisfy me." [He was] given [a] New Testament which he began to read avidly, "as if it were the most exciting novel." He came to see he was defiled, God loved him, Christ died for him, and "I accepted the Lord Jesus as my personal Saviour."

"For the true believer God becomes real. ... New habits of thought begin to take shape in his mind; he begins to have a new scale of values ... he has new norms, new motives, new ambitions. He acquires new spiritual tastes. ... A new power to overcome sin appears. ... These changes ... are signs of a new life given to us."

In brief, 2 Corinthians 5:17![29]

CONVERSION MAY COME IN MANY SHAPES

Themes: Conversion; Creativity

In *The Moon and Sixpence* (1919), Somerset Maugham portrays Charles Strickland, the dull London stockbroker, who left wife, family, home, and job because of an obsession to paint. Returning from Paris, where he tried to persuade him to return, the author

---

29. Tran Thuyen, *The End of the Search* (IVP, 1975).

reflects on how the creative instinct had seized him. He sees it as analogous to "the way in which the spirit of God has seized men, powerful and rich, pursuing them with stubborn vigilance till at last, conquered, they have abandoned the joy of the world and the love of women for the painful austerities of the cloister."

"Conversion may come under many shapes, and it may be brought about in many ways. With some men it needs a cataclysm, as a stone may be broken to fragments by the fury of a torrent; but with some it comes gradually, as a stone may be worn away by the ceaseless fall of a drop of water."[30]

FEAR OF HELL PROMPTED HIS CONVERSION

Themes: Conversion; Fear; Hell; Pride

Dr. Paul Wiesner, PhD of Vienna, of Jewish parentage, engaged in cancer research, described his experience to me on February 17, 1961: "I had no need of religion. I was *full* of self-confidence. My conceit was fantastic. I was bloated with conceit."

Then he was struck by an illness and paralyzed, and admitted to National Hospital for a brain operation. The night before, a great fear seized him. "I was frightened that I might be called to account for my life by some Superior Being. I was frankly terrified of hell. It was terrible." He sent for [a] parson friend but before [the] parson arrived, he found peace. "It all happened in 20 minutes." [He was] baptized after [an] operation which was largely successful.

---

30. W. Somerset Maugham, *The Moon and Sixpence* (Penguin, 1919), 53.

HAS ATHEISM CHANGED LIVES?

Themes: Atheism; Conversion

Dr. Harry Ironside, of Chicago, was once publicly challenged to debate by an atheist. He gave his reply as follows: "I accept on these conditions—first, that you promise to bring with you to the platform one man who was once an outcast, a slave to sinful habits but who heard you, or some other lecturer on agnosticism, was helped thereby and became a new man, and is today a respected member of society, all because of your unbelief. Second, that you agree to bring with you one woman who was once lost to all sense of decency, but who can now testify that agnosticism came to her while deep in sin and implanted in her mind a loathing of impurity and a love of holiness; put a new power into her life and delivered her from her base desires, so that she is now a sweet, clean, chaste woman, all through her belief in the Bible.

"Now, sir, if you will agree, I promise to be there with *one hundred* such men and women, once lost souls, who heard the Gospel of Jesus Christ, believed it, and have found new life and happiness in Him. Will you accept my terms?"[31]

"I WAS UNBELIEVABLY HAPPY"

Themes: Conversion; Forgiveness

A student at Newcastle University came to a meeting in the Debating Chamber in February 1973. He was not a Christian, but had been brought up in spiritualism. The following weekend the battle for his soul began in earnest, and on the Sunday (attending his Christian girlfriend's baptism) he confessed Christ publicly. But the next day he was still assailed by doubts and worries until, with a Christian

---

31. G. R. Beasley-Murray, *Can Honest Men Become Christians?* (1950).

friend, he cried in despair to Christ to save him. Then—"He really came to me. I felt actual, real love, I can't describe it. It was just pure beauty and serenity, and despite the fact that I knew nothing about salvation and sin, and did not even know what it meant, I just *knew* I was forgiven. ... I was unbelievably happy."[32]

LETTER FROM A MUSLIM INQUIRER

Themes: Conversion; Cults and Non-Christian Religions

Mohamed Mahmud Fahnmy, from the Maldive Islands, a Muslim whose late father was the chief justice, wrote January 1, 1970 (after attending watchnight service):

> I am writing to say that I feel a deep seated urge to be baptised as a Christian. ... I believe that Christianity alone can give a meaning to my life. I have not come to this decision on the spur of any moment. I have seen the light of Jesus Christ shining through the cob web woven by Mohammed. ... I face a serious crisis of personal identity and I need to make a public profession as early as possible ... yet I shudder to think of the step I am contemplating taking![33]

METAPHORS FOR GOD'S PURSUIT OF LEWIS

Themes: Conversion; Providence; Sovereignty of God

For some time before his conversion, C. S. Lewis was aware God was pursuing him. In *Surprised by Joy* he piles up metaphors to illustrate the divine pursuit:

1. God was "the great Angler" playing his fish, "and I never dreamed that the hook was in my tongue" (p. 199).

---

32. Letter to JRWS from David Whitton (March 3, 1973).
33. Letter to JRWS from Mohamed Mahmud Fahnmy (January 1, 1970).

2. God was like a cat chasing a mouse. "Amicable agnostics will talk cheerfully about 'man's search for God.' To me they might as well have talked about the mouse's search for the cat" (p. 214).

3. God [was] like a pack of hounds. "The fox had been dislodged from the Hegelian wood and was now running in the open. ... Bedraggled and weary, hounds barely a field behind. And nearly everyone was now (one way or another) in the pack" (p. 212).

4. God was the Divine Chessplayer, gradually maneuvering him into an impossible position. "All over the board my pieces were in the most disadvantaged positions. Soon I could no longer cherish even the illusion that the initiative lay with me. My Adversary began to make His final moves" (p. 205). So C. S. Lewis calls his penultimate chapter "Checkmate."[34]

"A NEW MAN IN A NEW WORLD"

Themes: Conversion

Dr. Ole Hallesby, professor of theology in the Free Faculty [of Theology] in Oslo for forty years, described his expression of new birth in [a] chapter headed "a new man in a new world": "An entirely new world was opened to me. Quietly and wonderfully I was lifted into the presence of God. As tho' I had been endowed with a sixth sense, I felt the world of invisible things which surrounded me. I see now that this invisible world had surrounded me before, but I lacked the faculties with which to apprehend it and to participate in its life."

---

34. C. S. Lewis, *Surprised by Joy* (Geoffrey Bles, 1955).

THE STORY OF A CONVERSION

Themes: Conversion; Doubt; Revelation

"About 2 years ago I began to seek God and was greatly helped by your book *Basic Christianity*. Until then I had been led to believe that doubt, honest or otherwise, made me unacceptable to God. The prayer on p. 19 spoke to me as though it had been written just for me. I made it my own, and challenged God to make himself known to me. Gradually I was brought face to face with Jesus Christ and in January 1977 accepted him as my Saviour and Lord. Praising him that he led you to write that book."[35]

THE TRANSFORMATION OF DAVID MENDEL

Themes: Conversion

David Mendel (b. 1789) was [the] son of a German Jewish peddler and moneylender. He was ungainly in figure, so that he was usually teased at school. But he had a brilliant mind. The year after leaving school (which was in 1805) at age seventeen he became a Christian and was baptized.

So great was the change in him that he assumed new names: "Johann August Wilhelm Neander," honoring by [the] first three friends who'd helped him to Christ, and in [the] last Christ, who'd made him a "New Man."

[He was] later professor of church history (1813) at [the] newly established University of Berlin.

---

35. Letter to JRWS from Miss C. Kimber of Battersea (October 19, 1978).

THE UNREPENTANT GANGSTER

Themes: Conversion; Discipleship; Repentance

By 1949 Mickey Cohen was "top man in the Los Angeles under-world," handling half a million dollars a day from his gambling casinos. "Nothing happened in that glittering town without his say-so."

Late that year Jim Vaus, one of Cohen's associates, told Cohen how he [had been] converted at Billy Graham's Los Angeles crusade. Jim made thorough restitution for his dishonesty, selling his house and car to pay back the $15,000 [in] electronic equipment he'd stolen. Cohen called him and offered [to] lend him a car. "I'm working for a new boss now, Mickey. There are new rules. I can't take something that somebody got through crime."

Then in 1951 Mickey was convicted and jailed for five years for tax evasion. Bill Jones, introduced to Mickey by Jim Vaus, visited him in jail and led him to Christ, but told him nothing of repentance. He flew to New York and attended a Madison Square Garden meeting in which Billy Graham stressed repentance. Cohen returned to Los Angeles but dropped Bill Jones and Jim Vaus. "He began hanging around with his underworld cronies again."

Bill Jones went to remonstrate with him. "Jones, you never told me that I had to give up my career. ... There are Christian movie stars, Christian athletes, Christian businessmen. So what's the matter with being a Christian gangster? If I have to give up all that—if that's Christianity—count me out."[36]

---

36. Charles Colson, *Loving God* (Zondervan, 1983), 81–92.

COST OF DISCIPLESHIP

"COUNT THE COST" ON A ROAD SIGN

Themes: Discipleship

A road safety campaign was organized in 1958 in Sydney. Seizing the opportunity afforded by the tollgates which give access onto the famous Harbour Bridge, the campaign displayed a huge poster for motorists to see. Underneath a big central clock were the words, "Time to think. Count the Cost. Safety is priceless."

FOLLOWING CHRIST REQUIRES "UPHEAVALLING"

Themes: Commitment; Discipleship

A first-year music student at University of Western Ontario, London, had been brought up in a convent but had no personal experience of Jesus Christ. She very much wanted this but realized it would be a costly business—"upheavalling" was her word to describe the changes Christ would have to make.[37]

THE GUERRILLA'S NEED FOR SELF-CONTROL AND SELF-SACRIFICE

Themes: Calling; Commitment; Discipleship; Discipline

Che Guevara outlined his ideals and practical policies of revolution in *Guerrilla Warfare* (1960). He sees the guerrilla as "a crusader for the people's freedom" and emphasizes the need for self-control and self-sacrifice. "He must be an ascetic … and must always aid the peasant technically, economically, morally and culturally." The guerrilla must be timeless, heroic, stoical, resilient, healthy. He must be ready

---

37. Letter to JRWS (November 1956).

to endure every privation, hunger, thirst, illness, wound, fatigue, and torture. The ideal which sustains him "must be simple, direct, not elaborate nor visionary. But it must be so firm and so clear that a man can, without the least hesitation, sacrifice his life for it."[38]

THE OLD TESTAMENT AS RADICAL LITERATURE

Themes: Commitment; Government

The Nazi police once asked Martin Buber, the Jewish scholar, whether he was harboring any radical literature. "Yes" replied Buber, and handed them a copy of the Jewish Scriptures.

PELLAT'S FOLLY

Themes: Commitment; Discipleship

Major-General Sir Henry Pellatt, CVO, DEL, VD, was a gallant and brilliant soldier, a champion athlete, and excellent marksman. His royalist sympathies were so great that he determined to build a magnificent castle in Toronto to accommodate royalty on their visits to Canada. The work began in 1911. Stonemasons were brought from Scotland and took a year to build the outside garden wall. Three bronze doors in [the] castle were made in exact replica of some in an Italian palace. The bathrooms were fitted with fourteen-karat gold taps. The stables had Spanish mahogany stalls with bronze fittings. The basement was supplied with a tiled swimming pool, a two-hundred-foot rifle range, and a bowling alley.

But Pellatt had miscalculated his fortune. He spent three million dollars on his castle and went bankrupt. The castle has never been finished, and no royal couple has ever entered it. Pellatt lived there by himself in one little room and died a miserable pauper. "Pellatt's

---

38. Andrew Sinclair, *Che Guevara* (Fontana, 1970), 34–35.

Folly" stands out prominently in Toronto today as a warning to those who forget to count the cost.

WILLING TO GIVE UP THE CANARY

Themes: Conversion; Love; Repentance

A boy had [a] canary of which [he was] very proud. But his mother fell ill, and the bird's singing disturbed her. [The] boy carried it to [the] top of [the] house, but [it] still could be heard. So [he] gave it away to [a] school friend. [The] mother [said]: "[I] thought you were so fond of Dicky."

"So I am, Mum, but I'm much fonder of you."

DEVOTIONAL LIFE

BASKING IN JOHN 14–15

Themes: Scripture

Extract from a letter to the Rev. J. R. W. Stott from a young architect in March 1967: "I am basking, nay wallowing drunkenly in John 14, 15 at the moment. I must have read these words and thrilled over them so many times, yet still they set the heart on fire."[39]

E. STANLEY JONES'S EXPERIENCE OF ABUNDANT LIFE

Themes: Faith; Prayer; Peace

Stanley Jones describes how eight years of strain as a missionary in India had broken him. Even after furlough he kept collapsing. He saw that unless he regained his health, his missionary career was in ruins.

---

39. Letter to JRWS from Chris Boyce (March 1967).

Then during a meeting at Lucknow, while in prayer, a Voice seemed to tell him to turn his problem over to the Lord. He did.

> A great peace settled into my heart and pervaded me. I knew it was done! Life—abundant life—had taken possession of me. I was so lifted up that I scarcely touched the road as I quietly walked home that night. Every inch was holy ground. For days after that I hardly knew I had a body. I went through the days, working all day and far into the night, and came down to bedtime wondering why in the world I should ever go to bed at all, for there was not the slightest trace of tiredness of any kind. I seemed possessed by Life and Peace and Rest—by Christ himself. … I seemed to have tapped new Life for body, mind and spirit. Life was on a permanently higher level. And I had done nothing but take it![40]

"HOW DO YOU GET YOUR QUIET TIME?"

Themes: Prayer

A Christian in the north of England tells of a woman who lived in one room in a poor part of that town. The Christian worker said to her, "How do you ever get your quiet time?" to which she replied, "I puts me apron over me head and shuts meself in with the Lord!"

THE LIFE OF BROTHER LAWRENCE

Themes: Presence of God; Prayer; Work

Brother Lawrence, or Nicholas Herman of Lorraine, who after working as soldier and then footman, was admitted a lay brother in Carmelite Community in Paris in 1666. "He was cook to the society"; he was a "great awkward fellow who broke everything"; and he was lame. But "in his business in the kitchen (to which he had naturally a great aversion)," he learned to practice the presence of God. "When the

---

40. E. Stanley Jones, *The Christ of the Indian Road* (Hodder and Stoughton, 1925), 29–31.

appointed times of prayer were past, he found no difference, because he still continued with God," until he could say: "I am come to a state wherein it would be as difficult for me not to think of God as it was at first to accustom myself to it." "In short, I am assured beyond all doubt that my soul has been with God above these thirty years."[41]

PASCAL'S "SECOND CONVERSION"

Themes: Conversion; Revelation; Vision

Blaise Pascal (b. 1623) had already mastered Greek and Latin aged twelve, and became [an] inventive mathematical genius. Nominally Roman Catholic, the family became Jansenists in 1646 within [the] Roman Catholic Church. When his father died in 1651 he became worldly but found no satisfaction. Then [as he] read John 17 on November 23, 1654, God revealed [him]self to him in fire from around 10:30 p.m.–12:30 a.m.

He wrote on parchment, and later [it was] sewn inside the lining of his coat (discovered after his death):

> God of Abraham, God of Isaac, God of Jacob, not of the philosophers and scholars. Certitude. Certitude. Feeling. Joy. Peace. God of Jesus Christ. "Thy God shall be my God." Forgetfulness of the world and of everything, except God … Joy, joy, joy, tears of joy. … This is eternal life (John 17:3). JESUS CHRIST … let me never be separated from Him. … Renunciation, total and sweet.
>
> Total submission to Jesus Christ and to my director. Eternally in joy for a day's training on earth. Amen!

[This was] often called his "second conversion." Thereafter [he] lived for God, not self, and became Jansenist solitary.

[He] died [in] 1662, aged thirty-nine.

---

41. Brother Lawrence, *The Practice of the Presence of God* (F. H. Revell, 1900).

A VERY PRACTICAL BOOK

Themes: Scripture

On my last day at Harvard University (February 19, 1957), I sat in Lowell House dining hall having breakfast. Several students and I were discussing getting up in the mornings, and quiet times. "I find the Bible a very practical book," said a fourth-year philosophy student. "I always keep it at my bedside, so that when my alarm clock goes off at the other end of [the] room, I have something to throw at it."

He later told me he used the Interpreter's Bible. I wondered if [the] reason was that it has twelve volumes, so that he had twelve rounds of ammunition by his bed!

WALKING WITH CHRIST IN LOVE

Themes: God's Love; Union with Christ

In 1805 Henry Martyn set sail from Falmouth for India. The voyage took nine months. He was only actually twenty-four and, cultured and delicate, not at all at home on board among rough crew, soldiers, etc. He had also left his love (Lydia Grenfell) behind.

"At last the Lord hath appeared for the comfort of His creature. In prayer launched sweetly into eternity. … Thy work may be prosecuted best by my soul's remaining in heaven. The transcendent sweetness of the privilege of being always with God would appear to me too great were it not for the blessed command 'set your affection on things above.' "

Again—"Separated from my friends and country for ever, there is nothing to distract me from hearing 'the voice of my Beloved,' a coming away from the world and walking with Him in love, amid the flowers that perfume the air of paradise."[42]

---

42. Henry Martyn, *Journals and Letters of the Rev. Henry Martyn: In Two Volumes*, ed. Samuel Wilberforce (Seeley and Burnside, 1837), 1:314, 384.

In 1805 Henry Martyn set sail from Falmouth for India. The voyage took 9 months. He was eng. aet. 24 and; cultured a delicate, not at all at home on board among rough crew, soldiers etc. He had also left his love (Lydia Grenfell) behind. "at last the L. hath appeared for the comfort of this creature. In prayer launched sweetly into eternity.... Thy work may be prosecuted best by my soul's remaining in heaven. The transcendent sweetness of the privilege of being always with God would appear to me too great, were it not for the blessed command 'Set your affection on things above'.[4] again — "Sep'. fr. my friends & country for ever, there is nothing to distract me fr. hearing 'the voice of my Beloved', a coming away fr. the world & walking with Him in love, amid the flowers that perfume the air of paradise". (Henry Martyn p. 73)

Abiding

EVANGELISM

AN EXAMPLE OF HENRY TRUMBULL'S APPROACH TO EVANGELISM

Themes: Alcohol; Evangelism

H. C. Trumbull was traveling one November from New York to Boston in [a] crowded train. [He] sat next to [a] red-faced young sea captain who presently took out a large bottle of whiskey and a metal drink cup and offered them to him. [He] declined. Later [this was] repeated. "Don't you ever drink, my friend?" "No, my friend, I do not." "Well, I guess you think I am a pretty rough fellow." Trumbull then, instead of rebuking him for evil ways, graciously replied, "I think you are a very generous hearted fellow."

They got into conversation. H. C. T. found he was going home to Massachusetts for Thanksgiving. "I asked him about his mother, and he spoke lovingly and tenderly of her. He said he knew she was praying for him constantly. This brought us into close quarters." (pp. 80–82).[43]

A FREEDOM FIGHTER OF A DIFFERENT KIND

Themes: Conversion; Evangelism

A German student at Heidelberg University called Peter had been active in 1968–1969 with his fellow students organizing strikes and demonstrations to change the establishment.

Six years later he wrote that his student friends of 1969 were now "either internationally-known terrorists in the underground or resigned." What had happened to him, however? Why didn't

---

43. C. G. Trumbull, *Taking Men Alive: Studies in the Principles and Practise of Individual Soul-Winning* (YMCA, 1907).

he continue in the way of violent revolution? Let him give his own answer: "It began one day when I met a credible Christian"—one who took him seriously, made time to listen, didn't contradict his theories, but asked searching questions about issues. Now he's a freedom-fighter of a different kind.[44]

RESOLVE TO PRACTICE EVANGELISM

Themes: Conversion; Evangelism

Charles G. Trumbull in *Taking Men Alive* devotes a whole chapter to what he calls "The Need of a Life Resolve." He relates how his father (Henry C. Trumbull) had been surprised as a young man of twenty-one that an intimate friend of his who was converted said nothing to him of it, and only wrote it to him some time later. The letter led to his conversion. He immediately spoke to an office associate and fellow boarder about his decision and discovered to his astonishment that his friend was a secret disciple!

These two incidents, involving the silence of two friends, greatly influenced Trumbull. They led him to make a purpose and resolve for life, namely that "wherever I am in such intimacy with a soul as to be justified in choosing my subject of conversation, the theme of themes shall have prominence between us, so that I may learn his need, and if possible meet it" (pp. 68–69).[45]

---

44. Bernstein, article in *On the Offensive,* organ of the Reichenberg Fellowship (1975/1976).

45. C. G. Trumbull, *Taking Men Alive: Studies in the Principles and Practise of Individual Soul-Winning* (YMCA, 1907), 68–69.

SPURGEON'S EARLY DEDICATION TO EVANGELISM

Themes: Evangelism; Joy

C. H. Spurgeon converted on January 6, 1850. On June 11, 1850, [he] wrote to his mother: "I have 70 people whom I regularly visit on Saturday. I do not give a tract and go away; but I sit down and endeavour to draw their attention to spiritual realities. I have great reason to believe the Lord is working" (p. 166). [This was] eight days before his sixteenth birthday!

His first convert gave him such rejoicing that he wrote: "If anybody said to me, 'Someone has left you £20,000,' I should not have given a snap of my fingers for it, compared with the joy I felt when I was told God had saved a soul through my ministry" (p. 167).[46]

THE TACT AND LOVE OF GEORGE WILLIAMS, FOUNDER OF THE YMCA

Themes: Evangelism; Love

Tact and love seem to have been notable characteristics of Sir George Williams, YMCA founder. When asked for advice as to how to tackle a young man, he'd say, "Don't argue; take him to supper" (p. 103).

G. W. used to tell [the] story of how they won a young fellow (Rogers) who was greatly opposed. When anyone converted, he'd pounce on him with "we'll soon take all that nonsense out of you." This fellow was [the] organizer and chairman of the "free-and-easy" held on Saturday evenings at [an] adjoining pub, The Goose and Gridiron. First they prayed. Many weeks. Hostility grew. G. W. asked if he was specially fond of anything: [he said he had] a passion for oysters. "Let's give him an oyster supper then," said G. W.

---

46. Richard E. Day, *The Shadow of the Broad Brim: The Life and Legacy of Charles Haddon Spurgeon* (Judson, 1955).

They selected [the] best man to invite him. [He] accepted. [It was a] lively evening. G. W. had given strict instructions that [there should be] no attempt at proselytizing.

He concluded these Christians [were] not so black as [they had been] painted. As [a] return for [their] hospitality, he later consented to attend one of their meetings. [He] converted. And his name is among the first twelve members of the YMCA (pp. 104–5).[47]

TWO STORIES OF HESITATING TO EVANGELIZE

Themes: Evangelism

On one occasion D. L. Moody played tennis a whole afternoon, without mentioning religion, with a young fellow who was expecting to be buttonholed at once, and was ready to resent it. It was after he had won the young fellow to himself that he won him for Christ (p. 44).

Frances Ridley Harvergal during the school holidays used to have some of the village girls at the rectory to teach them singing. But she never spoke to them on spiritual things. Years later, she was asked to visit a dying woman, whom she discovered to be a former pupil from her singing class. "I often wished in those days that you would speak to me about my soul, and I often lingered at the gate when the others had gone, hoping you would do so, but you never did. Sometime afterwards someone else led me to the Saviour, but I ought to have been yours, Miss Frances, I ought to have been yours" (p. 103).[48]

---

47. C. G. Trumbull, *Taking Men Alive: Studies in the Principles and Practise of Individual Soul-Winning* (YMCA, 1907).

48. Edward Last, *Hand-Gathered Fruit* (Prairie Book Room, 1963).

FAITH AND DOUBT

A BELIEF OF THE MIND DOESN'T ALWAYS LEAD TO A TRUST OF THE HEART

Themes: Doubt; Faith

[Charles] Blondin used to walk on [a] tightrope over Niagara Falls. Once he did so with [a] wheelbarrow. [He asked a] small boy on the bank, "Do you believe I could wheel you over?"

"Yes."

"Will you let me?"

"No!"

[Here is an instance of] a belief of the mind *not* leading to a trust of the heart!

BRINGING AN UMBRELLA TO THE PRAYER MEETING

Themes: Faith

Christians in Jamaica [were] called to prayer by [the] pastor [because the country] greatly needed rain. As [they] prayed, torrents fell. But only [one] little girl had really believed he would answer; she showed her faith by bringing her umbrella to [the] prayer meeting!

DIFFERENT KINDS OF EVIDENCE

Themes: Doubt; Faith

Writing in *A Lawyer Among the Theologians* about different kinds of evidence, admissible and inadmissible in a court of law, Norman Anderson points out that whereas in a *criminal* trial the accused's guilt must be proved "beyond reasonable doubt," in a *civil* case a "preponderance of probability" is sufficient. Moreover, in a *criminal* case, according to Lord Denning in *Miller v. Minister of Pensions*, "proof beyond a reasonable doubt does not mean proof beyond a shadow of doubt." Anderson adds, "This is something very different from conclusive proof."[49]

"NEARER, MY GOD, TO THEE"

Themes: Comfort; Doubt; Hope

Sarah Flower Adams wrote "Nearer, My God, to Thee" in 1840. It became a favorite of Queen Victoria and later King Edward VII ([and was] played at his funeral). And when on April 14, 1912 the "unsinkable" *Titanic* struck an iceberg in [the] North Atlantic and sank, Baptist pastor John Harper (who chose to remain on board because there were not enough lifeboats, once his daughter was safely on one) asked [the] ship's orchestra to play it. It's a hymn which has brought comfort and hope to many.

Yet few know that Sarah Flower Adams was tormented with doubts, and after her father's death in 1829 suffered for four years a complete breakdown. She once wrote to a Unitarian minister (W. J. Fox), "I have a firm belief in a Resurrection—at least I think I have—but my mind is in a sad state. ... I must endeavour to build up my decaying faith. How is it to be done? I would give worlds to [be] a sincere believer, to go to my Bible as I used to, but I cannot." That was in her twenties. She was thirty-five when she wrote the hymn.

REFUSING THE OFFERED TEA

Themes: Evangelism; Faith; Salvation

F. B. Meyer [went] out to tea with [a] lady. [When] offered a cup, [he] ignored it. She tried to draw his attention to it, but he took no notice. When she became impatient, he turned to her and said, "Madam, that

49. Norman Anderson, *A Lawyer Among the Theologians* (Hodder and Stoughton, 1973), 23–24.

is exactly what you are doing to God. He is offering you salvation, and you will not take it."

ROCK OF AGES

Themes: Faith

In Mendip Hills in Somerset (near [the] village of Blagdon), [a] road runs through [a] deep ravine called Burrington Coombe. At [one] end stands a great gray rock one hundred feet high, with [a] slanting cleft which forms a deep cave.

One day in 1762, Augustus Toplady, curate of Blagdon, [was] overtaken by [a] storm [and] took refuge in [the] cleft. While thunder rumbled and lightning flashed, and he was safe and dry, he remembered Isaiah 26:4: "Trust ye in the Lord forever, for the Lord is a Rock of ages." Looking round he saw [a] playing card ([the] six of diamonds) and wrote on it [the] first words of [the] hymn "Rock of Ages."

THREE TYPES OF BELIEF

Themes: Faith

[We] use [the] word "believe" loosely to convey several shades of meaning, for example:

i.   I believe in ghosts, fairies, God = Belief in Fact

ii.   I believe in aspirins, communism, Christianity = Belief in Value

Both [of the above are] intellectual.

iii.   I believe in Dr. Jones = such a belief in his existence (fact) and competence (value) that [makes one] ready to trust him

TWO STORIES OF FAITH LEADING TO OBEDIENCE

Themes: Faith; Obedience and Disobedience

1. [A] signalman's child [was] playing on [a] railway line. [His] father shouted from [the] signal box, "Lie down," and he did so, [the] express thundering over him. [The] boy's prompt obedience saved him. He obeyed, though he could not see [the] reason [cf. Jeremiah 38:20!] (p. 53).

2. [A] French general sent [a] man onto [the] bridge of Basle to stay one hour one afternoon, watch everyone closely, and report. [He] watched [a] girl selling flowers, soldiers, children, [a] man with [a] stick who tapped three times with it on [the] parapet as [he] crossed. [An] hour passed and [the] watcher returned, disappointed. But [the] general's eye brightened when he heard about three taps, for it was [the] prearranged signal telling him to attack [the] neighboring fortress that night. Neither [the] tapper nor [the] watcher knew why [he had been] sent. But both obeyed (p. 54).[50]

FALSE TEACHING

JIM BAKKER'S FALSE DOCTRINE

Themes: False Teaching; Greed; Money; Repentance

After years of Bible study in prison, Jim Bakker, the jailed televangelist, confessed, "I had been teaching false doctrine for years and hadn't even known it! ... I had been doing just the opposite of Jesus' words by teaching people to fall in love with money." He then proceeds to critique his own sermons.[51]

---

50. G. R. Balleine, *Children of the Church* (Home Words Publishing, 1950).

51. Jim Bakker with Ken Abraham, *I Was Wrong: The Untold Story of the Shocking Journey from PTL Power to Prison and Beyond* (Thomas Nelson, 1996).

FALSE GOSPELS ARE LIKE MULES

Themes: False Teaching

False gospels and half gospels, according to Peter Kuzmic at Lausanne II in Manila (July 1989), are like mules: They have "neither pride of ancestry nor hope of posterity."

FAMILY

BUILDING THE HOME AROUND THE CHRIST CHILD

Themes: Family; Birth of Jesus

It is said that in Switzerland while a newly planned wooden chalet is only a skeleton, a little trimmed Christmas tree is brought and placed up in [the] roof among the rafters. The little Christmas tree is a symbol of the Christ child, and as the house is built up around the tree, so the future occupants declare their resolve to build their home around the Christ child and let him have the prominent place.[52]

CHILDREN BETTER OFF WITH NO PARENTS

Themes: Family: Children; Family: Parents

"It would often be better if children had no parents at all."

—Earl of Shaftesbury

NB: Shaftesbury's father was a bully, his mother a "friend," and his childhood was very unhappy. His insecurity and depressions were probably attributable to this.[53]

---

52. Mrs. Laurie-Walker (1950).

53. Anthony Ashley Cooper, *Speeches of the Earl of Shaftesbury* (Chapman and Hall, 1868), 240.

HOW TO TURN A CHILD INTO A DELINQUENT

Themes: Family: Children; Family: Parents

A circular issued by the police department of Houston, Texas, which is both a warning and an accusation:

FOR PARENTS: HOW TO MAKE A CHILD
INTO A DELINQUENT—12 EASY RULES

1. Begin at infancy to give the child everything he wants. In this way he will grow up to believe the world owes him a living.

2. When he picks up bad language, laugh at him. This will make him think he's cute.

3. Never give him spiritual training. Wait until he is twenty-one and then [let] him "decide for himself."

4. Avoid the use of the word "wrong." It may develop a guilt complex. This will condition him to believe later, when he is arrested for stealing a car, that society is against him and he is being persecuted.

5. Pick up everything he leaves lying around: books, shoes, clothes. Do everything for him so that he will be experienced in throwing all responsibility on others.

6. Let him read any printed matter he can get his hands on. Be careful that the silverware and drinking glasses are sterilized, but let his mind feast on garbage.

7. Quarrel frequently in the presence of your children. In this way they will not be too shocked when the home is broken up later.

8. Give a child all the spending money he wants. Never let him earn his own. Why should he have things as tough as you had them?

9. Satisfy his every craving for food, drink, and comfort. See that every sensual desire is gratified. Denial may lead to harmful frustration.

10. Take his part against neighbors, teachers, policemen. They are all prejudiced against your child.

11. When he gets into real trouble, apologize for yourself by saying: "I never could do anything with him."

12. Prepare for a life of grief. You will be likely to have it.[54]

"NEVER LEAVE A CHILD IN THE DARK"

Themes: Health and Healing; Mission; Family: Parents

In Florence Nightingale's "Notes on Nursing" (1859) she mentions on the first page the evil effects of "the want of fresh air, or of light, or of warmth."

In [the] chapter "Health of Houses," the longest of her five sections deals with light. "A dark house is always an unhealthy house, an ill-aired house, a dirty house."

And in her added final chapter to girls on "Minding Baby," she writes: "Plenty of light, and sunlight particularly, is necessary to make a child active, and merry and clever. ... Never leave a child in the dark."

FORGIVENESS

GOD'S PARDON AND A PRESIDENTIAL PARDON

Themes: Forgiveness; Guilt; Repentance

In September 1974, President Gerald Ford announced that he was granting ex-President Nixon a "full, free and absolute pardon." He was doing so under Article II, Section 2 of the Constitution, which says

---

54. G. Ingle, *The Lord's Creed* (Collins, 1964), 40–41.

the president "shall have power to grant reprieves and pardon offences against the United States."

At first hearing, the pardon sounded very Christian, for doesn't pardon lie at the root of Christianity? But further thought raises questions and reveals fundamental differences between the pardon of God and the pardon granted by President Ford.

1. God's pardon covers offenses against law, and the presidential pardon too concerns "offenses v. the United States." But [the] ex-president has not confessed to any offenses, only to [an] error of judgment. So how can Ford pardon what Nixon says he has never committed?

2. God pardons those on whom his judgment justly rests. Traditionally the presidential pardon has been used to right wrongs, i.e., the injustice of someone wrongly convicted. But not only has Nixon not confessed to any offense, but he has never been tried, let alone convicted.

3. God does not pardon arbitrarily, but *offers* pardon to those who repent of their offense and accept it. How can Nixon accept a pardon for offenses he has never acknowledged?

Conclusion: A real offense, a real guilt, and a real repentance are required for a real pardon.

GUILT IN THE FAMILY REUNION

Themes: Guilt; Purity

In T. S. Eliot's verse play *The Family Reunion*, Harry, returning home for his mother's birthday, confesses how one night in [the] mid-Atlantic he'd pushed his wife overboard. His feelings of guilt are well nigh unbearable.

"It's not being alone that is the horror. ... What matters is the filthiness."

"I can clean my skin, purify my life, void my mind, but always the filthiness, that lies a little deeper."[55]

JOHN WESLEY ON FORGIVENESS AND SIN

Themes: Forgiveness; Sin

When John Wesley was serving as a missionary in Georgia, he was much opposed by General James E. Oglethorpe (founder of the colony of Georgia), who had a reputation for pride and stubbornness. "I never forgive," he once said, to which Wesley responded, "Then I hope, Sir, you never sin."

JOMO KENYATTA'S EMPHASIS ON FORGIVENESS

Themes: Forgiveness; Neighbors

After his final release from Maralal on August 14, 1961, after eight and a half years' detention and his return to Kikuyu land, some ten thousand Africans turned up to welcome Mzee Kenyatta to Gatundu. To reporters who crowded round he said: "I do not feel bitter towards anyone at all, because I know my cause and my activities were just. I regard everybody as my friends. You know the commandment 'love thy neighbour.' Well, the world is my neighbour."

Similarly, when independence came on December 12, 1963, there was no recrimination. Now the great task was Kenyan unity by "harambee," meaning "pull together."

Cf. also *Suffering without Bitterness* (1968), which contains Mzee Kenyatta's own account of events leading to independence and major speeches since 1963.

---

55. T. S. Eliot, *The Complete Poems and Plays* (1909–50) (Harcourt, Brace), 235–69.

At the state opening of parliament after Kenya became a republic in December 1964, Kenyatta said: "This is not a moment, Honorable Members, for Kenya to be bitter, or to seek retaliation or revenge" (p. 264).

In his foreword to *Suffering without Bitterness* he recalls his speech on Kenyatta Day 1964 in which he proclaimed "that the foundation of our future must lie in the theme forgive and forget" (p. xv).[56]

LADY MACBETH'S GUILT

Themes: Forgiveness; Guilt

Burdened with an intolerable weight of guilt, restless and sleepless, Lady Macbeth paces to and fro in the early hours of the morning. Obsessively and compulsively she rubs her hands and cries out: "Out, damned spot! out, I say! One: two: Why, then, 'tis time to do't: Hell is murky! ... Yet who would have thought the old man to have had so much blood in him? ... Here's the smell of the blood still: all the perfumes of Arabia will not sweeten this little hand. Oh! Oh! Oh!"

Her husband, on hearing the story later, questions the doctor:

Canst thou not minister to a mind diseas'd,
Pluck from the memory a rooted sorrow,
Raze out the written troubles of the brain,
And, with some sweet oblivious antidote
Cleanse the stuff'd bosom of that perilous stuff
Which weighs upon the heart?

The doctor replies that there is no remedy known to man: "Therein the patient must minister to himself."[57]

---

56. Jeremy Murray-Brown, *Kenyatta* (Allen and Unwin, 1972), 306–7.
57. William Shakespeare, *Macbeth*, Act 5, Scene 3.

PEOPLE WANT TO CONFESS

Themes: Confession; Forgiveness; Guilt

People with a guilty conscience have an urgent need to talk to someone who'll listen and to get their problem off their chest. When a new TV talk show opened in Los Angeles in 1988, the promoters were astounded that people called in not [to talk] about politics or to air their opinions but to get things off their chest. Within a week the program's name was changed to *Phone Confessions*. Soon two hundred people a day were phoning to confess or apologize to a mechanical answer machine. The confessions were then edited and played back, and between two thousand and fourteen thousand people called daily to eavesdrop on people baring their souls.

[On the show,] a soothing female voice says, "Have you ever done something you feel badly about? Call me at Phone Confessions, (213) 654-1055, to leave your own message. Tell someone how you feel or tell someone that you're sorry. Maybe apologize. And now let me play some more phone confessions." [The show was] so lucrative that soon a second Los Angeles service opened, and two in New York.

STEVE BIKO'S MOTHER ON FORGIVENESS

Themes: Forgiveness; Reconciliation; Truth

Steve Biko was killed in prison in 1977, beaten into a coma in Port Elizabeth by security police. He was thirty-eight, and South Africa's leading anti-apartheid campaigner. His mother Alice, shortly before her death in 1996, said: "Yes, I would forgive my son's killers. I am a Christian, and we Christians do forgive. But first I must know who to forgive and what to forgive, which means I must be told fully what happened and why." About a year after her death five men applied to South Africa's Truth and Reconciliation Commission for amnesty, confessing to his murder.[58]

FRIENDSHIP

THE BEST OF FRIENDSHIPS IS TEMPORARY

Themes: Friendship

In my parish (some years ago), there were two boys, one was [a] Greek boy from Cyprus, [the] other was [an] English boy. The Greek boy [was] called Andreas (Andrew), the English boy [was] called Philip. They both attended our church school. Andrew was tall; Philip was short. Andrew was dark, with glossy black hair; Philip was fair, with wavy blonde hair. They were seldom separated. Tall dark Andrew and short fair Philip were often seen walking through [the] streets.

Then one day suddenly [a] blow fell. I think Philip's father lost [his] job; anyway they had to pack up home in [a] hurry and move to [the] Midlands.

I can still see Andrew's tall dark figure walking alone through [the] streets. *Of course* they could visit each other and write. But it wasn't the same. The best of human friendships is temporary.

FRIENDSHIP IN *PILGRIM'S PROGRESS*

Themes: Friendship

Faithful: "I saw in my dream they went very lovingly on together, and had sweet discourse of all things that had happened to them in their pilgrimage."

After Faithful's martyrdom in Vanity Fair, his place was taken by Hopeful: "I saw in my dream that Christian went not forth alone; for

---

58. *Guardian Weekly* (February 9, 1997).

there was one whose name was Hopeful ... who joined himself unto him and, entering into a brotherly covenant, told him that he would be his companion"—which he was until they reached the end of their pilgrimage, crossed the river, and entered the Celestial City together.[59]

HUMAN NATURE

CHURCHILL'S AWARENESS OF HUMAN NATURE

Themes: Sin; Wisdom

In the memorial service for Sir Winston Churchill in York Minster on January 31, 1965, Donald Coggan mentioned his understanding of human nature: "He was conscious of the fact that man, who 'has conquered the wild beasts and ... even the insects and the microbes ... has only to conquer his last and worst enemy—himself.' These are not the words of a moralising preacher but of Sir Winston, shrewd enough to see not only the potential nobility of man but also his potential self-destructiveness."[60]

DAG HAMMARSKJÖLD'S UNDERSTANDING OF HIS OWN SIN

Themes: Pride; Sin; Service

Dag Hammarskjöld, secretary general of [the] UN, a deeply committed public servant, described by W. H. Auden as "a great, good and lovable man" (p. 24), had a different opinion of himself. He defined original sin as "that dark counter-centre of evil in our nature" (p. 128) and bemoaned it in himself. He wrote in his diary on April 7, 1957:

---

59. John Bunyan, *The Pilgrim's Progress* (Collins, 1953).
60. Donald Coggan, *Convictions* (Hodder and Stoughton, 1975), 302.

Not to brood over my pettiness with masochistic self-disgust, not to take a pride in admitting it—but to recognise it as a threat to my integrity of action, the moment I let it out of my sight.

How selfish and aesthetic our so-called "sympathy" usually is. There come times when, momentarily we can serve as the foundation for somebody else's faith in himself—a faith which is constantly being threatened in all of us. ... [This] makes our unselfish service of others the foundation for our own self-esteem.

Success—for the glory of God or for your own, for the peace of mankind or for your own? Upon the answer to this question depends the result of your actions (p. 128).

And on October 1, 1957: "You have allowed your hunger for 'justice' to make you self-conscious, so that, in the performance of your task, you no longer forget yourself" (p. 137).[61]

THE GREATNESS OF CYRIL GARBETT

Themes: Humility; Sin

On his eightieth birthday Cyril Garbett wrote at length in his diary (Feb 6, 1955). That day he received many greetings and tributes, including the GCVO: "People have been undeservedly kind, they have formed an ideal picture of myself—the devoted pastor, the kindly old gentleman, and the courageous prophet! They don't see me as I really am, selfish, self-centred, seeking and enjoying the praise of men, lazy, possessive, and timid."

Yet, comments Charles Smyth his biographer, none who knew him could "fail to recognise that in this, the truest and profoundest meaning of the phrase, he was indubitably 'a great man.' "[62]

---

61. Dag Hammarskjöld, *Markings* (Faber, 1964).

62. Charles Smyth, *Cyril Forster Garbett, Archbishop of York* (Hodder and Stoughton, 1959), 424.

THE HINDU UNDERSTANDING OF SIN

Themes: Cults and Non-Christian Religions; Salvation; Sin

Dr. Anandkumar said at Bermuda [in January 1978]: "A Hindu will never admit that he needs a Savior. Not because he doesn't acknowledge he's a sinner, but because he believes he can save himself—by Karma, by bhakti (devotion, dedication and duty to God) and by ceremonial washing. Vivekananda said, 'It's a sin to call a man a sinner.' "

"I LIKE TO TALK ABOUT MYSELF"

Themes: Pride

1. "I like to talk about myself. It's my favourite hobby." These are the first words of the biography of A. E. Matthews, the distinguished actor known as "Matty," published by Hutchinson in 1952.

2. James Agate, the literary critic, wrote his autobiography in eight volumes, entitled "Ego One," "Ego Two," and "Ego Three." The third volume was published in 1938, and Mr. Agate includes on the frontispiece the expostulation of a friend, "Really, James, you are becoming a megalomaniac!"

THE PROBLEM OF THE HUMAN SELF

Themes: Pride; Sin

Norman Mailer, an American political journalist, wrote [a] book called *Advertisements for Myself*. Reviewing his next book in [the] *Manchester Guardian Weekly, Cannibals and Christians*, Martin Green writes: "The self that Mailer advertises is a very contemporary-American thing, very aggressive and exhibitionist. ... Above all, it is a self intensely conscious of being a self."

In [the] same *MGW* Alex Comfort reviews Arthur Koestler's *The Ghost in the Machine*, which expounds man's dilemma "with the growth of primatology." Writes Comfort, "No animal is so irrationally belligerent, so easily provoked by wholly internal processes into self-destructive behaviour." The remedy he chooses is "a super-tranquilliser which will reconcile emotion with reason pharmacologically, an insight-giving drug."

UTOPIA, TEXAS, IS NO UTOPIA

Themes: Death and Dying; Sickness; Sin

Utopia is the name which Sir Thomas More gave to the imaginary island he described in his book (1516), which enjoyed unspoiled social perfection. Yet the Greek derivation of the word is οὐ "not" and τoπoς "place," i.e., no such place has ever existed, or will exist.

Yet there's a small town in West Texas (around sixty miles west of San Antonio) called Utopia. Its inhabitants adopted this name for their community at the instigation of a TB sufferer from Alabama who found its climate health-giving.

But Utopia, Texas, is no utopia. It has one jail, one hospital, and two cemeteries—i.e., sin, crime, disease, and death have not been banished from it.

WHAT IS MAN?

Themes: Sin

What Is Man? by Mark Twain purports to be a conversation between OM (old man) and YM (young man). The OM is a freethinker, expressing Mark Twain's opinions, while the YM is a naïve believer. The overriding concern is [to argue that] man's sole impulse is "the securing of his own approval" (p. 20). Every act springs from but one motive, viz. "the necessity of appeasing and contenting one's own spirit" (p. 29).

There's no such thing as self-sacrifice, only self-satisfaction. So his is the "gospel of self approval" (p. 45).[63]

HUMILITY

BAXTER, A PEN IN GOD'S HAND

Themes: Humility; Obedience and Disobedience

When on his deathbed a friend comforted Richard Baxter with the remembrance of the good many had received from his writings, he replied, "I was but a pen in God's hand, and what praise is due to a pen?"[64]

DEFENDING OTHERS, EXAMINING ONESELF

Themes: Anger; Humility

Holding a mission in Edinburgh, an evangelist fell to criticizing the resident ministers in the city and, among them, Dr. James Hood Wilson of the Barclay Church.

A man who heard the criticism called [the] next day on Dr. Alexander Whyte. "I went to hear the evangelist last night, Dr. Whyte," he began, "and do you know what he said? He said that Dr. Hood Wilson of the Barclay was not a converted man."

Alexander Whyte leapt from his chair in anger. His fine face went dark with indignation. "The rascal!" he said. "The rascal! Dr. Wilson not a converted man!" The visitor was amazed to see a saint so furious. So he went on. "That wasn't all he said, Dr. Whyte," he continued. "He said that you were not a converted man either!"

---

63. Mark Twain, *What Is Man?* (Watts for Rationalist Press Association, 1910).
64. J. C. Ryle, *Light from Old Times* (Evangelical Press, 1980), 339.

Whyte stopped in his stride. All the fire went out of him. Sinking into his chair, he put his face in his hands, and for a full long minute he did not speak. Then, looking up, he said to his visitor with awful earnestness: "Leave me, friend; leave me! I must examine my heart."[65]

THE FALSE HUMILITY OF URIAH HEEP

Themes: Humility; Pride

No one has depicted false humility better than Dickens in his description of Uriah Heep. Aged fifteen, when David Copperfield first set eyes on him, he had close-cropped red hair, a cadaverous face, no eyebrows or eyelashes, and "a long, lank skeleton hand" (p. 275). His characteristic saying was to call himself "very humble" (p. 291). He had a way of writhing (p. 292), and when he shook hands, "his hand felt like a fish in the dark" (p. 293). He seems to have learned his deferential servility from his mother, who said, "'Umble we are, 'umble we have been, 'umble we shall ever be" (p. 313).[66]

GOD CHOSE HUDSON TAYLOR BECAUSE HE WAS WEAK ENOUGH

Themes: Humility; Weakness

Looking back in 1894, at the age of sixty-two, on nearly thirty years of proving that "God is sufficient for God's work," Hudson Taylor, the leader of more than six hundred missionaries then active in China, said: "God chose me because I was weak enough. God does not do His great works by large committees. He trains somebody to be quiet enough, and little enough and then He uses him."[67]

---

65. W. E. Sangster, *The Pure in Heart* (Epworth, 1954), 161–62.
66. Charles Dickens, *David Copperfield* (Penguin, 1985).
67. John Pollock, *Hudson Taylor and Maria* (Hodder and Stoughton, 1962), 130.

THE GOSPEL ENTHRONES HUMILITY

Themes: Gospel; Humility

R. C. Trench in his *Synonyms of the New Testament* writes that since the gospel of Christ came into the world "to put down the mighty from their seat, and to exalt the humble and meek," it is not surprising that "it should dethrone the heathen virtue *megalopsuchia* and set up the despised Christian grace *tapeinophrosuné* in its room."

The very word *tapeinophrosuné* "is itself a birth of the gospel," since no Greek writer used it before Christ, nor after Christ apart from Christian influence, although it occurs in [the] LXX.[68]

"IF YOU ARE HUMBLE ENOUGH, YOU CAN DO ANYTHING"

Themes: Humility

The family crest of the Carlile family has one word on it: "Humilitate" [with humility]. Wilson Carlile faithfully lived up to it. In later years he used to say, "If you are humble enough, you can do anything."[69]

"LET THE NAME OF WHITEFIELD DIE"

Themes: Humility; Pride; Temptation

Converted in 1735 and ordained [in] 1736, aged only twenty-one, George Whitefield's preaching ministry was blessed from the start, large crowds attending and many experiencing new birth: "Morning, noon and night he was caught up in the unexpected revival. ... He was now carried along on a high tide of popularity until he grew

---

68. R. C. Trench, *Synonyms of the New Testament*, 8th revised ed. (Macmillan, 1876), 142–43.

69. Marie Carlile Hale, *Yours in the Fight, Wilson Carlile* (SPCK, 1945), 9.

terrified of pride and would steal away to plead, 'Lord, take me by the hand and lead me unhurt through this fiery furnace. Help me to see the vanity of all commendation but thine own' " (p. 47).

By 1749, "Men were now speaking of Wesleyans and not, as in the first flush of the revival, of Whitefieldians. George Whitefield did not mind. 'No, let the name of Whitefield die,' he wrote in the spring of 1749, 'so that the cause of Jesus Christ may live. I have had enough popularity to be sick of it' " (p. 239).[70]

THE LITTLE SERVANT OF AN ILLUSTRIOUS MASTER

Themes: Humility; Service

Hudson Taylor was being introduced by a Presbyterian moderator in Melbourne. He was the visiting missionary speaker. The introduction was effusive and ended with a reference to "our illustrious guest."

"Dear friends," began Hudson Taylor, "I am the little servant of an illustrious Master."[71]

THE PRICE OF J. B. PHILLIPS'S SUCCESS

Themes: Depression; Humility; Pride; Victory and Defeat

J. B. Phillips, celebrated author of *The New Testament in Modern English*, entitled his autobiography *The Price of Success* (Hodder and Stoughton, 1984). He writes with complete candor about the terrible depression which engulfed him (and nervous collapse) in the early '60s. He describes how "the springs of creativity were dried up and the ability to communicate disappeared overnight" (p. 197), and how

---

70. John Pollock, *George Whitefield and the Great Awakening* (Hodder and Stoughton, 1973).

71. Warren W. Wiersbe, *Walking with the Giants* (Baker, 1976), 61.

he experienced "hellish torments of mind" (p. 201). He is also brave enough to introduce his book with a section entitled "The Price of Success" (p. 9):

> I was in a state of ... excitement throughout the whole of 1955. ... I was tasting the sweets of success to an almost unimaginable degree ... my future prospects were rosier than my wildest dreams could ever suggest; applause, honour and appreciation met me wherever I went. ... I was not ... aware of the dangers of success. The subtle corrosion of character, the unconscious changing of values and the secret monstrous growth of a vastly inflated idea of myself seeped slowly into me ... it is very plain to me now why my one man kingdom of power and glory had to stop.[72]

SELF-PREOCCUPATION AND SELF-FORGETFULNESS

Themes: Humility; Pride

1. Alcibiades, the gifted but unscrupulous Greek, was noted as an unhappy man. Someone asked Socrates why it was that he, who had traveled so much, was such an unhappy man. Socrates replied: "Because wherever Alcibiades goes, he always takes himself with him."

2. Festo Kivengere, bishop designate of Kigezi, said at Keswick 1972: "You've only got to take the throne of your personality and sit yourself on it, and you see at once that you are conspicuously too small for it."

3. Consecrated December 1972 with nearly eleven thousand present, Festo was anxious regarding the splendor of his episcopal robes. He quoted his friend Hohama Omazi, when made first Archbishop of Tanzania: "I want to be like the little donkey our Lord chose to ride on to enter Jerusalem. They laid their robes on it and shouted, but the shouting was all for the Lord Jesus, whom it was carrying."

---

72. J. B. Phillips, *The Price of Success* (Hodder and Stoughton, 1984).

STILL BEGINNING AT EIGHTY

Themes: Humility; Work

Michelangelo was apprenticed to Ghirlandaio at [the] age of thirteen. So rapid was his progress that soon [he was] able to copy great masters without anyone easily telling [the] copy from [the] original. Despite the fact [that] he is known all over [the] world as the creator of the Sistine Chapel painting and as perhaps [the] greatest painter of history, he was never really satisfied with his achievements. All through his long life he never ceased to learn his craft. When asked at [the] age of eighty what he was doing with a sketching book in the Colosseum, he replied, "Beginning."

"THINK IT POSSIBLE YOU MAY BE MISTAKEN"

Themes: Humility

It was on August 3, 1650 that Oliver Cromwell wrote to the General Assembly of the Church of Scotland, "I beseech you, in the bowels of Christ, think it possible you may be mistaken."

WE LEARN HUMILITY IN WORSHIP

Themes: Humility; Worship

William Temple, like many other Christian leaders, was engaged in a lifelong struggle for humility, and found it in worship. "There is nothing big enough to hold a man's soul in detachment from the centre of himself through all the occupations of life except the majesty of God and his love; and it is in worship, worship given to God because he is God, that man will most learn the secret of real humility."[73]

---

73. F. A. Iremonger, *William Temple, Archbishop of Canterbury: His Life and Letters* (OUP, 1948), 503–4.

WOLSEY'S ADVICE TO FLING AWAY AMBITION

Themes: Humility; Pride

Wolsey to Thomas Cromwell: "Cromwell, I charge thee, fling away ambition: By that sin fell the angels, how can man then, the image of his Maker, hope to win by it?" (Shakespeare, *King Henry VIII*, Act III)

And Cardinal Wolsey knew from experience what he was talking about. For Wolsey must have been one of [the] most ambitious men who has ever lived. Indeed, pride and ambition were his downfall.

INTEGRITY

"WHAT IS GOOD ACTING BUT CONVINCING LYING?"

Themes: Character; Hypocrisy

Laurence Olivier, actor, producer, director of the National Theatre 1962–1973, was made [a] life peer [in] 1970 [and] died [in] 1989. "I have never been conscious of any need other than to show off." And "I am far from sure when I am acting and when I am not. For what is good acting but convincing lying?"

MCDONALD'S, GOD, FAMILY

Themes: Character; Hypocrisy; Work

The founder of McDonald's was an evangelical Christian. According to Os Guinness at Lausanne II in Manila (July 1989), he once said: "I believe in God, my family, and McDonald's. But when I go to the office, I reverse the order."

LEISURE

THE CHRISTIAN BEGINNINGS OF FOOTBALL CLUBS

Themes: Sabbath and Rest; Work

On Saturday afternoons, over a million spectators watch League matches. At 5:30 p.m. many more switch on [the] radio to hear [the] BBC announce football results.

But how many know that several of [the] best-known professional teams sprang from church clubs like ours?

1. Aston Villa, six-time winners of [the] FA Cup, was started by some young fellows [who were] members of Wesleyan Chapel, Aston Villa, Birmingham, [in] 1874.

2. St. Jude's Institute Football Club. Recognize it? Encouraged by [a] parson (Gordon White), [this] club started in 1885. If [I] tell you [they played in] Queen's Park, [you may] know [the] name changed in 1888 to Queen's Park Rangers.

3. Bolton Wanderers [was] begun by teachers and boys of Christ Church Sunday School Bolton. Paid one day a week football sub. First called "Bolton Wanderers" in 1877.

4. Southampton sprang from [a] side first connected with St. Mary's. Called "Southampton St. Mary's" in 1880s. Still called "The Saints."

So a saint can play football? Certainly! [It is a] fine, clean game—[a] game Christian fellows [would be] proud to play. As Paul said, "Present [your] bodies"—not corpses!

On Sat'y. p.m. over a million spectators watch League matches. At 5.30 p.m. many more switch on radio to hear B.B.C. announce Football results.

But how many know that several of best known professional teams sprang fr. clubs like ours?

(1) Aston Villa, 6 × winners of F.A. cup, was started by some young fellows members of Wesleyan Chapel, Aston Villa, Birmham 1874.

(2) St. Jude's Institute Football club. Recognize it? Encouraged by parson (Gordon White) club started in 1885. If tell you Queen's Pk, know name changed in 1888 to Q.P. Rangers.

(3) Bolton Wanderers begun by teachers + boys of ch. Sunday School Bolton. Paid 1ᵈ a week football sub. Re-called "B.W." in 1877.

(4) Southampton sprang fr. side 1ˢᵗ connected with St. Mary's. called "Southampton St. Mary's" in 1880ˢ. Still called "the Saints".

So a saint can play football? Certainly! Fine, clean game. Game Xtian fellow proud to play. As Paul said "Present bodies" — Not corpses!

Football

EXPLAINING CRICKET TO AN AMERICAN

Themes: Sabbath and Rest

Brian Johnston, the well-known cricket commentator, tells the story
of an Englishman trying to explain a game of cricket to an American:

> You have two sides. One out on the field and one in. Each
> man on the side that's in, goes out; and when he's "out" he
> comes in, and the next man goes in until he's "out." When
> they're all "out," the side that's out on the field comes in, and
> the side that's been in goes out and tries to get "out" those
> coming in. Sometimes you get men still in and "not out."
> When both sides have been in and out, including the "not
> outs," that's the end of the game.

THE VOWS OF THE ANCIENT OLYMPICS

Themes: Character; Discipline; Perseverance

The Greek games were held in Delphi, Nemea, Olympia, and
Poseidon. Before they began, each athlete, with his father or trainer,
would enter the arena, stand before a huge statue of Zeus, and make
three vows: that

1. he had trained for ten months (discipline)

2. he would compete according to the rules (fairness)

3. he would endure (perseverance)

MARRIAGE

BACK PAIN AND DIVORCE

Themes: Divorce; Marriage; Stress

In the waiting room of a Harley Street oculist in December 1976, I was skimming through one of the Sunday color supplements and found an article on backs and back pain. It included this sentence: "If we accept that back pain can be the outbreak of psychological tension, some people will cure their pain by changing their jobs, their husbands, and their wives."

THE DECLINE OF MARRIAGE IN THE TWENTY-FIRST CENTURY

Themes: Homosexuality; Marriage

Peter Tatchell, director of OutRage!, on why homosexual relationships should not attempt to mimic marriage: "In the twenty-first century, marriage is losing its relevance, even to heterosexual men and women. It belongs to an earlier, bygone era. Moreover, *there is no moral or practical reason why it should remain the sole, exclusive basis* on which legal rights are conferred on partnerships.

"Marriage is often touted as a symbol of love and commitment. But love and commitment can exist both inside and outside marriage. Wedding vows merely formalise pre-existing feelings of affection and loyalty, but they play no part in creating or sustaining those feelings."[74]

---

74. Peter Tatchell, *Church of England Newspaper* (July 2001).

THE FOUR THINGS MARTIN LUTHER
KING JR. LOOKED FOR IN A WIFE

Themes: Family: Husbands; Family: Wives; Marriage

The second time Martin Luther King Jr. met his future wife Coretta, while they were both students in Boston, he said to her in the car:

> "You have everything I have ever wanted in a wife. There are only four things, and you have them all." Somewhat flurried, I said, "I don't see how you can say that. You don't even know me."
>
> "Yes, I can tell," he said. "The four things that I look for in a wife are character, intelligence, personality, and beauty. And you have them all. I want to see you again. When can I?"[75]

IS DIVORCE PERMITTED?

Themes: Counseling; Divorce; Marriage

As a young pastor at the beginning of the twentieth century, Otto Dibelius found that "the most common form of pastoral counselling in the west end of Berlin was to assist people when their marriages had come to grief. ... At first I was inclined to regard dissolution as the only course where a marriage had long ceased to be a marriage—though I never actually counseled divorce. But with experience I became firmer and more decided as the years went by. Finally I said this: 'Divorce, except for adultery, is forbidden by our Lord Jesus Christ, and anyone purposing to seek divorce is guilty before God. If the other party has committed adultery, then the duty of love is to forgive. The marriage vow is binding beyond all estrangement.

75. Coretta Scott King, *My Life with Martin Luther King, Jr.* (Hodder and Stoughton, 1970), 69.

Separation, yes, if nothing else works; divorce, no.' As a pastor I cannot say more on the basis of God's word."[76]

PROBLEMS WITH COHABITATION

Themes: Courtship; Dating and Romantic Relationships; Marriage

On November 14, 1987, the *Los Angeles Herald Examiner* carried an article about the growing disenchantment with premarital cohabitation. It begins, "Living together is out." "Area psychologists agree that the social experiment that reached its zenith in the early 1970s is coming to an end."

Walter Brackelmanns, an associate professor of clinical psychiatry at UCLA, who has watched the situation for twenty years, says: "Living together doesn't work. ... There really is no commitment until marriage. It has been thought that it would better prepare one for marriage. But in many cases it has worked the opposite way. It has been a way of avoiding commitment."

Especially the woman in the partnership wants to define the relationship. Women are increasingly "impatient with their partner's inability to make a long term commitment." "It's almost an anti-commitment, living together," said one of them.

THE RISE OF OPEN MARRIAGE

Themes: Divorce; Marriage

George and Nena O'Neill write in *Open Marriage: A New Life Style for Couples* (New York: Evans, 1972) that monogamous marriage is now obsolete. They urge their readers to replace an "archaic, rigid,

---

76. Otto Dibelius, *In the Service of the Lord* (Holt, Rinehart and Winston, 1964), 95.

outmoded, oppressive, static, decaying, Victorian" institution with one that is "free, dynamic, honest, spontaneous, creative."[77]

MARRIAGE IS "A SCHOOL FOR CHARACTER"

Themes: Character; Marriage

Luther, who married a former nun called Katharina von Bora, called marriage "a school for character."

THE MARRIAGE THEOLOGY OF SUN MYUNG MOON

Themes: Adultery; Family: Children; Marriage

Sun Myung Moon of [the] Unification Church teaches blessing through marriage and pronounces Jesus a failure because he never married and had children. By contrast Moon had two by his first wife, one illegitimate child when he was young, and thirteen by his second wife. This fathering of children was to reverse [the] consequences of [the] fall = adultery.

In 1982 in Madison Square Garden, New York, he married around two thousand couples, and later [the] same year nearly six thousand in Seoul, Korea. These are arranged and are cemented first by a wine ceremony ([with] twenty ingredients, including [the] blood of Moon and his wife) and then a blessing ceremony. By these marriages Moon hopes to overcome racial and national barriers and unify humanity. But around 90 percent of Moonies eventually secede.

---

77. Quoted in George Gilder, *Sexual Suicide* (Quadrangle, 1973), 46ff.

MISSION

AFFLUENCE AS A MISSIONARY PROBLEM

Themes: Mission; Money

In his *Missions and Money: Affluence as a Western Missionary Problem* (Orbis, 1991), Jonathan J. Bonk, a Mennonite from Winnipeg Theological Seminary, argues that missionary affluence alienates missionaries, contradicts the incarnational model, and hinders the spread of the gospel.

In 1938 Tambaram recognized the problem of missionary wealth, and in the '30s Donald McGavran founded a "Fellowship for Ventures in Simpler Living," which lasted only two or three years; it created too much friction. "Affluent missions are becoming increasingly marginalized in the great spirit mission of the church."

CONDUCTING MISSION ON INDIGENOUS PRINCIPLES

Themes: Mission

In an official statement issued about 1850, Henry Venn, general secretary of CMS, described the ultimate object of a missionary as [the] creation of "a Native Church under Native pastors upon a self-supporting, self-governing and self-extending system." When this goal is reached, he went on, "the Mission will have attained its *euthanasia*."

NB: this "euthanasia" means the death of [the] mission/missionary in their original role. Such a death may, however, lead to a rebirth, either (a) in a changed role ("fraternal worker," "service organization"); or (b) in another pioneer missionary situation.

One man guided by these principles was Alfred Tucker, the third bishop of Eastern Equatorial Africa (consecrated 1890). He was an unusual combination of artist and athlete, and for more than two decades sought to guide the young Uganda Church according to indigenous principles. He wanted an African church with an African

Bible and an African ministry, supported by African money. In 1909 the "Uganda Native African Church" was established, and by the time Tucker retired in 1911 the number of Ugandan Christians had grown from 200 to about 75,000.

"I HAVE A CANDLE IN MY HEART"

Themes: Mission; Power

During the 1978 Lambeth Conference John Falope, bishop of Ilesa diocese in Nigeria, spoke of his strong desire for the gospel to spread. "I have a candle in my heart," he said, with his hand on his chest, "and I bring it to the Lord Jesus to light. Then I call my three archdeacons, and they light their candles from mine. Then they take their lighted candles to the clergy, and the clergy take theirs to the laity. So the light and the fire will spread."

INCARNATION IN MISSIONS

Themes: Birth of Jesus; Mission; Service

In a guide to would-be candidates [to become missionaries,] Hudson Taylor wrote, "Let us, in everything not sinful, become Chinese, that by all means we may save some. Let us adopt their costume, acquire their language, study to imitate their habits, and approximate to their diet as far as health and constitution will allow. Let me live in their houses, making no unnecessary alterations in external form, and only so far modifying their internal arrangements as attention to health and efficiency for work absolutely require.

"This cannot of course be attained without some measure of inconvenience. ... But will anyone reflect on what He gave up who left heaven's throne to be cradled in a manger ... and yet hesitate to make the trifling sacrifice to which we have alluded?"[78]

---

78. Marshall Broomhall, *The Man Who Believed God* (China Inland Mission, 1946), 125.

JESUS' COMMANDS TO COME AND GO

Themes: Discipleship; Evangelism; Mission

[The] first command of Jesus to which we must respond is "Come!" But as soon as we have come to him, we hear his second command, "Go! Go home to your friends and tell them. … Go and make all nations my disciples." Thus the Christian life is always one of "coming and going"—coming to him for salvation, for refreshment, for direction, and then going for him into the world as his representative or ambassador.

Max Warren quotes from Elizabeth Goudge's autobiography entitled *The Joy of the Snow:* "If we go home like the Prodigal Son, we must go out again as the Good Samaritan."[79]

MISSION IN THE NEW SECULAR EUROPE

Themes: Evangelism; Mission

Peter Kuzmic has written about essential features of mission in the new secular Europe:

> We must renew the credibility of the Christian mission. Missions and evangelism are not primarily a question of methodology, money, management and numbers, but rather a question of authenticity, credibility and spiritual power.
>
> In going out to evangelize in Yugoslavia, I frequently tell our seminary students that our main task may be simply to "wash the face of Jesus," for it has been dirtied and distorted by both the compromises of institutional Christianity through the centuries and antagonistic propaganda of atheistic communism in recent decades.

---

79. Max Warren, *I Believe in the Great Commission* (Hodder and Stoughton, 1976), 185.

The mayor of Bihać, a cultural Muslim, gave permission for Agape, the evangelical equivalent to Roman Catholic Caritas. When Peter Kuzmic asked him why he trusted him, he replied: "You are credible with us because you became vulnerable with us" (LLCC Nov 2000).[80]

MISSIONARIES SHOULD LIVE WITH THOSE TO WHOM THEY MINISTER

Themes: Birth of Jesus; Mission

At the BMMF's united conference in Karachi in early 1978, Bashir Jiwan said of missionaries: "Let them live among us, like Bishop Young's son and his wife. They picked cotton in the fields, lived in a village hut, and his wife dutifully cooked meals like any other village wife. They blended with and served the village community to such a degree that the people wept when they left."

THE MONEY IS FINE, BUT THE JOB ISN'T BIG ENOUGH

Themes: Calling; Mission; Money; Work

I heard Paul Little in December 1973 tell the story of an American missionary engineer in Indonesia who had expert knowledge of the country's oil deposits. Standard Oil heard of him and cabled him an offer of $20,000 a year if he'd work for them. He declined. They called [with] a second offer of $30,000. He declined again. Then came a third offer of $40,000, together with a request to say if the offer still wasn't big enough. He cabled back his answer: "You don't understand. The money's fine. But the job isn't big enough."

---

80. Peter Kuzmic, "A Credible Response to Secular Europe," *Evangelical Review of Theology* (June 1994).

PASTOR AND CHURCH FIT ON TWO CAMELS

Themes: Church; Evangelism; Mission

David Gitari, bishop of Mount Kenya East since November 1975, is very concerned about the evangelization of the sixteen thousand Gabbra people near Kenya's northern border with Ethiopia. They are 99 percent animist. The Rev. Andrew Adano is one of them. Bishop Gitari appealed for money to buy two camels—one for Andrew and the other to carry the church! Now, when these nomads move on to look for water, their church and their pastor go with them!

REASONS WHY PEOPLE DISCOURAGE EVANGELISM

Themes: Evangelism; Mission; Truth

Reasons why people urge us to leave others alone and not interfere:

1. *Individual*—A person's religion is part of his identity; don't undermine it.

2. *Social*—Religion is a strong social cement, especially in a pluralist community. Don't disturb this harmony.

3. *Historical*—Christianity is Western. To seek to impose it is paternalistic.

4. *Intellectual*—No system can claim to be absolute and therefore have a monopoly of truth.

5. *Emotional*—How can we bring ourselves to declare others wrong or condemn them?

SEEKING THE LOST IN SHINKAWA

Themes: Mission

Toyohiko Kagawa chose to live for Christ in the squalor of Shinkawa, one of the world's worst slums. Among his neighbors were thieves, murderers, and prostitutes. Everybody lived in indescribable misery and filth. The place was slippery with sewage, was infested with rats, and stank to high heaven. But here Kagawa sought men and women for Christ.

TAKING CARE OF BABIES AND NEW BELIEVERS

Themes: Nature of the Church; Family: Children

Florence Nightingale's *Notes on Nursing* first appeared in December 1859. It has fifteen chapters on matters like ventilation, housing, noise, food, bedding, light, [and] cleanliness. But [the] last chapter is called "Minding Baby," and is written for eldest daughters who have the job of [taking care of younger children.]

It begins, "And now, girls, I have a word for you." Later, "do you know that one half of all the nurses in service are girls of from five to twenty years old? You see you are very important little people. Then there are all the girls who are nursing mother's baby at home. ... I need hardly say, what a charge! ... You, all of you, want to make baby grow up well and happy, if you knew how."

So she gives and elaborates seven conditions:

1. Fresh air

2. Proper warmth

3. Cleanliness for its little body, its clothes, its bed, its room and house

4. Feeding it with proper food, at regular times

5.   Not startling it or shaking either its little body or its little nerves

6.   Light & cheerfulness

7.   Proper clothes in bed and up

And management in *all these* things. "I would add one thing. It is as easy to put out a sick baby's life as it is to put out the flame of a candle."

There are some parallels here to how we care for brand-new believers.[81]

TO KILL A MOCKINGBIRD'S LESSON FOR MISSIONARIES

Themes: Mission

To Kill a Mockingbird was a Pulitzer Prize winner and has sold many millions. Set in the Deep South of [the] US in [the] 1930s, it exposes the racial prejudice of the small town of Maycomb, Alabama. The hero is Atticus, a lawyer, who tries to teach his children (Jem and Scout) that "you can never really understand a person until you consider things from his point of view; … until you climb into his skin and walk around in it."[82]

THE WEST IS THE "MOST CHALLENGING MISSIONARY FRONTIER OF OUR TIME"

Themes: Gospel; Idolatry; Mission

Foolishness to the Greeks asks what'd be involved in such an encounter "between the gospel and this whole way of perceiving, thinking and living that we call 'modern western culture' " (p. 1), since this is "the most challenging missionary frontier of our time." He laments [the]

---

81. Florence Nightingale, *Notes on Nursing: What It Is, and What It Is Not* (D. Appleton and Co., 1860).

82. Harper Lee, *To Kill a Mockingbird* (William Heinemann, 1960), 33.

way Christians abandoned [the] public arena and withdrew into [a] privatized world (pp. 15–19), and urges us to go over to the offensive. The church must affirm "that the central shrine of a nation's life cannot remain empty" and "that, if Christ is not there, an idol will certainly take his place" (p. 123).[83]

PERSEVERANCE

"ALL YOU NEED IS A BIG POT OF GLUE"

Themes: Perseverance; Work

Irwin C. Hansen, CEO of Porter Memorial Hospital, Denver: "All you need is a big pot of glue. You smear some on your chair, and some on the seat of your pants, you sit down, and you stick with every project until you've done the best you can do." Alan Loy McGinnis (family therapist, corporate consultant, author), who quotes this, adds: "Average achievers stay glued to their chairs and postpone pleasure so they can reap future dividends."

NB: in [the] UK, we call this "stickability." McGinnis also quotes a lady [who says,] "The best ability is dependability."[84]

CRAWLING TO HEAR JOHN STOTT

Themes: Commitment

"Jolly John" of Jacksonville Florida: "When I first read a book by John Stott, I said to myself I would crawl on my knees 500 miles to listen to that man." [When he did, he] fell asleep and snored. [Apparently the] crawl [was] too much for him.

---

83. Lesslie Newbigin, *Foolishness to the Greeks* (SPCK, 1986).
84. *Reader's Digest* (August 1992), 73, 76.

THE DIFFERENCE DISCIPLINE MAKES

Themes: Discipline

When Paderewski became president of Poland and resolved not to give up public duties until his country was liberated, he had little or no time for music. He confessed that if he stopped practicing piano:

for one day, he noticed [the] difference;

for two days, his family noticed [the] difference;

for three days, his friends noticed [the] difference;

for a week, the public noticed [the] difference.

DOUGLAS BADER ON NEVER LOOKING BACK

Themes: Encouragement; Hope; Perseverance

Douglas Bader (died September 1982 aged seventy-two) was twenty-one, [an] Oxford scholar and athlete, when as [a] young RAF officer on December 14, 1931, he crashed a Bulldog fighter and lost both his legs. It was his own fault (a misjudgment), as he admitted.

"You can't change what has happened," he often said, "but what you can do is make the best of what you've got." Defiantly rejecting resignation and self-pity, he determined to build a new life and mocked at his adversities. He became a much-decorated ace of the Battle of Britain; he bailed out over enemy territory, leaving one of his two artificial legs in his Spitfire cockpit; escaped from prison, was recaptured, and had his legs confiscated. After the war he worked for the disabled in many countries. "I've never looked back," he said. "That's the point. I've never looked back, nor have I ever allowed myself to think negatively."[85]

---

85. Laddie Lucas, *Flying Colours: The Epic Story of Douglas Bader* (Hutchinson, 1981).

"IF YOU HAVE A DREAM YOU CAN MAKE IT HAPPEN"

Themes: Perseverance

In February 2001, Ellen MacArthur completed her circumnavigation of the world in the Bay of Biscay. An ecstatic crowd of more than 200,000 people welcomed her with fireworks, floodlights, and flares, as she was the youngest (24) and smallest (157 cm) competitor and completed the race in 94 days, 4 hours, 25 minutes, and 40 seconds—12 days faster than the previous record. There had been some days out there, she confessed, when she feared for her life, "but the most important message," she continued, "is that if you have a dream you can make it happen." Her 18.3-meter yacht was called *Kingfisher*. (She came second in the race, one day behind the winner.)

IT IS THE LONG STRAIGHT ROAD THAT TIRES

Themes: Perseverance; Work

Once, when talking to a farmer, I was pitying his horses at the plough. It was a very upland farm, the fields were very steep, the horses had to struggle up the brae. But the farmer told me that these hilly fields were not nearly so trying to the horses as the long steady pull upon the level. In walking, as every walker knows, it is the long straight road that tires.

IT IS NOT THE BEGINNING BUT THE CONTINUING THAT MATTERS

Themes: Encouragement; Perseverance; Prayer

Sir Francis Drake's prayer on the day he sailed into Cádiz harbor [in] 1587: "O Lord God, when thou givest to thy servants to endeavour any great matter, grant us also to know that it is not the beginning, but the continuing of the same, until it be thoroughly finished, which yieldeth the true glory: through Him that for the finishing of thy work laid down His life, our Redeemer, Jesus Christ."

JESUS IS HOLDING ON WITH BOTH HANDS

Themes: Assurance; Perseverance; Satan

I once heard of two little girls who had a conversation. Mary said to Marjorie, "If you died, how do you know you would be saved?" Marjorie replied instantly, "Because I am holding on to Jesus with both my hands." "Ah! But supposing Satan cut off your hands," was the unexpected rejoinder.

Marjorie thought and then said, "But Jesus is holding on to me with both His hands and the devil can't cut off Jesus' hands."[86]

NEVER DETERRED BY DISAPPOINTMENTS

Themes: Discouragement; Perseverance

Squadron Leader L. D. A. Hussey, a member of Sir Ernest Shackleton's last two polar expeditions, wrote in [the] March 1945 *Listener* regarding his 1914–1916 expedition south: "It was typical of Shackleton that he named his little wooden sailing ship *Endurance*. He himself was never driven from his course by his disappointments—and he had plenty of them."

THE PERSEVERANCE OF MUNGO PARK

Themes: Perseverance

It was Sir Joseph Banks, the botanist and patron of exploration, [who became a] Fellow of the Royal Society aged only twenty-three [and was] later its president for forty-plus years and sailed round [the]

---

86. Lionel B. Fletcher, *Step by Step in the Christian Life*, 1930s.

world with Captain Cook, who sent Mungo Park, [a] young Scottish doctor, in 1795, aged twenty-four, to West Africa to trace [the] source of [the] River Niger. [Park] arrived on [the] Gambia River and learned Mandingo. At last, after many setbacks, including captivity and robbery by Muslims, and much hunger, thirst, and fever, he saw "the majestic, long sought Niger, glittering in the morning sun" ... to his surprise, flowing *eastward*.

[He] struggled on nearly one hundred miles, seeking to trace its course. But rains defeated him, and he returned three hundred miles, and then five hundred more to [his] starting point on [the] Gambia.

[He was] back in England [in] 1797. In 1799 his book *Travel in the Interior Districts of Africa* was published. In 1805 he left [his] wife and three kids to begin [his] second expedition, sponsored by [the] British government.

Delays meant he arrived later than intended, with forty Europeans. By [the] time he reached [the] Niger, only eleven had survived sunstroke and disease. "I once more saw the Niger rolling its immense streams along the plain."

Six more died, including his brother-in-law. He felt "lonely and friendless amid the wilds of Africa." Despite lions, crocodiles, robbers, and dysentery, he went on, and wrote to [the] Colonial Secretary: "Though all the Europeans who are with me should die, though I was myself half dead, *I would still persevere*; and if I could not succeed in the object of my journey, I would at last die in the Niger"—which he did by drowning, having sailed around one thousand miles, and with only 720 left to [the] mouth of [the] river.[87]

87. Josephine Kamm, *Men Who Served Africa* (Harrap, 1957), 15–31.

THE RIGHT STUFF

Themes: Courage; Men; Perseverance; Pride

Tom Wolfe's electrifying bestseller *The Right Stuff* tells the story of the
Mercury program, which put the first Americans into space, and of
seven of the eight astronauts involved. Combining technical accuracy,
psychological insight, and sensational description, he analyzes the
driving forces that made these astronauts risk their lives—a fusion
of outside and inside forces, patriotism, and ambition.

1. *Patriotism.* The Russians were far ahead, launching
   unmanned Sputnik I in 1957 and Yuri Gagarin's Vostok
   I, which performed a single orbit in April 1961 (the same
   month as the Bay of Pigs fiasco). In the United States,
   there was a sense of panic and shame. Senator Lyndon B.
   Johnson said [the] Roman Empire controlled [the] roads,
   [the] British [the] sea, and now the question was who'd
   control "the high ground," that is, space. The survival
   of the free world was at stake.

   Then there was a series of technical failures that made
   Soviet premier Khrushchev mock. But when the United States
   pulled it off, Americans experienced the greatest surge of
   patriotism since the Second World War. They responded to
   "the presence, the aura, the radiation of the right stuff" (p. 291).

2. *Ambition.* Wolfe writes of the "titanic ego" of the test
   pilots (p. 31), of astronauts "ravenous for glory," and
   of their indignation when they discovered "a monkey's
   gonna make the first flight" and that they were to be
   more passengers than pilots. Wolfe likens them to gallant knights of olden days, men of dash and daring, of
   lances and plumes, "knights of the right stuff" (p. 33).

The "right stuff" is never defined, but it's a mixture of manliness,
courage, professionalism, and achievement that made these astronauts objects of public awe. Even John Glenn (whose turn came in

January 1962, who'd trained with utter dedication, but Wolfe obviously doesn't like) was "getting ready to do precisely what his enormous Presbyterian Pilot self-esteem had been dying to do for 15 years: demonstrate to the world his righteous stuff" (p. 266).[88]

THE STORY OF TERRY FOX

Themes: Courage; Perseverance; Sickness

Terry Fox was a young Canadian athlete who contracted cancer and had to have a leg amputated. Then, one-legged and aged twenty-two, he ran 3,340 miles along the Trans-Canada Highway to raise money for cancer research, until he was forced by the spread of the disease to give up. Yet by this courageous marathon he raised over $25 million.

THOMAS CRANMER'S FINAL STATEMENT AND PRAYER

Themes: God's Mercy; Persecution; Perseverance; Repentance

When Cranmer had been in prison two and a half years, his isolation from friends and books and even (mostly) from means of writing told on him. Ridley and Latimer had been burned; and no doubt in the loneliness of the Bocardo he dreaded a similar fate. At last he subscribed his name to a statement drawn up in advance.

After brief freedom and much flattery (before his recantation) he was now thrown back into Bocardo. [There was a] procession to St. Mary's for service before execution. Called upon to make [a] final profession of Catholic faith, Crammer read and stated [his] Reformed convictions! "I renounce and refuse ... things written with my hand contrary to the truth which I thought in my heart, and written for fear of death ... for as much as my hand offended in writing contrary to

88. Tom Wolfe, *The Right Stuff* (Jonathan Cape, 1980; Bantam, 1981).

my heart, therefore my hand shall first be punished; for if I may come to the fire, it shall be first burned."

But before this statement he prayed aloud for himself, "Thou didst not give Thy Son unto death for small sins only, but for all the greatest sins of the world: so that the sinners return to Thee with his whole heart as I do here at this present. Wherefore, have mercy on me, O God, whose property is always to have mercy. Have mercy upon me, O Lord, for Thy great mercy."[89]

PRAYER

DISMISSING EXPERIENCES OF GOD IN PRAYER

Themes: Prayer

In *The Human Face of God* by J. A. T. Robinson (SCM, 1973), he dismisses all claims to a direct experience of God in prayer as "the naive theism in which God is directly present to the religious consciousness"—which David Jenkins (reviewing the book in *MGW* March 31, 1973) calls "a quite horribly condescending remark."

LATIMER'S REQUEST FOR PRAYER

Themes: Commitment; Courage; Fear; Prayer

Latimer was committed to the Tower in September 1553, two months after Mary Tudor came to the throne. Ridley was there too, and they corresponded, Ridley arming Latimer with arguments for the coming trial. Latimer wrote less but asked for Ridley's prayer. "Pray for me, I say; for I am sometimes so fearful that I would creep into a mousehole.

---

89. Marcus Loane, *Masters of the English Reformation* (Church Book Room, 1954), 236–39.

Fare you well once again, and be you steadfast and unmovable in the Lord."[90]

PRAYER FUNDAMENTAL TO THEOLOGICAL WORK

Themes: Humility; Prayer

Karl Barth, at [the] end of [a] long service in Basel University, said: "The first and most fundamental act of theological work is prayer." For then the theologian who prays comes before God in humility, which is the only perspective from which to approach God.[91]

PREACHING

LOOK AT CHRIST MORE THAN THE PREACHER

Themes: Church Leadership; Jesus: Death

[In] September 1955 the American magazine *Look* carried [a] striking colored photo of Billy Graham on [the] cover.

It was taken in All Souls Church, and I was there when it was taken. Billy Graham stands on [the] steps by [the] communion table. [His] hand [is] lifted, [his] mouth open as he preaches. Above [him] is [the] word, "Look." At what? At Billy Graham? Yes, but beside him is [the] top of [a] golden cross, and behind him is [the] shadowy figure of [the] Lord Jesus Christ. Shall we look at Billy Graham? No, but at Christ and his cross!

---

90. Marcus Loane, *Masters of the English Reformation* (Church Book Room, 1954), 124.

91. Karl Barth, *Evangelical Theology: An Introduction* (Holt, Rinehart and Winston, 1963), 160.

SO MUCH THE WORSE FOR CALVIN!

Themes: Church Leadership; Truth

H. W. Beecher delivered the first Lyman Beecher Lectures on Preaching at Yale in 1872. After [the] first lecture on "What Is Preaching?" a student asked him a question whether preachers would not be well advised to teach Calvinism. His reply included that extraordinary statement: "I consider myself Calvinistic, you know; and in this way: I believe what John Calvin would have believed if he had lived in my time and seen things as I see them. My first desire is to know what is true; and then I am very glad if John Calvin agrees with me; but if he doesn't, so much the worse for him!"

Henry Ward Beecher was minister of Plymouth Congregational Church, Brooklyn, for over twenty-five years [and a] popular preacher.[92]

SACRAMENTS

ANGLICAN UNDERSTANDING OF THE SACRAMENTS

Themes: Baptism; Lord's Supper

- "All receive not the grace of God who receive the sacrament of His grace."—Richard Hooker

- "Visible signs to which are annexed promises."—"Homily of Common Prayer and Sacraments" from Book II (1571), possibly Bishop John Jewel: "The exact signification of a sacrament" is "visible signs expressly commanded in the New Testament, whereunto is annexed the promise of free forgiveness of our sin."

- "Verba visibilia."—Augustine

---

92. Henry Ward Beecher, *Yale Lectures on Preaching* (Nelson, 1872), 35.

- "The real presence of Christ's most blessed body and blood is not ... to be sought for in the sacrament, but in the worthy receiver of the sacrament."—Richard Hooker, Book V, ch. 67, 6.

BAPTIZED IN PRISON WITH CHOPSTICKS

Themes: Baptism; Conversion

During the 1950s and '60s many Roman Catholic priests and lay preachers were imprisoned for their faith in China. One Roman Catholic layman (interviewed in 1984) shared how he had led a fellow prisoner to faith even while in solitary confinement. "Every day I was given two bowls of rice and a kettle of water. The latter was for drinking and washing. ... The guards did not pay much attention to those in solitary confinement. So I was able to speak to a young man in the cell next door by making a hole in the wall and speaking through it. Eventually he wanted to believe in Christ. So I dipped my chopsticks in the remaining water I had used to brush my teeth, and baptized him on the forehead through the hole! Later this friend was killed during the Cultural Revolution."[93]

BAPTIZING ONESELF

Themes: Baptism

1. A certain John Smith in 1604, in exile in Holland, unable to find anyone to baptize him as an adult believer, took what seemed to him the only course left and baptized himself.

2. A man from Shanghai returned home (from Hong Kong) for [the] first time in seventeen years to visit his son,

---

93. Tony Lambert, *The Resurrection of the Chinese Church* (Hodder and Stoughton, 1991), 178.

and led him to Christ. At that time Christians were only meeting by twos and threes, and listening to Okinawa broadcasts. Later the son wrote that he wanted to be baptized but none was willing. So during a storm of rain and snow he walked out into the street, lifted his face to heaven and asked God to do so![94]

CALVIN: SCRIPTURE DOES NOT COMMAND THE MASS

Themes: Lord's Supper; Scripture

"One day" at Poitiers in 1534, "when a discussion had arisen on the Lord's Supper," Calvin having his Bible before him said, "Here is my mass." And, throwing the hood of his cloak onto the table and raising his eyes to heaven, he exclaimed, "Lord, if on the day of judgment you hold it against me that I never went to mass and that I left it, I shall say and with reason, Lord, you did not command it. Here is your law, here is Scripture which is the rule you have given me, in which I have not been able to find any sacrifice other than that which was offered on the altar of the cross" (p. 53).[95]

JOHN FRITH ON THE LORD'S SUPPER

Themes: Lord's Supper

John Frith (1503–1533) was explicit in his assertion that the saying, *Hoc est Corpus Meum*, must be understood, not in a literal, but in a spiritual sense, and he went on to say: "For as verily as that bread is broken among them, so verily was Christ's body broken for their sins; and as verily as they receive that bread into their belly through eating

---

94. Robert Bowman of the Far East Broadcasting Company, talk to OMF staff (October 1968).

95. Florimond de Raemond, *Histoire de la naissance, progrès et décadence de l'hérésie de ce siècle* (1623), 906; quoted by Jean Cadier in *The Man God Mastered: A Brief Biography of John Calvin*, trans. O. R. Johnston (Inter-Varsity, 1960), 53.

it, so verily do they receive the fruit of His death into their souls by believing in Him" (John Frith, *Works*, p. 120–21).

On Friday, June 20, 1533, John Frith appeared before Stokesley, Longland, and Gardiner in St. Paul's Cathedral. He summed up the points at issue in a paper which was dated on June 23 and which bears the title "The Articles Wherefore John Frith Died." He was asked if he believed that the Sacramental bread and wine were "the very body of Christ or no," and he answered, "As verily as the outward man receiveth the Sacrament with his teeth and mouth, so verily doth the inward man, through faith receive Christ's body and the fruit of His Passion, and is as sure of it as of the bread which he eateth."[96]

AN UNCLAIMED PENSION

Themes: Baptism; Promises

Many years ago an old Indian died of starvation in [the] United States. When dead, [there was] found round his neck a little bag containing an old yellow parchment. He'd kept it as a charm. When deciphered, [it] turned out to be a document granting a pension to the man's grandfather for bravery in [the] War of Independence. [The] terms of [the] deed made [this] pension available to [the] first recipient, his son—and grandson, the man who died of starvation! [The] document [was] signed by George Washington. Here was an instrument conveying a pension, [and the] old man never claimed it!

That pathetic old man represents the hundreds of thousands of baptized church members who have received [the] document, the instrument, the sacrament, but never personally claimed the benefits which it promises.

---

96. Marcus Loane, *Pioneers of the Reformation in England* (Church Book Room, 1964).

SATAN

THE CHRISTIAN LIFE IN MILITARY TERMS

Themes: Satan; Spiritual Warfare

"Gvozden Simić" was a partisan fighter under Tito in the Yugoslavian Liberation War. Converted soon after its conclusion (because [he became] disillusioned with the greed of the Communist leaders), he thought and spoke of the Christian life in military terms. Jesus Christ is our commander-in-chief, he would say; "we are his officers, and need to fight the enemy together, and seek the liberation of Satan's slaves."

His simple lifestyle, unselfish public service, and outspoken witness to Communist leaders have attracted attention and been the subject of articles in major newspapers. He speaks of the helplessness of unregenerate man under the power of the devil, who has put two of his fingers into his eyes to blind him, two more into his ears to make him deaf, and the fifth into his mouth to stop him from calling out for help.

THE DEVIL IS THE MOST DILIGENT BISHOP IN ENGLAND

Themes: Satan; Spiritual Warfare

On January 1, 1538 (after the coronation of [the] boy king Edward VI, [Hugh] Latimer being now released from prison), he resumed his career as a preacher with a sermon at Paul's Cross, where he preached weekly during the month. The fourth is the famous "Sermon on the Plow" (in which he likened "preaching to a plowman's labour, and a prelate to a plowman").

After deploring the fact that little affective preaching was being done, he continued: "And now I would ask a strange question: who is the most diligent bishop or prelate in all England? … I can tell you, for I know who it is; I know him well. But now I think I see you listening and hearkening that I should name him. Then it is one that passeth all the others, and is the most diligent preacher and prelate in all England. And will ye know who it is? I will tell you: it is the devil. He is the most diligent preacher of all others; he is never out of his diocess; he is never from his cure; ye shall never find him non occupied; he is ever in his parish. … Ye shall never find him idle, I warrant you."[97]

OUR FEELINGS OF SUPERIORITY TO THE DEVIL

Themes: Evil; Pride; Satan

Charles Williams thinks the popularity of Milton's legend of fallen angels "has perhaps been assisted by the excuse it has seemed to offer for mankind," i.e., in explaining our revolt against the good, "and by its provision of a figure or figures against whom men can, on the highest principles, launch their capacities of indignant hate and romantic fear. The devil, even if he is a fact, has been an indulgence. … While he exists there is always something to which we can be superior."[98]

SERVICE

"ALWAYS UNDER SENTENCE OF DEATH"

Themes: Commitment; Death and Dying

A German Jew named Eugen Leviné organized the Workers' and Soldiers' Soviets in the Bavarian Soviet Republic of 1919. When the Republic was suppressed, Leviné was captured and court-martialed. The court came to its inevitable conclusion. "You are under sentence of

---

97. Marcus Loane, *Masters of the English Reformation* (Church Book Room, 1954), 96.
98. Charles Williams, *He Came Down from Heaven* (Eerdmans, 1984 [1938]), 15–16.

death," they told him. Leviné answered: "We Communists are always under sentence of death."[99]

BILLY GRAHAM WILL SLOW DOWN IN HEAVEN

Themes: Calling; Heaven; Service

At Urbana '76 Billy Graham developed a leg clot. In March 1977 he wrote me: "The clot in my left leg has disappeared, but I still am suffering from an inflammation of a vein, so am on rather heavy medication, plus I must wear the Jobst stockings, and of course as always the doctors say 'slow down'—which I intend to do in Heaven, the Lord willing!"[100]

BLESSING OF A DOCTOR'S HANDS

Themes: Blessing; Heath and Healing; Service

Some years ago we had as a member of All Souls a petite but very hardworking American lady doctor. She'd lived many years in the UK and had a practice in Cavendish Square.

She was a mixture of chiropractor and physiotherapist, so [she] worked with her hands. Once a year without fail she'd ask and come to church for [the] blessing of her hands.

One of us would kneel with her at the communion rail and together we'd present her hands to God, and pray that he would perform his work of healing through them.

---

99. W. E. Sangster, *The Pure in Heart* (Epworth, 1954), xiv.
100. Letter to JRWS from Billy Graham (March 1977).

"DISCOVER WHAT YOU ARE MADE TO DO"

Themes: Calling; Commitment; Service; Work

In December 1964, in London on his way to receive his Nobel Peace Prize in Oslo, Martin Luther King preached in St. Paul's Cathedral. "He preached one of his favorite sermons that day—'Three Dimensions of a Complete Life.' ... The text was from Revelation 21:16, 'the length and the breadth and height of it are equal.' ... The first dimension of a complete life is the development of a person's inner powers. He must work tirelessly to achieve excellence in his field of endeavor, no matter how humble. 'Set yourself earnestly to discover what you are made to do and then give yourself passionately to the doing of it. This clear onward drive towards self-fulfilment is the length of a man's life.' "[101]

"DISPOSE OF ME HOW YOU WISH"

Themes: Service; Submission

When I was an undergraduate at Cambridge, one of [the] college librarians [was a] refugee from Poland. He was polite to [the] point of obsequiousness, but his command of [the] English language [was] defective. Whenever one entered [the] library, he would come forward, make [a] deep bow and say, "Please dispose of me how you wish." One had visions of picking him up between [the] forefinger and the thumb and disposing of him in [a] wastepaper basket or rubbish bin!

What he meant was (he was) at our disposal. But bad English was good theology, because if we are at Christ's disposal, he may dispose of us as he wishes!

---

101. Coretta Scott King, *My Life with Martin Luther King, Jr.* (Hodder and Stoughton, 1970), 20–21.

THE FOUR Q'S

Themes: Humility; Service; Submission

In one of his ordination charges, Archbishop Michael Ramsey said he'd often been helped by a prayer which is included in the old edition of the *Priest's Book of Private Devotion* (attributed to "a not very inspiring person, Pope Clement VI"):

> *Volo quidquid vis*
> *Volo quia vis*
> *Volo quomodo vis*
> *Volo quamdiu vis.*

"I commend to you the 'Four Qs.' They often help me when duties are irksome. … *Quidquid*, if God wills it, God's presence will be in it, however tiresome it may be. *Quia*, if God wills it, this becomes the motive. *Quomodo*, we are to do it not just in the way we might ourselves have planned, for the *how* is in God's hands. *Quamdiu*, I must be ready to do this for as long as God wills that I should."[102]

"LET SERVICE BE THE INSPIRATION OF OUR FUTURE"

Themes: Giving; Poverty; Service

Jomo Kenyatta was sworn in as president of the Republic of Kenya on December 12, 1964. In a broadcast to the nation he said: "The Republic is the people. And just as I called on you all to enter the Republic in the Spirit of Harambee, so I call on you now to enrich the Republic with the spirit of Community. Commencing with this coming year, let every man who is educated teach a man to read and write. Let every man who is healthy help … a man who is sick. Let every man who has work and position find some prospect for a man who is unemployed

---

102. Michael Ramsey, *The Christian Priest Today* (SPCK, 1972), 63–64.

and poor. Let service be the inspiration of our future, so our future can be made worthwhile."[103]

METHODIST WORDS OF DEDICATION

Themes: Commitment; Service; Submission

In the Methodist Covenant Service, first urged by John Wesley on Methodists Christmas Day 1747, the words of dedication are: "I am no longer my own, but thine. Put me to what Thou wilt, rank me with whom Thou wilt; put me to doing, put me to suffering; let me be employed for Thee or laid aside for Thee; exalted for Thee or brought low for Thee; let me be full; let me be empty; let me have all things; let me have nothing; I freely and heartily yield all things to Thy pleasure and disposal.

"And now, O glorious and blessed God, Father, Son and Holy Spirit, Thou art mine, and I am Thine. So be it. And the covenant which I have made on earth, let it be ratified in heaven. Amen."

(NB: John Wesley borrowed these words from Richard Alleine, the Puritan.)

NO CHRISTIAN PRIVILEGE WITHOUT OBLIGATION

Themes: Discipleship; Gospel; Service

Handley Moule, when principal of Ridley Hall, was also evening lecturer at Holy Trinity. He held university Bible readings on Sunday evenings after Evening Prayer. For years he continued expounding the Greek New Testament, verse by verse. His lectures centered on what he called "the golden alphabet of the Gospel, the mighty first things—Christ for thee, thy acceptance; Christ in thee, thy life and power."

We can't have Christian privilege without Christian obligation.[104]

---

103. Jomo Kenyatta, *Suffering without Bitterness* (East African Publishing House, 1968), 255.

104. John Pollock, *A Cambridge Movement* (Murray, 1953), 90.

QUEEN ELIZABETH II'S EDUCATIONAL PRINCIPLES FOR HER CHILDREN

Themes: Education; Family: Children; Family: Mothers; Service; Victory and Defeat

Queen Elizabeth II has (1954) seven clear principles of education for Prince Charles and Princess Anne. Three of them are:

1. Let both face both triumph and defeat.

2. Give them the opportunity to efface themselves for a public common cause.

3. Make them understand that their birth brings them many duties and few rights.

QUOTATIONS ON SERVICE FROM HISTORY

Themes: Service; Suffering

- Francis Xavier: "Yet more; oh, my God, more toil, more agony; more suffering for Thee."

- David Brainerd: "I declare, now that I am dying, I would not have spent my life otherwise for the whole world."

- The Moravians' Declaration: "God's place of service for me is my home, not, my home is God's place of service."

A SMILE COSTS NOTHING

Themes: Mercy

Found in The Normandy, a café in Vancouver:

> A smile costs nothing, but gives much. It enriches who receive, without making poorer those who give. It takes but a moment, but the memory of it sometimes lasts for ever. None is so rich

or mighty that he can get along without it, and none is so poor but that he can be made rich by it. …

Yet it cannot be bought, begged, borrowed, or stolen, for it is something that is of no value to anyone until it is given away. Some people are too tired to give you a smile. Give them one of yours, as none needs a smile so much as he who has no more to give.

SIN

AUGUSTINE ON TRYING TO FIND THE REASON FOR ADAM'S SIN

Themes: Sin

Struggling to understand what it was that caused Adam to make the original wrong choice, since God had created him without sin, Augustine came to the conclusion that this was "like trying to see darkness or hear silence, so no one must try to get to know from me what I know that I do not know."[105]

BEING TOLD YOU'RE A SINNER IS OFFENSIVE AND INSULTING

Themes: Pride; Sin

Eighteenth-century England was still socially feudal, in that the different classes were regarded as necessarily separated from each other. For example, the Duchess of Buckingham wrote to the Countess of Huntingdon:

> I thank your ladyship for the information concerning the Methodist preachers. Their doctrines are most repulsive, and strongly tinctured with impertinence and disrespect towards

---

105. Augustine, *City of God*, xii.6–8.

their superiors, in perpetually endeavouring to level all ranks and do away with distinctions. It is monstrous to be told that you have a heart sinful as the common wretches that crawl on the earth. This is highly offensive and insulting, and I cannot but wonder that your ladyship should relish any sentiments so much at variance with high rank and good breeding.[106]

HAVING TO GO TO GOD EMPTY-HANDED

Themes: Good Works; Guilt; Sin

The anonymous whisky priest, who is the tainted hero of Graham Greene's *The Power and the Glory* (1940), during the violent persecution of the Roman Catholic Church in Mexico, wakes up in prison on the morning on which he is to be shot by a firing squad. He reviews his life and is ashamed of his failures. "He felt only an immense disappointment because he had to go to God empty handed, with nothing done at all."[107]

JOHN WESLEY'S MOTHER ON MAINTAINING HOLINESS

Themes: Holiness; Sin

Mrs. Wesley's advice to her son John: "Whatever weakens your reason, impairs the tenderness of your conscience, obscures your sense of God, or takes off the relish of spiritual things, in short, whatever increases the strength and authority of your body over your mind, that thing is sin to you, however innocent it may be in itself."[108]

---

106. Alfred Plummer, *The Church of England in the Eighteenth Century* (1909), 124.

107. Graham Greene, *The Power and the Glory* (Penguin, 1940), 210.

108. C. C. Southey, *Life of Wesley* (Longman, Hurst, Rees, Orme and Brown, 1820), 25.

LUTHER'S DESCRIPTION OF
UNREGENERATE HUMANITY

Themes: Sin

Luther described unregenerate man as *in se incurvatus*—man turned in on himself, or better, "bent, crookedly bent" in on himself. The phrase seems to combine the two ideas that man is twisted and that his twist is self-centered, self-imprisoning. "The natural man seeks himself in his own and his own interests in everything. He never seeks God … this is Scriptural teaching. Which describes a man as curved in upon himself. … This curvature is a natural crookedness. It is a natural defect … natural evil."[109]

"SIN IS THE HOOK"

Themes: Evil; Satan; Sin

Thomas Manton on John 17:15, whether "evil" there is "evil" or "the evil one." Manton opts for both together: "Satan he is the author; the world is the bait. Sin is the hook."[110]

SPIRITUAL BATTLES

"JESUS LOVER OF MY SOUL"

Themes: Faith; God's Love; Temptation; Victory and Defeat

Charles Wesley [was] staying [in a] Cornish fishing village. [There was a] gale, [and he was] watching from [an] open window [a] fishing boat making for [the] harbor. Would [the] captain guide it safe into [the] haven? [A] little bird, battling with [the] storm, exhausted, darted

---

109. Martin Luther, *Weimarer Ausgabe* 56, 355.

110. Thomas Manton, *An Exposition of John 17* (Sovereign Grace Book Club, 1958), 268.

through [the] window and hid for shelter in [the] bosom of his coat. [The] boat reached [the] harbor; [the] bird [was] safe in [his] bosom.

[Following this, he] wrote [the] hymn "Jesus, lover of my soul, let me to thy Bosom fly," and headed it "In Temptation."

"Other refuge have I none"!

THE VIGILANCE OF THE SECRET SERVICE

Themes: Commitment; Discipline; Watchfulness

When President Roosevelt attended Peter Marshall's church, one of the things which most impressed Mrs. Marshall was [the] "eternal vigilance of the secret-service men. I could watch one of them closely. He stood in the left front section of the church during the entire service. Never once did he allow himself to become interested in any part of the service. His eyes were never still. They searched tirelessly back and forth across the gathering for any unusual or suspicious movement. I have never witnessed such faithful and disciplined attention to duty."[111]

SUFFERING

ANDREW BONAR'S DEPRESSION

Themes: Depression

[Andrew Bonar was] born [in] 1810, converted [in] 1830.

- July 9, 1834: "Sorrow this day came in like an oozing tide" (p. 22).

- February 15, 1835: "A strange flood of sorrow and vexation, from earthly cisterns being dry to me, often comes upon me on Saturday and Sabbath" (p. 25).

---

111. Catherine Marshall, *A Man Called Peter* (Peter Davies, 1955), 113.

- July 4, 1857: "I was very, very melancholy, I may say, on Saturday evening" (p. 186).

- September 19, 1858: "Feeling somewhat cast down ..." (p. 191).[112]

"O, LOVE THAT WILL NOT LET ME GO"

Themes: Providence; Suffering

"O, Love That Will Not Let Me Go" was written by the Rev. George Matheson, seventy-five years ago, in 1882. His eyesight was defective from childhood and grew worse until by the time he entered Glasgow University he was quite blind.

For the first eighteen years of his ministry he was minister of Innellan in Argyllshire and came to be known as "Matheson of Innellan." The church where he served is now known as Matheson Church. He used to memorize the whole service and preached with great power.

He says that he composed the hymn in the manse of Innellan on the evening of June 6, 1882, when he was alone. He writes, "Something had happened to me which was known only to myself and which caused me the most severe mental sufferings. The hymn was the fruit of that suffering. It was the quickest bit of work I ever did in my life. I had the impression rather of having it dictated to me by some inward voice, than of working it out myself."

"WHAT IS A CANDLE MADE FOR, BUT TO BE BURNT?"

Themes: Submission; Suffering

- "What have we our time and strength for, but to lay both out for God? What is a candle made for, but to be burnt?"—Richard Baxter

---

112. Andrew Bonar, *Andrew Bonar: Diary and Life*, ed. Marjorie Bonar (Banner of Truth, 1960).

- When extremity of pain made Richard Baxter long for death, he would check himself and say: "It is not fit for me to prescribe, when Thou wilt—what Thou wilt—how Thou wilt!"[113]

THANKFULNESS

BART SIMPSON, DOSTOEVSKY, AND GRATITUDE

Themes: Thankfulness

Bart Simpson, America's favorite cartoon kid, when asked to say grace before supper, said, "Dear God, we pay for all this ourselves. So thanks for nothing."

As Dostoevsky wrote regarding humanity in *Notes from Underground* (1864): "If man is not stupid, he is monstrously ungrateful. … In fact I believe that the best definition of man is the ungrateful biped."[114]

"NOW THANK WE ALL OUR GOD"

Themes: Holidays: Thanksgiving; Thankfulness

During the Thirty Years' War, the walled city of Eilenburg in Saxony was besieged. Eight thousand people died from pestilence and famine, including the Lutheran minister's wife. When peace came in 1648, the minister, Martin Rinckart, read from [the] pulpit Ecclesiastes 1:22–24: "Now bless ye the God of all who everywhere doeth great things; may He grant us joyful hearts and may peace be in our days forever."

Later, inspired by this text, he wrote [the] immortal hymn "Now Thank We All Our God."

---

113. J. C. Ryle, *Light from Old Times* (Evangelical Press, 1980), 340.
114. Os Guinness, *The Call* (Thomas Nelson, 1998).

UNION WITH CHRIST

ANDREW BONAR ON CHRIST AND BEING ALONE

Themes: Grief; Loneliness; Union with Christ

Andrew Bonar lost his wife in 1864, his "dear, dear Isabella." "O what a wound," he cried. Eighteen years later he could write: "I thought then that life could never again be lightsome, but I find that the more of Christ we enjoy, the more we are able to bear. When we have truly found Christ, we can go through the world alone."[115]

CHRIST'S PRESENCE TO THE ELDERLY

Themes: Presence of God; Loneliness; Union with Christ

1. After listening to a "Lift Up Your Hearts" broadcast [in January 1958], an old age pensioner of ninety-two (Mrs. A. E. Collins) wrote from Clapham that she had been housebound for ten years, and continued: "I live alone except for His presence always."

2. Another (Miss Putman, S.E. 20) wrote: "Jesus Christ has been my friend ever since I was a child and still is. I am now seventy-two."

3. A lady from Exeter with seven grandchildren wrote after listening to "Lift Up Your Hearts": "I am a widow of seventy-eight and have not been able to go out to any place of worship for ten years, because of infirmity of body. I have known Christ as my Saviour since I was a child."

---

115. Andrew Bonar, *Andrew Bonar: Diary and Life,* ed. Marjorie Bonar (Banner of Truth, 1960), 501.

CHRIST'S PRESENCE TO HUDSON
TAYLOR IN HIS OLD AGE

Themes: Death and Dying; Presence of God;
Grief; Joy; Loneliness; Union with Christ

In 1870 Hudson Taylor wrote, "A few months ago my home was full, now so silent and lonely—Samuel, Noel, my precious wife, with Jesus; the elder children far, far away, and even little T'ien-pao (Charles) in Yang Chow. Often, of late years, has duty called me from my loved ones, but I have returned, and so warm has been the welcome. Now I am alone. Can it be that there is no return from this journey, no home gathering to look forward to! Is it real, and not a sorrowful dream, that those dearest to me lie beneath the cold sod? Ah, it is indeed true."

Three months later he wrote: "No language can express what He has been and is to me. *Never does He leave me; constantly does He cheer me with His love.* … His own rest, His own peace, His own joy, He gives me. … Often I find myself wondering whether it is possible for her, who is taken, to have more joy in His presence than He has given me."[116]

WHOLE-LIFE DISCIPLESHIP

THE CHRISTIAN'S TWO CALLINGS

Themes: Calling; Work

Cotton Mather, the Boston Puritan (d. 1728), taught the Christians two callings—"general" ("to serve the Lord Jesus Christ") and "personal" ("a particular employment by which his usefulness in his

---

116. Marshall Broomhall, *Hudson Taylor: The Man Who Believed God* (Moody, 1929), 161.

neighbourhood is distinguished"). "Every man ordinarily should be able to say, 'I have something wherein I am occupied for the good of other men.' " The two callings should be pursued in balance. In this the Christian is like a man in a boat rowing toward heaven and pulling hard on *both* oars.[117]

FREEDOM AND WORK

Themes: Freedom; Providence; Laziness; Work

During his speech on Uhuru Day, December 12, 1963, to the newly independent nation of Kenya, Mze Jomo Kenyatta said: "We must all work hard with our hands ... when the children of Israel were crying, saying 'God, why did you bring us to this wilderness, where there is no water or sustenance,' God said He would bring them something called manna. This cannot happen again. ... He said He had closed the door with a lock, and had thrown the key into the ocean. That the door would never open again and there would be no more manna in the world. ... From today onwards I want one Uhuru to mean 'Uhuru na Kazi ... Freedom and work' " (p. 216).

In his foreword to the book he wrote (p. xiii), "I have always believed that the best way to achieve worthwhile human ambitions is through hard work. To me, 'Uhuru na Kazi' is a living reality. Of all the deadly sins, that of sloth seems to be the most contemptible, a flaunting of the very purpose of creation."[118]

---

117. Cotton Mather, *A Christian at His Calling* (Green and Allen, 1701).

118. Jomo Kenyatta, *Suffering without Bitterness* (East African Publishing House, 1968).

THE HALLOWING PLACES OF COVENTRY CATHEDRAL

Themes: Creativity; Health and Healing; Holiness; Work

In November 1940 Coventry was devastated by aerial bombardment, including its fourteenth-century cathedral. After the war, the ruins of the old cathedral were preserved, while a new cathedral was built beside it.

Ever since the Middle Ages, Coventry has been famous for its crafts and craftsmen's guilds. Although the old cathedral's guild chapels were destroyed, in their place "hallowing places" have been set round the ruined walls, expressing implications of the prayer "Hallowed Be Your Name":

> In industry, God be in my hands and in my making
> In the arts, God be in my senses and in my creating
> In the home, God be in my heart and in my loving
> In commerce, God be in my desk and in my trading
> In healing, God be in my skill and in my touching
> In government, God be in my plans and in my deciding
> In education, God be in my mind and in my growing
> In recreation, God be in my limbs and in my leisure.

WHOLEHEARTEDNESS

BAPTIZED EXCEPT FOR THEIR FIGHTING ARMS

Themes: Baptism; Commitment; Violence; War

Stanley Jones describes how the warlike Saxons were practically compelled by Charlemagne to become Christians. They consented on a condition they would make plain at their baptism. They were baptized by immersion. But when [the] time came, these warriors were totally immersed except for their right arms; these they held out of the waters above their heads. For their right arm was their fighting arm, and they refused to surrender it to Christ.[119]

GIVING CHRIST A PASSKEY

Themes: Commitment; Discipleship

"Instead of giving Christ a whole set of different keys to the many rooms of the house, some keys of which may become worn or sticky under adverse conditions, I have given Him a pass key to the whole lot."

> —Marc Bell, fourth-year forestry student and Chairman of University Clubs Committee, Member of Student Council, University of British Columbia, Vancouver[120]

GOD WILL USE ANYONE WHO IS COMPLETELY AT HIS FEET

Themes: Commitment; Laziness

Daddy Hall ("Bishop of Wall Street," who died in 1950 aged eighty-five) used to say that "when God wanted to shock the world out of its complacency and show what He could do with a man fully surrendered to Him, He went to Sing Sing Prison to get the man, an unlearned one—Jerry McAuley. He laid His hands on him, took him out, and set him on fire for God. His influence has gone around the world. We learn from this that no one is hopeless or helpless. God can and will use any man or woman who is completely in His hands and at His feet."

---

119. E. Stanley Jones, *The Christ of the Indian Road* (Hodder and Stoughton, 1926), 21.

120. Letter to JRWS (February 1957).

Many of the friends of Dad Hall felt that he exalted this truth too much. "But," he said, "I get so disgusted with men and women who have received all kinds of training, have a string of degrees to their names, and yet have accomplished so little for God. Few people even want to hear them preach. To be a successful worker for Christ you must be fully surrendered and separated from the world, the flesh and the Devil and living at Jesus' feet, and I firmly believe anyone can qualify under these conditions."[121]

HENRY MARTYN'S DEDICATION TO GOD

Themes: Commitment; Discouragement; Submission

[In] 1805–1806 Henry Martyn spent nine months at sea, via Cape Town. Leaving Africa, [he suffered through] storms and seasickness. "I pray that this may be my state, neither to be anxious to escape from this stormy sea that was round the Cape, nor to change the tedious scene of the ship for Madras ... but to glorify God where I am and where He puts me" (p. 83).

Arriving in the Hooghly river: "I feel pressed in spirit to do study for God. ... I have hitherto lived to little purpose, more like a clod than a servant of God; now let me burn out for God" (p. 175).

When Lydia Grenfell finally refused in October 1807 to come out to Henry Martyn in India, his heart was "bursting with grief and disappointment." Yet he wrote: "I wish to have my whole soul swallowed up in the will of God" (p. 178).[122]

---

121. Sara C. Palmer, *Daddy Hall, "Bishop of Wall Street"* (Moody, 1954), 83–84.

122. Henry Martyn, *Journals and Letters of the Rev. Henry Martyn: In Two Volumes,* ed. Samuel Wilberforce (Seeley and Burnside, 1837).

OFFER YOUR HEART TO GOD

Themes: Commitment; Prayer; Submission

- "Offer thy heart to God in a soft and tractable state, lest thou lose the impress of His fingers, lest by being hardened thou might miss both His craftsmanship and thy life" (Irenaeus).

- "Lord, take my heart from me, for I cannot give it to Thee. Keep it for Thyself for I cannot keep it for Thee; and save me in spite of myself" (Augustine).

[The above were] quoted by Dr. Michael Ramsey at the end of his enthronement sermon in Canterbury Cathedral (1961). [The] text of the sermon was 1 Samuel 10:26. He suggested that these prayers, which were his, should be ours also.

THE RESOLVE OF JONATHAN EDWARDS

Themes: Commitment; Discipleship

Jonathan Edwards, the philosopher-theologian, was born in 1703, entered Yale aged thirteen and before that had learned Latin, Greek, and Hebrew.

He was [a] friend of George Whitefield, God's instrument in the Great Awakening of 1734–1735, became president of Princeton [in] 1758, and died one month later.

[He was] converted aged eighteen in spring, 1721. In the seventieth of his famous Resolutions, written on August 17, 1723, just before [his] twentieth birthday, these words occur: "Resolved: Never to lose one moment of time, but to improve it in the most profitable way I possibly can. Resolved: To live with all my might, while I do live. Resolved: To study the Scriptures so steadily, constantly and frequently, as that I may find myself to have grown in the knowledge of the same."

WISDOM

WHILE LEADERS ARGUE, ORDINARY FOLK NEED TO THINK FOR THEMSELVES

Themes: Government, Politics and National Identity; Wisdom

In October 1960, the heads of many states assembled in New York for General Assembly of the United Nations—Khrushchev, Tito, Nasser, Castro, and others were there.

Harold Macmillan made a great impression in a memorable speech. In [the] course of it he said that while the leaders of the world were quarrelling, "ordinary folk" needed "the chance to think for themselves about the deepest problems on which man has to meditate during his short individual sojourn on earth—the relations between man and man, and the relation between man and God."

THE WILL OF MISS X AND THE WILL OF GOD

Themes: Guidance; Wisdom

At the 1966 London Diocesan Conference, the archdeacon of London (Martin Sullivan, later dean of St. Paul's) told the following story:

> I remember sitting in a synod under a bishop, and it was reported to the synod that an elderly spinster whose name was Miss X had left £70,000 to build a cathedral on condition that the foundation stone should be laid within seven years of the reception of the gift. Every layman in this synod knew that this was impossible, and one after another they got up to say so.
>
> The bishop who was presiding could see that cheque fluttering out of the west door on the way to some charity, so he drew himself to his full purple height and he said, "Now let us lift this on to a spiritual level. It is the will of God that we should take this money. It is the will of God that we should

lay this foundation stone. It is the will of God that we should build this cathedral."

One clergyman, to his eternal credit, with high courage got up and said, "My Lord, a point of order." And irascibly my Lord said, "What is the point of order?" And the clergyman said, "We are discussing the will of Miss X, not the will of God!"

WITNESS

THE BEST POETRY IS LIVED

Themes: Calling; Mission

Rupert Brooke, the handsome, popular poet at [the] beginning [of the] twentieth century, who died in Greece during World War I: "It is good to read poetry; it is better to write it; but the best is to live it."

FROM PITYING THE METHODISTS TO ENVYING THEM

Themes: Conversion; Happiness

Robert Robinson, who later wrote [the] hymn "Come Thou Fount of Every Blessing," was converted through George Whitefield's preaching. "I confess it was to spy the nakedness of the land I came, to pity the folly of the preacher, the infatuation of the hearers and to abhor the doctrine. I went pitying the poor, deluded Methodists, but came away envying their happiness."

THE POOR WITNESS OF THE CONQUISTADORS

Themes: Heaven; Mission

Indian people witnessed the appalling cruelty of the Spanish *conquistadores*. One proud Cuban *cacique* or Indian chief named Hatuey, condemned to be burned alive, was exhorted by his confessor to be converted and go to heaven. "Are there Christians in heaven?" he asked. "Why, of course," came the reply. "Well," said the *cacique*, "I don't want to go to any place where I shall have any chance of meeting them."[123]

THE POWER OF TYNDALE'S DOCTRINE AND SINCERITY

Themes: Conversion; Evangelism

William Tyndale was arrested in Antwerp in May 1535 and consigned to the castle of Vilvorde, the government state prison of the Low Countries. Foxe writes: "Such was the power of his doctrine and the sincerity of his life that … he converted his keeper, the keeper's daughter, and others of his household; also the rest that were with Tyndale conversant in the Castle reported of him that if he were not a good Christian man, they could not tell whom to trust."[124]

QUESTION FROM A HINDU REFORMER

Themes: Evangelism; Hypocrisy; Mission

Dr. S. Radhakrishnan, the modern Hindu reformer, once said to a missionary, Professor Dewick: "You Christians seem to us Hindus to be rather ordinary people, making very extraordinary claims!" He replied, "We make these claims not for ourselves, but for Jesus Christ." The retort came back quickly: "If your Christ has not succeeded in making *you* into better men and women, have we any reason to suppose that He would do more for us if we became Christians?"

---

123. John A. Mackey, *The Other Spanish Christ* (SCM, 1932), 37.

124. Marcus Loane, *Masters of the English Reformation* (Church Book Room, 1954), 81.

STANLEY JONES ON CHRISTIAN WITNESS IN INDIA

Themes: Hypocrisy; Mission

1. A Hindu in one of India's great cities once said to Stanley Jones, "If you can show me one real Christian in this city, I'll be a Christian" (p. 131).

2. A penetrating but kindly old philosopher of India, Bara Dada, the brother of Dr. Rabindranath Tagore, once said to Stanley Jones: "Jesus is ideal and wonderful, but you Christians—you are not like him" (p. 141).

3. A Hindu lecturer on educational subjects, addressing an audience of educationalists in southern India, said: "I see that a good many of you here are Christians. Now this is not a religious lecture, but I would like to pause long enough to say that, if you (Christians) would live like Jesus Christ, India would be at your feet tomorrow" (pp. 141–42).[125]

WE CAN STILL SPEAK BY ACTION

Themes: Evangelism; Mission; Speech

A Christian Chinese working in communist-occupied territory in 1949 said, "We may not be allowed to preach by mouth, but if we should be silenced, we can yet speak by being ourselves and by action. Jesus is the Word of God, we too are words."

---

125. E. Stanley Jones, *The Christ of the Indian Road* (Hodder and Stoughton, 1935).

WORSHIP

CHRISTOPHER BOOKER'S SPIRITUAL JOURNEY

Themes: Atheism; Conversion; Worship

Christopher Booker (first editor of *Private Eye*, scriptwriter for *That Was the Week That Was*, author of *The Neophiliacs* and *The Seventies: Portrait of a Decade*, columnist for *The Spectator*) says he became an atheist aged three. Then in 1965 "I suddenly fell through the floor. … I knew that I and most of the people around me were living in a complete fantasy." The world had not only lost a sense of meaning, but was celebrating meaninglessness. Then in February 1966 he had "a religious experience." Standing looking out of [the] window of his Victoria flat one evening, feeling acutely disillusioned, "Suddenly I heard a voice within me, as it were, proclaiming 'There is another way, I am that other way.' " From that moment he ceased [to] be [an] atheist, and has been trying to come to terms with it since. [He] went to the Church of England but it didn't express the all-pervasive sense he had of [the] sacredness of anything. He has an awareness of a transcendent reality, and a conviction that man's ultimate purpose is to live in relation to this.[126]

A CONVERT'S ASSESSMENT OF CHRISTIAN WORSHIP

Themes: Cults and Non-Christian Religions; Worship

A Christian convert from Islam gave his frank impressions of Christian worship. "The Christian worship I saw was unclean, irreverent, arrogant, idolatrous and immoral." He then explained: "You neither wash yourselves nor take off your shoes before entering God's house. You

---

126. Steve Turner, "Christopher Booker—Fighting against Fantasy," *Third Way* (January 1980), 6.

gossip irreverently and never cover your heads when you pray. You put so much furniture in the place of prayer that no one can prostrate himself before God. You make pictures of Christ—something God has forbidden. And you mix women and men, making it impossible to have a pure thought life or concentrate on God."[127]

---

127. Letter to JRWS.

3

WORLD AND WORLDVIEWS

ADDICTIONS

THE BEGINNING OF SMOKING
WARNING LABELS IN THE UK

Themes: Addiction; Health and Healing

In 1971 the Royal College of Physicians calculated that in the age bracket 35–64 some 27,500 UK deaths per annum can be put down to smoking. As a result of such statistics, Sir Keith Joseph has secured the tobacco companies' agreement to label cigarette packets with the warning "Smoking can damage your health." But American experience of similar warnings has led only about one in fifty smokers to give up smoking.[1]

---

1. *Guardian Weekly* (March 20, 1971).

THE DISAPPEARING STIGMA ON GAMBLING

Themes: Addiction; Stewardship

According to George Washington, gambling is "the child of avarice, the brother of iniquity, and the father of mischief." But now it permeates American culture. Thirty-seven states now have lotteries as opposed to one in 1978, and twenty-three have legalized casinos. Evidently the moral stigma which used to attach to gambling has been eroded.[2]

GAMBLING AS A CAUSE OF NEGLECT

Themes: Addiction; Family: Children; Greed; Stewardship

During 1960 the National Society for the Prevention of Cruelty to Children helped 112,000 children—5,000 more than in 1959. Most of them—70,805—were suffering from neglect.

The Society's annual report says that in a substantial number of cases the prime cause of the children's sufferings is gambling by one or both parents. "Related to this scourge of gambling is the temptation, often quite unscrupulously extended to parents, to undertake hire purchase commitments which are far beyond their resources to meet."

NOTES ON ALCOHOLISM

Themes: Addiction; Alcohol

Alcoholism (as opposed to drunkenness) has been defined by Alcoholics Anonymous as "a constitutional disorder allied to a personality maladjustment."

---

2. Martin Woollacott, *Guardian Weekly* (September 18, 1994).

An alcoholic has been defined by a well-known American psychiatrist as "a person who drinks when he knows he should not, or wishes he would not."

Alcoholics have been classified by a specialist into four types:

1. Good previous personality (80 percent successful recoveries)

2. Basically neurotic personality (30 percent)

3. Basically psychotic personality (prognosis depends on the psychosis)

4. Basically psychopathic personality (little can be done)

Ministry of Health memo (1962) requested hospital boards to set up special units for treatment of alcoholics. By 1964 nine centers [had been] established (in mental hospitals). The recommended stay in them [is] three months.[3]

---

3. Medical Correspondent, *The Times Leader* (November 13, 1964).

'Alcoholism' (as opposed to drunkenness) has been defined by Alcoholics Anonymous as 'a constitutional disorder allied to a personality maladjustment'.

An alcoholic has been defined by a wellknown American psychiatrist as 'a person who drinks when he knows he should not, or wishes he would not'.

Alcoholics have been classified by a specialist into 4 types:
1) Good previous personality
   (80% successful recoveries)
2) Basically neurotic personality
   (30%)
3)   "   psychotic   "   (prognosis depends on the psychosis)
4)   "   psychopathic personality
           (little can be done)

Ministry of Health memo (1962) requested hospital boards to set up special units for treatment of alcoholics. By 1964 nine centres established (in mental hospitals). The recommended stay in them = 3 months.

(Times Leader by Medical Correspondent, 13 Nov.1964)

ALCOHOL

NOTES ON DRUG DEPENDENCE

Themes: Addiction

For "drug dependence," cf. [the] words of Bill Paton, professor of pharmacology [at] Oxford. NB:

1. *"Dependence"* can be enriching to personality (marriage, e.g.) or body (food). Other dependencies are destructive.

2. *[The] drug itself* [is] not an evil; what is important [is the] human problem.

3. *Causality* is very varied:

    a. availability (supermarket) and off license

    b. advertisers, e.g., sexual prowess

    c. inner compulsive drive (feeling of rejection is key)

    d. epidemiology, e.g., when heroin became available in New Towns, … explosive epidemic. But [it] reached [a] saturation point, i.e., a susceptible group was engulfed

    e. social habit/ritual (pipe, syringe, toasts)

4. *Cure.* [The] great need is [a] positive alternative (conversion, marriage, hobby, pet) as [a] substitute.

POPULAR TYPES OF DRUGS

Themes: Addiction

1. *Marijuana* ("pot" or "dope") = Indian hemp leaves smoked in [a] cigarette or sucked through [a] waterpipe (hashish = marijuana resin). Narcotic, mind-expanding.

2. *Cocaine* ("coke"/"snow") = white powder. Either sniffed (like snuff) or injected. Anesthetic, euphoria.

3. *LSD* ("acid"). Drop on sugar lump or blotting paper. Mind-expanding, hallucinatory, but nonaddictive.

4. *Heroin* ("skag"). White powder, derived from morphine, melted in [a] spoon and injected. Sedative.

USING TOBACCO TO FIGHT DRUNKENNESS

Themes: Addiction; Alcohol

When Wilfred Grenfell worked among men of the deep-sea fisheries in the North Sea, one of their greatest temptations was drunkenness, through the innumerable quayside inns and floating "hells."

He had the rather unconventional idea of using tobacco "to fight the floating grog traffic." The rum sellers used cheap tobacco to lure men to their destruction on the "hells." "We sold it cheaper, even at a loss, to lure them away."

Justifying this policy, he adds: "A man does not beat his wife, wreck his home, fight his neighbours, or part with his reason and his money because he has been smoking tobacco."[4]

BOOKS

THE BLACK PANTHERS' COMMITMENT TO STUDY

Themes: Education; Government, Politics and National Identity

The Black Panther Party was founded in 1966. In October 1966 they issued a ten-point party program reminiscent of the Communist Manifesto and then drew up twenty-six Party Rules to be memorized by BPP members. These include: "Everyone in a leadership position must read at least two hours per day to keep abreast of the changing political situation."[5]

---

4. Wilfred Grenfell, *What Christ Means to Me* (Hodder and Stoughton, 1964), 45.
5. Maurice Cranston, ed., *The New Left* (Bodley Head, 1970), 161–62.

ELIZABETH GOUDGE ON THE DIFFICULTY OF WRITING

Themes: Work

Elizabeth Goudge (1900–1984) wrote of how she would "sit down at the appointed time for work and stare in terror at the empty sheet of paper before me." She added: "What a crazy way to earn a living, making dirty marks on clean paper."

(NB: her father Rev. Henry Goudge was successively Principal of Wells and Ely theological colleges and Regius Professor, Oxford).

COMPARATIVE RELIGION

DIFFERENT RELIGIONS' ADVICE TO A DROWNING MAN

Themes: Cults and Non-Christian Religions;
Good Works; Salvation; Sin; Suffering

Someone has summarized [the] difference between some of [the] religions of [the] world by comparing [the] advice [they would give] to [a] drowning man (in [the] sea). [The] sinner is like [a] drowning man, floundering helplessly, unable [to swim]:

- Confucius: "Learn by your experience."

- Mohammed: "Islam (resignation); it is the will of Allah."

- Buddha: "Struggle!" ("Walk the noble eightfold path.")

- Zoroaster: "You must suffer the penalty of evil you've done."

- Hinduism: "You will be reincarnated."

- Mary Baker Eddy: "There isn't any sea anyway."

- Only Jesus Christ: "Take my hand; I will lift you out and save you."

That is, every other religion is a system of human effort and merit. Christianity alone is a religion of grace, of [the] initiative of God who comes in Christ to seek and save the lost.

THE HINDU BELIEF IN REINCARNATION

Themes: Cults and Non-Christian Religions; Killing

In the *Bhagavad Gita*, Krishna reminds Prince Arjuna of his duty to fight, because he belongs to the *Kshatriya* (warrior) caste, and that in any case he won't hurt [the] souls of his relatives by killing them. For the souls wear successive bodies of reincarnation.

As a man casts off his worn out clothes
And takes on other new ones in their place
So does the embodied soul cast off his worn out bodies
And enters others new.

"NO SYSTEM CAN SWALLOW UP JESUS"

Themes: Cults and Non-Christian Religions;
Jesus: Divinity; Philosophy

At Lausanne July 1974, Samuel Kamaleson said: "No system can swallow up Jesus Christ without having indigestion problems."

THE PARTICULAR THING IS CHRIST

Themes: Cults and Non-Christian Religions; Jesus

Sadhu Sundar Singh was once asked by an agnostic professor of comparative religions in a Hindu college what he had found in Christianity which he had not found in his old religion. "I have Christ," he replied. "Yes, I know," said the professor rather impatiently ... "but what particular principle or doctrine have you found that you did not have before?"

"The particular thing I have found" he replied, "is Christ."[6]

IN ROME, ALL RELIGIONS ARE EQUAL FOR DIFFERENT REASONS

Themes: Government, Politics and National Identity; Philosophy

It was eighteenth-century Edward Gibbon in his *Decline and Fall of the Roman Empire* who said that in Roman society, all religions were to the people equally true, to the philosophers equally false, and to the government/magistrate equally useful.[7]

THREE SYNCRETISTS: PARAMAHAMSA, VIVEKANANDA, AND GANDHI

Themes: Cults and Non-Christian Religions

- *Ramakrishna Paramahamsa.* The nineteenth-century Hindu mystic (1836–1886), originally a pujari in a Calcutta temple, taught that what mattered was not the outward forms of religion but the one inner reality they all express. "Every man should follow his own religion." He spoke of himself as "the same soul that had been born before as Rama, as Krishna, as Jesus, or as Buddha, born again as Ramakrishna" (*No Other Name*, pp. 36–37).

- *Swami Vivekananda* (1863–1902). One of [the] founders of Ramakrishna Mission, [who said that] all religions are ways to the one Supreme Reality. So he preached in 1893 at Parliament of Religions in Chicago.

---

6. E. Stanley Jones, *The Christ of the Indian Road* (Hodder and Stoughton, 1926), 64.

7. Edward Gibbon, *Decline and Fall of the Roman Empire*.

- *Gandhi* (1869–1948) said in 1928: "After long study and experience I have come to these conclusions: that (1) all religions are true; (2) all religions have some error in them and (3) all religions are almost as dear to me as my own Hinduism. My veneration for other faiths is the same as for my own faith. Consequently, the thought of conversion is impossible" (in *The Discovery of India* by Nehru, p. 340). And in his ashram prayer meetings he would read two extracts from scriptures of many faiths.

TWO PERSPECTIVES ON HUNGER IN INDIA

Themes: Cults and Non-Christian Religions; Poverty

- "For the millions who go without two meals a day, the only form in which God dare appear is food."— Mahatma Gandhi

- "There are about 2.4 billion rats in India. Each year they consume 12 million tons of food, about as much as India receives in outside assistance. The Indian Government would like to kill the rats but the nation's 350 million Hindus are largely opposed to extermination programmes.

   "The Indian's respect for the sacredness of all life extends to ants, monkeys, buzzards and especially cows. There are almost as many cows in India as there are people in the United States. Efforts to institute bovine birth control have been unsuccessful."—S. C. Rose of the World Council of Churches

CREATIVITY

C. S. LEWIS'S ADVICE ON WRITING

Themes: Creativity; Education; Work

[C. S. Lewis wrote] to a schoolgirl in America, who had written (at her teacher's suggestion) to request advice on writing (December 14, 1959):

> It is very hard to give any general advice about writing. Here's my attempt.
>
> 1. Turn off the Radio.
>
> 2. Read all the good books you can, and avoid nearly all magazines.
>
> 3. Always write (and read) with the ear, not the eye. You should hear every sentence you write as if it was being read aloud or spoken. If it does not sound nice, try again.
>
> 4. Write about what really interests you, whether it is real things or imaginary things, and nothing else …
>
> 5. Take great pains to be clear. Remember that though you start by knowing what you mean, the reader doesn't, and a single ill-chosen word may lead him to a total misunderstanding …
>
> 6. When you give up a bit of work don't (unless it is hopelessly bad) throw it away. Put it in a drawer. It may come in useful later. Much of my best work, or what I think my best, is the re-writing of things begun and abandoned years earlier.
>
> 7. Don't use a typewriter. The noise will destroy your sense of rhythm, which still needs years of training.

8. Be sure you know the meaning (or meanings) of every word you use.[8]

MUSIC, JOY, AND FREEDOM

Themes: Beauty; Creativity; Music; Freedom

When Joseph Knecht as a boy first watched the elderly Master of the Glass Bead Game (Magister Ludi) play the piano, he was overcome with awe: "His ear drank in the fugue; it seemed to him that he was hearing music for the first time in his life. Behind the music being created in his presence he sensed the world of mind, the joy-giving harmony of law and freedom, of service and rule. … In those few minutes he saw himself and his life, saw the whole cosmos guided, ordered and interpreted by the spirit of music."[9]

POETRY IS ACQUIRED BY LEARNING AND PRACTICE

Themes: Creativity; Education

[Arthur] Koestler quotes from a lecture by a party instructor to a literary circle of workers in a Soviet factory regarding the production of poetry: "To regard poetry as a special talent which some men possess and others don't is a bourgeois metaphysic. Poetry, like any other skill, is acquired by learning and practice. We need more class-conscious proletarian poetry; we must increase our poetry out-put on the literary front. Beginners should start with five or ten lines a day and then set themselves a target of twenty or thirty lines, and gradually increase the quantity and quality of their productions."[10]

---

8. C. S. Lewis, *The Letters of C. S. Lewis,* ed. W. H. Lewis (Geoffrey Bles, 1966), 291–92.

9. Hermann Hesse, *The Glass Bead Game* (Penguin, 1972 [1943]), 54.

10. Quoted in Stuart W. McWilliam, *Called to Preach* (St. Andrew Press, 1969), 35.

THE RENAISSANCE AND HUMAN AUTONOMY

Themes: Creativity; Freedom

The Renaissance proclaimed the autonomy of all departments of human activity, in rebellion against the Queen of [the] Sciences or the sovereignty of religion. For example, "'Art for Art's Sake' means that an artist's business is to express himself without regard to the question of whether he has a self worth, or even fit to be expressed."[11]

CULTURE

THE CHRISTIAN ADOPTION OF THE POTTU

Themes: Mission

"Pottu" is the red spot worn by Hindu ladies on their forehead. Now [it is] also used by many Indian Christian ladies as a cosmetic or beauty adornment without any religious significance. Cf. drums in Africa.

FROM SOLA SCRIPTURA TO SOLA CULTURA

Themes: Evil; Philosophy; Scripture

Os Guinness in *Prophetic Untimeliness* (Baker, 2003) warns that our passion for relevance too easily degenerates into a surrender to contemporary culture. Much of the evangelical community, he writes, "has transferred authority from *sola scriptura* to *sola cultura*" (p. 65). We're in danger of becoming "kissing Judases" (Kierkegaard), pretending to embrace Jesus even while we destroy him (p. 67).[12]

---

11. William Temple, *Citizen and Churchman* (Eyre and Spottiswoode, 1941), 3.
12. Os Guinness, *Prophetic Untimeliness* (Baker, 2003).

MISLEADING USES OF ENGLISH

Themes: Mission

The official European Community translators have collected examples of misleading uses of English:

- A Paris hotel told its guests to leave their "values" at the front desk.

- A Hong Kong dentist advertised tooth extraction "using the latest Methodists."

- An airline at Copenhagen airport vowed to "take your bags and send them in all directions."[13]

WHITE SKIN, BLACK HEART

Themes: Birth of Jesus; Mission; Service

The Rev. J. A. Persson from Sweden, working among the Tswa people of South Africa and Mozambique, so identified himself with those whom he went to serve that at a farewell dinner given in his honor before a furlough, one Tswa man arose and paid the highest tribute a white man could ever receive in Africa: "Mr. Persson may have a white skin, but his heart is as black as any of us."[14]

---

13. Paul-Gordon Chandler, *Divine Mosaic: Windows on God from Around the World* (SPCK, 1997), chapter 7.

14. Eugene A. Nida, *God's Word in Man's Language* (Harper and Brothers, 1952), 117.

EDUCATION

THE CHRISTIAN TEACHER

Themes: Education

In *Christian Education Reviewed* by Spencer Leeson, headmaster of Merchant Taylors and Winchester and Bishop of Peterborough (1957): "The Christian teacher, therefore, has the stage of his work set in eternity, and he is in the most literal sense a fellow worker with Christ for the souls of his pupils."

Again, "the teacher as he opens the classroom door is confronted with human personalities capable of growth and needing the best food he can give them. In what spirit will he address himself to his tasks?"[15]

DEFINING CHRISTIAN EDUCATION

Themes: Education; Truth

Scottish Presbyterian Alexander Duff was one of India's pioneer missionary-educators. Soon after he arrived in India in 1830 he decided to open a school for high-caste Bengali youths, teaching them in English. Dr. C. E. Abraham, principal of India's Serampore College today, comments: "By Christian education, Duff did not mean secular education plus a period of Scripture teaching but education given in the setting of the Christian religion, education inspired by Christian ideals, education imparted by Christian men who believed in Christianity as a way of life and Christ as the sum of all truths."

---

15. Spencer Leeson, *Christian Education Reviewed* (Longmans, Green, 1957).

EDUCATING AS CATALYZING

Themes: Education

Arthur Koestler has described his dissatisfaction with the OED's definition of "to educate" as to "give intellectual and moral training to,"
"to train (person) … train (animals)" because these imply "asserting
one's mental powers over another person's mind—in the present context, a younger person's." He challenges "the ethics of this procedure."
Instead he defines the purpose of education as "catalysing the mind."
This is how he points [out] the difference between the two concepts:
"To influence is to intrude; a catalyst, on the other hand, is defined as
an agent that triggers or speeds up a chemical reaction without being
involved in the product. So the ideal educator acts as a catalyst, not
as a conditioning influence."[16]

THE EXCITING EDUCATION OF JAMES WOODFORDE

Themes: Education

James Woodforde, who went up to New College Oxford from
Winchester in 1758 age eighteen, records these purchases on arrival:
"A pair of curling tongs 2/8d; 2 logick books 6/-; 2 bottles of port wine
3/4d; a sack of coal 4/9d; a new wigg 1 guinea; nosegays 1d; 2 white
waistcoats £1.16s," and a "superfine blue suit of cloathes £4.10s."

He spent much of his time playing cricket in the summer and
skating in the winter, bear-baiting, shooting, coursing hares, and in
particular drinking large quantities of ale, wine, and punch. He had
two girlfriends, who were sisters, to each of whom he gave a silver
thimble.[17]

---

16. Arthur Koestler, *Rebellion in a Vacuum*, quoted in *Protest and Discontent*,
ed. Crick and Robson (Penguin, 1970), 14.

17. James Woodforde, *A Country Parson: James Woodforde's Diary 1759–1802*
(OUP, 1985), 11.

FRANCIS ASBURY'S COMMITMENT TO LEARNING

Themes: Education

Francis Asbury was a Staffordshire peasant who became [a] Methodist local preacher aged eighteen, and aged twenty-one was appointed by John Wesley [as] an itinerant evangelist. Five years later he volunteered for America, where he toiled unremittingly for forty-five years (1771–1816). Homeless, riding on horseback around five thousand miles per annum, earning most of life less than £20 per annum, he traveled through much of America, winning converts, building up Methodist class meetings and societies, and so (as bishop) establishing the Methodist Episcopal Church, which now has over five million members.

He rose daily at four, taught himself Latin, Hebrew, and Greek, and made a rule to read at least one hundred pages of good literature daily.[18]

OLD ARABIAN PROVERB

Themes: Education; Foolishness; Wisdom

> A man who *knows not* and knows not that he knows not is a *fool*; shun him.
> A man who *knows not* and knows that he knows not is *simple*; teach him.
> A man who *knows* and knows not that he knows is *asleep*; wake him.
> A man who *knows* and knows that he knows is a *wise man*; follow him.[19]

---

18. J. Wesley Bready, *England: Before and After Wesley* (Hodder and Stoughton, 1939), 431–37.

19. T. B. Rees (July 6, 1950).

ETHICS

GEORGE CAREY ON MORAL RELATIVISM AND PRIVATIZED MORALITY

Themes: Character; Family: Children; Law

In July 1996 George Carey, Archbishop of Canterbury, initiated a debate in [the] House of Lords. The motion was "to call attention to the importance of society's moral and spiritual well being."

One of his "most consistent concerns" since he became Archbishop of Canterbury has been "to highlight the dangers of moral relativism and privatised morality. There is a widespread tendency to view what is good and right as a matter of private taste and individual opinion only.

"We take it for granted that you cannot play a game of football without rules. Rules do not get in the way of the game, they make the game possible. It is strange that what we take as so obvious for games we deem unnecessary for life."

He went on to speak of the influence on children of schools, families, the media, and the wider community, and called for a partnership in developing shared values.

GUILT IN CRIMES AND MISDEMEANORS

Themes: Freedom; Guilt; Judgment; Law

In the Woody Allen film *Crimes and Misdemeanors*, Judah, an oph-thalmologist, is persecuted by his clinging mistress, and yields to the temptation to solve his problem by having her murdered. Judah is now torn between traditional morality and modern individualism. In flashbacks of imagination he returns to his Jewish school and to an early Passover at home, when he was taught that God sees and judges everything. But he no longer believes it. His rabbi friend slowly goes blind, which is surely meant to be understood as symbolic. If there is now (since the Holocaust) no God, are we free to do as we like? Is there nothing to stop us but the police (externally) and our unliberated conscience, which is a relic of an old morality? Clearly he sees his crime as nothing but a misdemeanor.

FREEDOM

THE CHARACTERISTICS OF ACADEMIC FREEDOM

Themes: Education; Freedom

An institution's academic freedom is its freedom to teach, research, and learn without interference.

For the individual (student or teacher) this includes the opportunity to think, read, hear, speak, write what he wants, and to assemble for the exchange of ideas.

Such freedom is destroyed when anybody:

1. tries to persuade by pressure instead of argument;

2. treats another's views with ridicule instead of respect;

3. prevents others from expressing their views.[20]

FREEDOM TO BE LONELY

Themes: Freedom; Loneliness; Responsibility

The "freedom" offered by existentialism comes from the courage to face up to the meaninglessness of existence. According to Nietzsche, "The superman is the free man, and this is the essence of his freedom, that he has had the courage to decide for himself alone." That is why,

---

20. John Alexander, paper at American IVCF (1970).

much later, Sartre wrote: "Total responsibility in total solitude—is not this the very definition of liberty?"

Similarly Martin Heidegger argues that only a man who accepts meaninglessness enters "authentic existence." As Tom Kitwood expresses it, such a man "enters a new liberty in which he is truly responsible for his actions and opinions, and is unafraid to stand alone. Thus, freedom in existential terms means something like 'the power to take decisions completely alone and utterly without compulsion.' … To become and to be oneself, that is everything."[21]

FREEDOM IN THE CHOSEN

Themes: Education; Freedom

In Chaim Potok's *The Chosen*, Rabbi Saunders's son Danny is given a strict Talmudic upbringing. He feels trapped in the Hasidic traditions of his family. "It's the most hellish, choking, constricting feeling in the world. I scream with every bone in my body to get out of it. My mind cries to get out of it. But I can't. Not now. One day I will though" (p. 200).

Gradually he widens his reading, especially of psychology. At the end of the book his rabbi father releases him from the expectation that he would succeed him as rabbi and gives permission for him to become a psychologist instead. "He rose slowly, painfully, to his feet. 'Today is the—the Festival of Freedom. … Today my Daniel is free' " (p. 278). On the last page Danny [is] on his way to Columbia. "His beard and earlocks were gone, and his face looked pale. But there was a light in his eyes that was almost blinding" (p. 280).[22]

---

21. T. M. Kitwood, *What Is Human?* (IVP, 1970), 82–84.
22. Chaim Potok, *The Chosen* (Penguin, 1967).

FROM A PAKISTAN PRISON

Themes: Conversion; Freedom; Forgiveness

Dear Mr. Masih,

I got the Bible and your letter. I have read more in this month in the Bible than I have ever read in all my life outside. I have even tried praying for the first time, and I took your advice and asked God to forgive me and take away that feeling that makes me want to kill all those people. I could never sleep because I stayed awake planning escapes and figuring out how I could kill everyone I hated and blamed.

I planned to kill every witness who appeared in court against me.

But now I have learned the Jesus secret of forgiveness. I had not really understood that I had to forgive those I hated, and then I received God's pardon. Now I sleep like a child at night.

I may be in prison all my life, but in my heart I am free. I even like to sing now. Thanks for the wonderful gift of the Bible. If I ever get out I will come to visit you. I love you. Greetings and heartfelt thanks.

Goodbye and thank you.   —J.B.

PS: I wish other prisoners could know what I have discovered.[23]

"I CAN'T COMPLAIN"

Themes: Complaining; Freedom

The story is told of a Romanian who decided to make inquiries about emigrating to England. "What's the matter?" asked the official. "Hasn't the state given you a comfortable flat?"

"I can't complain," answered the Romanian.

"Haven't you got a good job?"

"I can't complain."

"Then why on earth do you want to emigrate to England?"

"Because there I can complain."

---

23. British Forces Broadcasting Service.

JEAN-PAUL SARTRE AND FREEDOM

Themes: Atheism; Freedom; Philosophy

Jean-Paul Sartre died in 1980, aged seventy-five. For him the very essence of life was to be found in freedom—man's freedom to reshape his past and to respond to the challenge of the present, creating his own values as he does so.

L'Être et le Néant (Being and Nothingness) was published in 1943. In it he depicted man, as a French writer put it, "as a godless, free, responsible, and unashamed agent." This was the only antidote to unremitting angst. He rejected marriage as a bourgeois institution, yet lived for fifty years with Simone de Beauvoir.

JOHN CHRYSOSTOM'S RIDICULE OF SUPERSTITION

Themes: Fear; Slavery; Superstition

When John Chrysostom was preaching in Antioch at the end of the fourth century, he denounced the people's dread of omens and use of charms. He referred to superstition as "this most dangerous and ridiculous prison," and caricatured its prisoner:

> "My cursed slave, while giving me my shoes, held out the left one first; this means dread disasters and outrages for me." And again: "When I left the house, I stepped down with my left foot first; this is a sign of disaster." … If a mule brays or a cock crows, or if someone sneezes, or anything at all happens, as if they were bound by ten thousand chains, they hold all things under suspicion, as do those who live in darkness; they are more enslaved than ten thousand slaves.
>
> Let us not act in this way. Let us ridicule all these things, as do those who live in the light; let us have our citizenship in heaven and have nothing in common with this world; let us consider that we have only one thing to fear, namely, offending God by sin.[24]

---

24. John Chrysostom, "Ephesians Homily 12."

Jean-Paul Sartre died in 1980 aet. 75. For him the very essence of life was to be found in _freedom_, — man's freedom to reshape his past and to respond to the challenge of the present, creating his own values as he does so. L'Être et Le Néant | Being Nothingness was pub' in 1943. In it he depicted man, as a French writer puts it, 'as a godless, free, responsible o unashamed agent'. This was the only antidote to universal _angst_. He rejected marriage as a bourgeois institution, yet lived for 50 years with Simone de Beauvoir.

Freedom.

JOHN FOWLES'S SEARCH FOR FREEDOM

Themes: Freedom

John Fowles was once asked if there was any special theme in his books. "Yes," he replied, "freedom. How you achieve freedom. That obsesses me. All my books are about that."

But is he looking for true freedom in the right place? For in his foreword to his novel *The Magus* (1966; revised 1977), he writes, "God and freedom are totally antipathetic concepts."[25]

LOVE INHIBITS LIBERTY?

Themes: Freedom; Love

Françoise Sagan, the French novelist, was interviewed by *Le Monde* just before her fiftieth birthday in June 1985. She said she was perfectly satisfied with her life and had no regrets: "You have had the freedom you wanted?" "Yes." Then she qualified, "I was obviously less free when I was in love with someone. ... But one's not in love all the time. Apart from that, and in spite of love and illness—I've had some experience of both—I have been happy. ... I'm free."

The implication is clear: love inhibits liberty. The more you love, the less free you are. Presumably, then, the way to be completely free is not to love.[26]

MALCOLM X'S QUEST FOR FREEDOM

Themes: Education; Freedom

In 1943, aged only seventeen, Malcolm Little (alias Detroit Red or Malcolm X) became a Harlem hustler, peddling reefer (marijuana) especially to Negro musicians. "A roll of money was in my pocket. Every day,

---

25. John Fowles, *The Magus* (Triad Panther, 1977), 10.
26. *Guardian Weekly* (June 23, 1985).

I cleared at least fifty or sixty dollars … this was a fortune to a seventeen-year-old Negro. I felt, for the first time in my life, that great feeling of *free! … Free now to do what I pleased, upon an impulse I went to Boston"* (p. 99).

In prison later, on a ten-year sentence, he asked for a dictionary and steadily copied it out, perhaps a million words. A new world opened to him. He spent all his spare time reading in [the] library or on [his] bunk. As [a] result, "months passed without my even thinking about being imprisoned. In fact, up to then, I never had been so truly free" (p. 188).[27]

"MAXIMUM FREEDOM SHOULD BE THE YARDSTICK"

Themes: Freedom; Sex

Jean Carpentier, the celebrated thirty-six-year-old French doctor, wrote in February 1971 a tract entitled *Let's Learn to Make Love* and distributed it to schoolchildren at the gates of the Lycée in Corbeil-Essonnes, forty kilometers SE of Paris. In June '72 he was suspended by [the] regional council of L'Ordre des Médecins, and in October by [the] national council. The tract is published by the *Action Committee for Sexual Liberation* and is based on the premise that sex is "the path to happiness" and with the stated purpose of encouraging sexual relations and "all sexual activity."

> It should here be stressed—briefly but all the more forcefully—that notions of "normal" and "abnormal" have absolutely no foundation. In any sexual act what counts is the desire you have to participate in it and the pleasure you find in it. Maximum freedom should be the yardstick for our variety of choice. There's only one danger, the repression of our desires. There is nothing that is abnormal.[28]

---

27. Malcolm X, *The Autobiography of Malcolm X*, ed. Alex Haley (Ballantine, 1965).

28. *Le Monde*, English section in the *Guardian Weekly* (March 24, 1973).

MORE FREEDOM WITH FEWER LORDS?

Themes: Doubt; Freedom; Resurrection

Terho Hämeenkorpi was a third-year theology [student] at [the] University of Helsinki. [He] came from [a] village where religion was strong, but at university [he] studied Marxist theory. [His] hair [had] not [been] cut for months, nor washed and brushed for weeks— [it was] held together by [a] tortoiseshell slide. [But] through [the] undergrowth [he] seemed to be [a] gentle soul.

[He] began by assuring me [that he was] not an atheist or a communist, but agnostic. He believed Jesus Christ lived and died, but no more. Resurrection seemed to him unnatural. Besides, he had no god. Why should he need God? How could he use God in his life? *"I'm longing for freedom. But I'm getting more free since I gave up God."* God was a "lord" to him, and the less lords, the more there is freedom, he thought.

HEALTH

THE INTENSITY OF THIRST

Themes: Health and Healing

Probably no craving of the human body is more intense than thirst. When Shackleton left twenty-one of his men under the command of Frank Wild on Elephant Island, he took five with him on the twenty-foot lifeboat *James Caird*. It took them sixteen days to cross the most tempestuous seas to reach South Georgia. After about twelve, their water supply was very low and had become brackish. "Thirst took possession of us. ... The wind was still strong and the heavy sea forced us to navigate carefully, but any thought of our peril from the waves was buried beneath the consciousness of our raging thirst" (pp. 175–76).

Yet they had to endure four more days before they made it to land. Then suddenly, "We heard a gurgling sound that was sweet music in our ears, and, peering around, found a stream of fresh water almost at our feet. A moment later we were down on our knees drinking the pure ice-cold water in long draughts that put new life into us. It was a splendid moment" (pp. 179–80).[29]

LESS MENTAL ILLNESS IN CITIES

Themes: Health and Healing

[In] 1977 Columbia University sociologist Leo Srole, after studying comparative psychological texts between those living in big urban centers and in small towns of less than fifty thousand, discovered that people living in less densely populated areas suffer more from paranoia, insomnia and nervous trouble than those in urban areas.

PRAYER AND LAUGHTER WORK

Themes: Healing; Prayer

Warren Harvey (consultant dental surgeon in Scotland) writing to Mary Sorrell in hospital March 1969: "Remember that prayer and laughter (though not in the British Pharmacopoeia) are cheap, work, are priceless and highly infectious."

---

29. Ernest Shackleton, *South: The Story of Shackleton's Last Expedition (1914–1917)* (Century Press, 1919).

HISTORY

KEY EVENTS IN CHINA IN THE TWENTIETH CENTURY

Themes: Government, Politics and National Identity; Mission

- 1966: Cultural Revolution

- 1966–1979: For thirteen years the institutional church disappeared (except for expats in Beijing), churches closed, Bibles burned, pastors imprisoned—as in [the] third century

- 1976: Mao died and Gang of Four toppled

- 1978: Deng Xiaoping gains power and talks of modernization

- 1979: Religious freedom announced, though controlled by TSPM and CCC; churches reopened

- 1980–1985: Many house-church leaders imprisoned for itinerant prayers, distributions of Bibles and literature, contact [with] overseas churches, etc.

- June 1989: Beijing massacre

THE STATUS OF CHRISTIANITY IN CHINA (1985)

Themes: Government, Politics and National Identity; Mission

By 1985, [there are] around fifty million Protestant Christians and around twenty million Roman Catholics [in China]. In Hunan, ten out of seventy-five million are Protestants.

1. *1949–1955: Destruction of Institutional Church*

    » 1949: Six thousand missionaries and less than one million Christians

> » 1950: Three-Self Patriotic Movement's manifesto acknowledging Christianity [as a] tool of cultural aggression and support for New China

> » 1955: Arrests. Pastors recanted.

2. *1958–1966: Rise of House-Church Movement*

> » 1958: Two hundred churches [in] Shanghai reduced to eight. Sixty-six churches [in] Peking reduced to four.

> » Leaderless Christians met in homes. Church can survive without buildings or pastors!

3. *1966–1969: Cultural Revolution*

> » Red guards attack everybody including Three-Self.

> » Faithful pastors safe in prison!

> » Christians grew through suffering.

4. *1969–1976: Rebuilding through Prayer and Spirit*

> » Some house churches grew to four hundred members.

> » Signs and miracles (larger meetings)

> » Few preachers

5. *1978–1982: Open Door Policy*

> » Religious Affairs Bureau reestablished Three-Self.

> » Two thousand open churches claimed; Nanking and eight regional seminaries. Religion no longer illegal. Elders released from prison; house churches grew.

> » Revival and missions, also heresy and immorality

6. *1982–*

> » Pressure to join Three-Self [Patriotic Movement]

> » Four modernizations (industry, agriculture, scientific technologies and defense), no arrests; religion part of culture, capitalism encouraged[30]

"THOSE WHO IGNORE HISTORY"

Themes: Wisdom

"Those who ignore history are condemned to repeat it." This epigram is probably a popular corruption of a longer saying by George Santayana, the Spanish American (poet, novelist, philosopher, d. 1952): "Progress, far from consisting in change, depends on retentiveness. ... Those who cannot remember the past are condemned to fulfil it."

JUSTICE

THE BRIDGEWATER THREE

Themes: Justice; Killing

Following "The Guildford Four" and "The Birmingham Six" came "The Bridgewater Three" (1997): Jim Robinson, Vincent Hickey, and Michael Hickey, who were wrongfully convicted in 1979 for the murder of thirteen-year-old newspaper boy Carl Bridgewater at Yew Tree Farm in Staffordshire, and sentenced to life imprisonment.

Their conviction rested on one main evidence, the "confession" of Pat Molloy, which he soon after said had been extracted from him by police torture. Pat died in prison. The other three spent eighteen years in prison unjustly. If capital punishment were still being

---

30. Jonathan Chao, talk at LICC (August 1985).

practiced, they would of course have been executed for a crime they never committed.

LEADERSHIP

GOD GENERALLY BEGINS SMALL

Themes: Church Leadership; Providence;
Kingdom of God; Leadership

On January 28, 1770 (eight months before he died), the governor of Georgia came to George Whitefield's orphanage, Bethesda, ten miles from Savannah, for the official opening of two wings which were to house a college and seminary. George Whitefield preached on "Who hath despised the day of small things?"

"He showed them from the Bible that 'whenever God intends to bring about any great thing, he generally begins with a day of small things.' He warmed to this theme and spoke of Greece and Rome, and 'I can hardly forbear mentioning the small beginnings of Great Britain, now so distinguished for liberty, opulence and renown. And the rise and rapid progress of the American Colonies, which promises to be one of the most opulent and powerful empires in the world.'

"Eventually, after ranging through Scriptures and reminding his audience how the despised carpenter's Son rose from the dead, he came to the despised, impoverished beginnings of Georgia as he had found it in 1738," thirty-two years previously. "He gloried in recalling God's unfailing provision. ... He led them to a final rapturous adoration of Christ who had laid the foundation and would finish the work."[31]

---

31. John Pollock, *George Whitefield and the Great Awakening* (Hodder and Stoughton, 1973), 258–60.

LORD FISHER'S ADVICE TO YOUNG MIDSHIPMEN

Themes: Church Leadership; Counseling; Leadership; Prayer; Vision

A young midshipman, greatly daring, wrote [the] late Lord Fisher [a] letter on behalf of [the] junior officers in his gunroom to this effect: "My Lord, you were once a midshipman like ourselves; and now you are at the head of our profession. Can you tell us how you did it?"

[Fisher responded,] "Get a vision of the great thing you want to accomplish. Get a *plan* of the way in which you hope to achieve it. Be prepared to *battle* for it. Pray earnestly to God to give you the victory."[32]

POWER TENDS TO CORRUPT

Themes: Church Leadership; Leadership; Power

'Twas Lord Acton who composed the epigram "Power tends to corrupt, and absolute power corrupts absolutely."

He was [a] nineteenth-century British politician, a friend and adviser of Gladstone (four times prime minister). He was very disturbed to see democracy undermined by power styles. He was Roman Catholic, but in 1870 he strongly opposed [the] decision of [the] First Vatican Council to attribute infallibility to [the] pope. He saw it as *power corrupting* [the] *church.*

REASONS FOR LINCOLN'S POPULARITY

Themes: Leadership; Vision

Several presidential polls since World War II have ranked Abraham Lincoln (despite his known faults) the best chief executive in American history. Why? "Because he had a moral vision of where his country must go to preserve and enlarge the rights of all her people"; because

---

32. *Christian World Digest* (Winter 1946).

he had the "ability ... to articulate the promise that held for the liberation of oppressed humanity the world over"; and because "he made momentous *moral* decisions that affected the course of humankind"—especially, of course, in the emancipation of the slaves.[33]

THE SECRET OF WINNING THE SIX-DAY WAR

Themes: Church Leadership; Leadership; Victory and Defeat

The so-called Six-Day War was won by Israel over Egypt in June 1967. When Colonel Ariel Sharon, commanding officer of the leading tank battalion, was asked the secret of their victory, he answered, "We never say to our men, 'Forward! March!' We always say, 'Follow me!' "

WHAT TRANSFORMED BOB GELDOF

Themes: Conversion; Guilt; Leadership

What happened to transform the "scruffy Irish pop singer" into "St. Bob," the cult hero who alerted [the] world to the famine holocaust in Africa? Toward [the] end [of] 1984 he had a kind of "secular conversion." He watched on TV the news report on [the] famine in Ethiopia. The pictures were of people who were "so shrunken by starvation that they looked like beings from another planet" (p. 269). "I felt disgusted, enraged and outraged, but more than all those, I felt deep shame" (p. 271). "A horror like this could not occur without our consent. ... I had to withdraw my consent" (p. 271).

Out of that experience came [the] first Band Aid ([with] record sales of £8m), then on July 13, 1985 Live Aid, [the] biggest satellite TV event ever, [the] greatest assembly of rock musicians, with two billion in [the] audience (raising $100m).

---

33. Stephen B. Oates, *Abraham Lincoln: The Man behind the Myths* (New American Library, 1984), 57.

What drove him? A combination of "pity and disgust" (p. 386).[34]

MONARCHY

CHRISTIANS ARE SUBJECTS OF AN
EVERLASTING KINGDOM

Themes: Eternity; Government, Politics and
National Identity; Kingdom of God

When Her Majesty the Queen visited Australia in October 1973 for the opening of the Sydney Opera House, she attended a service in St. Andrew's Cathedral at which Archbishop Marcus Loane preached. He began by affirming the loyalty and affection of Australians to the queen, and the ties which bind Australia to England and the Commonwealth, but continued: "The inmost significance of a Service like this is to remind ourselves that there is another Sovereign to whom we owe obedience and another Kingdom to which we ought to belong." Christians "are subjects of an everlasting kingdom which cannot be shaken," pilgrims traveling to the eternal city: "And the central Figure in that city will be Jesus the Lord, whose Deity and Dominion will then be owned by all."

GIVING HOMAGE TO THE QUEEN

Themes: Sovereignty of God; Kingdom of God; Submission

During [the] coronation in Westminster Abbey, the Archbishop of Canterbury called four times toward the four points of [the] compass: "Sirs, I present unto you the undoubted Queen of this realm. Are you willing to do her homage?"

---

34. Bob Geldof (with Paul Vallely), *Is That It?* (Penguin, 1986).

Not until a great affirmative shout had thundered down the Abbey nave four times was the crown brought out and placed on [the] sovereign's head. Then came the Enthronement, and then the Homage.

All the princes and the peers then present were then to do their homage. Each ascended the steps of [the] throne, removed his own coronet, knelt before Her Majesty, placed his hand between hers, and said, "I ... Duke, or Earl, etc., of ... do become your liege man of life and limb, and of earthly worship; and faith and truth I will bear unto you, to live and die, against all manner of folks. So help me God."

When the homage is ended, the drums shall beat and the trumpets sound, and all the people shout, crying out: "God save Queen Elizabeth ... Long live Queen Elizabeth ... May the Queen live for ever."

A VIKING KING HUMBLED BY THE SEA

Themes: Sovereignty of God; Humility; Kingdom of God

Knut Sveinsson (son of Forkbeard) invaded England from Denmark in 1015 and became king of England in 1016. For twenty years he brought peace, order, and justice to England. The famous story of his trying to resist the sea first occurs in Henry of Huntingdon's *Historia Anglorum* (c. 1130). Knut "gave orders for his throne to be placed on the seashore as the tide came in" (traditionally at Bosham Beach near Chichester). He then addressed the rising tide: "'You are within my jurisdiction. No one has ever resisted my command with impunity. I therefore command you not to rise over my land and not to presume to wet the clothes or limbs of your lord.' But the sea rose as usual, and wetted the King's feet and legs without respect."

Henry of Huntingdon goes to make a moral out of it, viz. that King Knut *intended* his court to see the waters disobey him. Jumping back onto dry land he said: "'Be it known to all inhabitants of the world that the power of kings is empty and superficial, and that no one is worthy of the name of king except for Him whose will is obeyed by Heaven, earth and sea, in accordance with eternal laws.' And with that he took off his golden crown and never put it on his head again."[35]

OLD AGE

GREAT ACCOMPLISHMENTS AFTER FIFTY

Themes: Work

- At fifty-three Beethoven wrote the Ninth Symphony.

- At fifty-seven Handel wrote the *Messiah*.

- Louis Pasteur discovered the vaccination for rabies at sixty-two.

- Michelangelo didn't begin his work on St. Peter's Cathedral until he was over seventy and kept working on it until his death at eighty-nine.

- Among writers, age knows no limits. Tolstoy, Shaw, Victor Hugo, and Bertrand Russell all did their best work after seventy-five.[36]

NO AGE LIMIT ON SERVICE

Themes: Eschatology: Second Coming; Service; Work

Daddy Hall (who died in 1950 aged eighty-five) began at the age of seventy-five his renowned telephone ministry in New York City, and at the age of eighty acquired St. Paul's House near Madison Square Garden as an evangelism center:

I am now convinced that God has no age limit on service. A countless host of men and women of great age have been used

---

35. Magnus Magnusson, *Vikings!* (Bodley Head and BBC, 1980), 275–76.
36. *Eternity* (November 1978).

of God to do mighty things—Moses, Abraham, etc., and I am doing all I can to steer old people to feel and realize that they are not retired nor on the shelf, but are yet able and capable of doing many wonderful things. I am sure I would not last long if I dropped back into the rocking chair or sat under the juniper tree hunting a breeze wherever I could. I do not belong to the Church of the Heavenly Rest, but to the Chapel of the Holy Effort. The former is full of men and women awaiting the undertaker and causing many of their friends to wish he would not delay his coming.[37]

AN OLD MAN'S CHRISTMAS LETTER

Themes: Weakness

Christmas letter from [an] eighty-four-year-old man:

- "If the toothbrush is wet in the morning, you have brushed your teeth."

- "If the radio is warm, you left it on all night."

- "I stagger when I walk. Small boys gather behind me and bet which way I will lurch next. I don't like this: children should not gamble."

- "If I have a black shoe on one foot and a brown on the other, I know I have a matching pair somewhere in my closet."

- "My wife and I spend a great deal of time in front of the TV. We rarely turn it on."

---

37. Sara C. Palmer, *Daddy Hall, "Bishop of Wall Street"* (Moody, 1954), 127.

PEACE

BRINGING TRANQUILITY TO EARTH

Themes: Peace

Soon after 4 a.m. on Monday, July 21, 1969, when man first landed on [the] moon, President Nixon radioed to them: "As you talk to us from the Sea of Tranquility, it inspires us to redouble our efforts to bring peace and tranquility to earth."

THE ELUSIVENESS OF PEACE IN SOUTH AMERICA

Themes: Peace

Argentina and Chile made a pact with each other in 1902, and afterwards erected a huge statue of Christ on the frontier above La Cumbre Pass. The inscription reads: "Sooner shall these mountains crumble into dust than Argentines and Chileans break the peace which at the feet of Christ the Redeemer they have sworn to maintain."

La Paz, capital of Bolivia, is Spanish for "peace," though it has experienced 150+ uprisings since Bolivia became independent in 1825!

MARXIST OPPOSITION TO RELIGION

Themes: Atheism; Government, Politics and National Identity; Philosophy

The Marxist vision is to create a society [that is] both classless and religionless. Hence the ruthless atheistic program developed in [the] Soviet Union.

- *1925:* League of Militant Atheists founded to propagate [atheism].

- *1929:* Law limiting religious organizations. Enforced by Stalin until 1941, but disregarded 1941–1959, until Khrushchev enforced it 1959 onwards. I.e., no religious organization (e.g., Sunday Schools) for children. No libraries, no clergy work *outside* church, no publication of books, no under-eighteens allowed to worship.

- *By 1935* (?) [the] Soviet government claimed around 90 percent of sixteen- to nineteen-year-olds were atheists. Twelve university departments [were] formed to promote "scientific atheism." Also around 160 newspapers dedicated to spread atheism.

- *From 1959* onward, anti-religious literature published, and widespread closing of churches and monasteries.[38]

THE NOBEL PEACE PRIZE

Themes: Peace

Alfred Bernhard Nobel was a nineteenth-century Swedish engineer and chemist. It was he who first produced a patented dynamite. [He] made [a] fortune out of [the] manufacture of explosives, and Baku oil fields; and directed in his will that [the] interest [be] used for five prizes—physics, chemistry, medicine, literature, and peace, [which is given to] "the person who shall have most or best promoted the fraternity of nations, and the abolition or diminution of standing armies, and the formation and increase of peace congresses."

[The] first four [are] awarded in Sweden; [the] fifth by [a] committee of [the] Norwegian Storting. [Nobel requested that] "no consideration whatever be paid to the nationality of the candidates."

[Among others, the] peace prize [has been] awarded to Austen Chamberlain (1925), Theodore Roosevelt (1906), Woodrow Wilson (1919), Philip Noel-Baker (1959).

---

38. From Peter Kuzmic's papers.

SUNDAR SINGH'S PERSECUTION BY HIS FAMILY

Themes: Conversion; Persecution

Sundar Singh was born into a Sikh family and converted to Christ by a vision when [he was] fifteen. He immediately told his family. "Some said I was mad; some that I had dreamed; but, when they saw that I was not to be turned, they began to persecute me. But the persecution was nothing compared with that miserable unrest I had had when I was without Christ; and it was not difficult for me to endure the troubles and persecution which now began" (p. 102).

Soon after, he left home and became a Sadhu. When a little later he returned home,

> at first my father refused to see me, or to let me in, because by becoming a Christian, I had dishonoured the family. But after a little while he came out and said: "Very well, you can stay here tonight; but you must get out early in the morning; don't show me your face again." I remained silent, and that night he made me sit at a distance that I might not pollute them or their vessels, and then he brought me food, and gave me water to drink by pouring it into my hands from a vessel held high above, as one does to an outcaste.
>
> When I saw this treatment, I could not restrain the tears from flowing from my eyes that my father, who used to love me so much, now hated me as if I was untouchable. In spite of all this, my heart was filled with inexpressible peace. (pp. 108–9)

NB: Years later his father also turned to Christ.[39]

---

39. Sundar Singh, *With and Without Christ* (Cassell, 1929).

WANG MING-TAO'S COURAGE IN
THE FACE OF PERSECUTION

Themes: Compromise; Courage; Persecution; Truth

The Rev. Wang Ming-Tao was pastor of [a] church in East Peking [and] actively engaged in [the] ministry of preaching and writing. When Communists captured Peking, he continued.

In 1951, he wrote in his *Spiritual Food Quarterly*, as [the] opposition of [the] Three-Self reform movement [was] growing: "The One who faithfully preaches the word of God cannot but expect to meet opposition. ... I know that this will come to pass. I am prepared to meet it. I covet the courage and faithfulness of Martin Luther ..." and quoted one of his prayers.

In 1954 Mr. Wang suffered the ordeal of a vast public accusation meeting. But he continued without fear.

In 1955 [he] wrote [in a] pamphlet: "We are ready to pay any price to preserve the Word of God, and we are equally willing to sacrifice anything in order to preach the Word of God. ... Dear Brothers and Sisters, let us be strong through the mighty power of the Lord. ... Don't be cowards! Don't be weary! Don't give way! Don't compromise! The battle is indeed furious and the battlefield certainly full of dangers; but God's glory will be manifest there. ... My dear brothers and sisters, let us follow in the steps of the Lord, and holding aloft His banner, go forward courageously for His Gospel's sake."

That was, I think, in May 1955. On August 7, 1955 [he] preached [his] last sermon, on "[the] Son of man is betrayed into [the] hands of sinners," regarding [the] betrayal of Christianity by [the] Three-Self movement. That night at 1 a.m. [he was] roused from sleep by police. [He was] bound with ropes and taken to prison. "Mr. Valiant-for-truth."[40]

---

40. Leslie Lyall, *Come Wind, Come Weather: The Present Experience of the Church in China* (Hodder and Stoughton).

POLITICS

ADVOCATES OF VIOLENCE

Themes: Violence

1. The Black Panther slogan regarding 1968, "The Year of the Pig": "The Death of the Ballot, the Birth of the Bullet" (p. 10).

2. Lenin on [the] eve of [the] 1917 Revolution: "The substitution of the proletariat State for the bourgeois State is impossible without a violent revolution" (p. 14).

3. Frantz Fanon in *The Wretched of the Earth*, championing the native peasant versus the settlers in Algeria, rationalizes violence by three arguments:

    a. Only violence can overcome violence.

    b. Violence integrates and unifies the oppressed.

    c. Violence is cathartic, liberating the oppressed from their inferiority complex, despair, and inactivity, and restoring self respect.

4. In his intro to [the] book, Sartre [writes]: "The irrepressible violence is neither sound nor fury, nor the restoration of savage instincts, nor even the effect of resentment; it is man re-creating himself. ... To shoot a European is to kill two birds with one stone, to destroy an oppressor and the man he oppresses at the same time; there remains a dead man and a free man" (pp. 15–17).[41]

---

41. Quoted in Brian Griffiths, *Is Revolution Change?* (IVP, 1972).

POLITICS IS "CALCULATED CHEATING"

Themes: Government, Politics and National
Identity; Honesty and Dishonesty

"Politics represents the art of calculated cheating, or, more precisely, how to cheat without really being caught."

The author of that cynical maxim was James R. Schlesinger in 1968 in a prestigious law journal, while still an academic and before he became (in 1977) Jimmy Carter's secretary of energy.[42]

SOLZHENITSYN ON THE FALSEHOOD OF ALL REVOLUTIONS

Themes: Character; Evil; Government, Politics and National Identity

Solzhenitsyn describes how he came gradually to see that "the line separating good and evil passes not through states, nor between classes, nor between political parties either—but right through every human heart." Thus all religions "struggle with the *evil inside a human being (inside* every human being). ... And since that time I have come to understand the falsehood of all revolutions of history: they destroy only *those carriers* of evil contemporary with them. ... And they then take to themselves as their heritage the actual evil itself, magnified still more."[43]

THE TRUE REVOLUTIONARY GUIDED BY LOVE

Themes: Freedom; Government, Politics and National Identity; Love

Che Guevara: "Let me say, with the risk of appearing ridiculous, that the true revolutionary is guided by strong feelings of love. It is impossible to think of an authentic revolutionary without this quality" (p. 62).

---

42. *Guardian Weekly* (September 17, 1978).

43. Aleksandr Solzhenitsyn, *The Gulag Archipelago III–IV* (Harper and Row, 1975), 615–16.

The tragedy is that "the oppressed find in the oppressor their model of 'manhood' " (p. 23). But "the oppressed must not ... become in turn oppressors of the oppressors, but rather restorers of the humanity of both. This, then, is the great humanistic and historical task of the oppressed: to liberate themselves and their oppressors as well" (p. 21).

Thus the oppressed must avoid four mistakes:

1. fatalism (self-depreciation, capable of nothing, passivity);

2. fear of bosses and of freedom;

3. envy (wishing to become an oppressor); and

4. revenge.[44]

VIOLENCE AND THE AFRICAN NATIONAL CONGRESS

Themes: Government, Politics and National Identity; Violence

The ANC was a response to the apartheid legislation of 1948 onwards under chief Albert Luthuli and later Nelson Mandela. In 1959 Robert Sobukwe broke with Mandela and formed the PAC (Pan-Africanist Congress). In 1961 both ANC and PAC were banned, and Mandela and Sobukwe jailed. In his statement to court on April 20, 1964, Mandela explained how ANC had espoused violence as the only way of effective protest against "many years of tyranny, exploitation and oppression of my people by whites" (p. 25).

All lawful methods of expressing opposition to this principle [of white supremacy] had been closed by legislation, and we were placed in a position in which we had either to accept a permanent state of inferiority, or to defy the government. We chose to defy the law. We first broke the law in a way which avoided any recourse to violence; when this form was legislated against, and the government resorted to a show of force

---

44. Paulo Freire, *Pedagogy of the Oppressed* (Penguin, 1992), 62.

to crush opposition to its policies, only then did we decide to answer violence with violence.

But this was sabotage (e.g., of power plants, … to scare away capital from the country), and neither terrorism nor guerrilla warfare nor open revolution (p. 26).[45]

RACE

BRAMWELL BOOTH'S RESPONSE TO PREJUDICE DURING WORLD WAR I

Themes: Church Fellowship and Unity; Prejudice

During World War I "a fever of hatred for all things German gripped Britain. The Duke of Edinburgh's great-uncle, Prince Louis of Battenberg, was driven from his post as First Lord of the Admiralty. Only the personal intervention of King George V scotched the barely credible suggestion of Lord Fisher: for every air raid on Britain, batches of German prisoners should be systematically shot. Dachshunds were stoned through the streets."

But Bramwell Booth, general of the international Salvation Army since his father's death in 1912, took an unflinching stand. "'An army which recognised no barriers of colour or sex must rise above racial hatred.' As in World War Two, sub-editors slashed the word 'enemy' from every page-proof of Army copy. 'Keep it in mind that you are international,' Bramwell briefed one editor, 'as Jesus Christ was.' … At the close of 1915 he rallied his troops with the reminder: 'Every land is my Fatherland, for all lands are my Father's.' "[46]

---

45. Donald Woods, *Biko*, revised ed. (Penguin, 1987).
46. Richard Collier, *The General Next to God* (Collins, 1965), 249–50.

CHRISTMAS 1969 IN MENDENHALL, MISSISSIPPI

Themes: Injustice; Birth of Jesus; Prejudice

In December 1969 in Mendenhall, Mississippi, "whites and blacks alike began their usual—separate—preparations to celebrate the birth of the Prince of Peace" (p. 130).

Two days before Christmas the black leader John Perkins and his young white friend Doug Huemmer drove down Main Street: "Christmas lights glowed on the town square and on the stately, domed county courthouse. ... Christmas music seemed to be everywhere, filling the air. Silent night, holy night ... all is calm, all is bright" (p. 131). It sounded a mockery as they drove past the road signs: "White people unite, defeat Jew/Communist race mixers" (p. 132).

In the city, after trying to rescue a young black who had been drinking and was arguing angrily with a white shopkeeper, Perkins and Huemmer were flashed down by a police car and the slightly tipsy black was rudely and unwarrantably arrested and jailed. Later when Perkins visited him, he too was arrested and jailed. An angry black crowd gathered outside, but through the bars of his cell window Perkins pleaded with them not to return hate for hate, anger for anger, or violence for violence (p. 141).

Around two or three in the morning of Christmas Eve, John and Doug were officially charged and locked up, and the crowd dispersed. "The cell was bare. And the floor was hard. No Christmas carols now—except in memory. All is calm, all is bright. I had trouble sleeping" (p. 144).[47]

---

47. John Perkins, *Let Justice Roll Down* (Regal, 1976).

MALCOLM X ON CHRISTIANITY AS
THE WHITE MAN'S RELIGION

Themes: Cults and Non-Christian Religions; Jesus

Malcolm X, son of a Baptist preacher, renounced Christianity for Islam because he was persuaded that Islam was the black man's "natural religion." Christianity, by contrast, was the white man's religion, indeed the white slave owner's, so that the Negro was taught to worship "an alien God having the same blond hair, pale skin and blue eyes as the slave master" (p. 163). When Malcolm X became the minister of a Muslim "temple," this was a frequent theme of his preaching: "Brothers and sisters, the white man has brainwashed us black people to fasten our gaze upon a blond-haired, blue-eyed Jesus! ... The blond-haired, blue-eyed white man has taught you and me to worship a White Jesus" (p. 220).[48]

WHAT INSPIRED MZEE JOMO KENYATTA

Themes: Freedom; Injustice; Justice; Peace

[In the] foreword by Mzee Jomo Kenyatta to *Suffering without Bitterness*: "If asked to define what causes have inspired my life and striving, I would say that I have stood always for the purposes of human dignity in freedom, and for the values of tolerance and peace. ... One of the great affronts to human dignity which I have always opposed, is that of racialism."

At a political rally at Wundanyi on January 27, 1962, he said about his attitude to Europeans: "I am not against anyone. I am only against *Ubwang*, the boss mentality."[49]

---

48. Malcolm X, *The Autobiography of Malcolm X*, ed. Alex Haley (Grove Press, 1964).

49. Jomo Kenyatta, *Suffering without Bitterness* (East African Publishing House, 1968), xi, 166.

SANCTITY OF LIFE

BABY DOE

Themes: Sanctity of Life; Suffering

In 1982 in Bloomington, Indiana, an infant born with both Down syndrome and an esophagus detached from [the] stomach (correctable by surgery) was allowed to die, on the ground that he would have a "minimally acceptable quality of life." This was "Baby Doe," whose birth sparked furious controversy, and led in 1984 to Reagan's Child Abuse Amendment Act, which makes it a criminal offense not to treat handicapped infants except in cases where the condition is so serious that treatment would only prolong the death process. It also provides for a societal-based committee structure to review medical decisions. United States Surgeon General C. Everett Koop said in September 1984 to the American Academy of Pediatrics Committee on Hospital Care: "When we say, 'Baby Doe has a life that's not worth living,' are we not really saying, 'It's not worth our effort to care for him'?"

BETTER OFF DEAD?

Themes: Sanctity of Life; Suffering

At a pro-life, anti-abortion rally in Hyde Park in June 1973, I met Alison Davis, who described herself as a "happy spina bifida adult" [and] spoke from a wheelchair. I can think of few concepts more terrifying than saying that certain persons are better off dead, or may therefore be killed for their own good. One doctor, on hearing her say that she was glad to be alive, "made the incredible observation that none can judge their own quality of life." Some doctors try to persuade themselves that starving handicapped babies to death is not killing them.

THE CASE AGAINST CLONING

Themes: Sanctity of Life

Leon Kass (University of Chicago medical ethics professor and head of [George W.] Bush's bioethics commission) summarizes the case against cloning:

1. Cloning is a form of experimentation on a nonconsenting subject.

2. Cloning threatens human identity by permitting genetic replication of a person already in being.

3. Cloning turns procreating into manufacturing.

4. Cloning is an act of despotism which perverts parenthood by turning children into possessions.[50]

TERTULLIAN ON THE CHRISTIAN RESPONSE TO INFANTICIDE

Themes: Killing; Sanctity of Life

In his *Apology* Tertullian accuses the Romans of infanticide, and continues: "But to us, to whom homicide has been once for all forbidden, it is not permitted to break up even what has been conceived in the womb, while as yet the blood is being drawn (from the parent body) for a human life. Prevention of birth is premature murder, and it makes no difference whether it is a life already born that one snatches away, or a life in the act of being born that one destroys; that which is to be a human being is also human; the whole fruit is already actually present in the seed."

---

50. David P. Gushee, "A Matter of Life and Death," *Christianity Today* (October 2001), 39.

SATISFACTION

AN ACTRESS WHO FOUND MEANING IN CHRIST

Themes: Contentment; Conversion;
Depression; Happiness; Loneliness

Joan Winmill (Mrs. Bill Brown) wrote in *New York Crusade News*
November 1956: "I was an actress on the London stage—the fulfilment of all my childhood dreams … [I'd been] chosen for the leading role in a very successful show which ran for almost two years in
London. With this came everything I had ever dreamed of: parties,
gay functions, flowers, and all that goes with being an actress. But I
began to experience a *deep inner loneliness* that I could not understand.
Here I was, the envy of many of my friends, in the place I had always
longed for, and yet I was not happy."

She then described the nervous strain and anxiety and "contin-
ual fight for the big break." "My nerves went to pieces … I began to
contemplate suicide. Night after night I would lie awake longing for
rest from all my problems. … Two and a half years ago my life was
meaningless and I had nothing to live for. Now, with thanksgiving
to Christ who has granted me salvation, I know the true meaning of
the verse 'Seek ye first the Kingdom of God.' "[51]

EATING WITH NO SATISFACTION

Themes: Contentment; Idolatry

[A] strange plant called nardoo grows in [the] deserts of Central
Australia. [It is] like a fern, and natives eat its seeds when they can
obtain no other food. One peculiar property [is that] it satisfies and
produces [a] pleasant feeling of comfort, but it does not nourish.

---

51. Joan Winmill Brown, *New York Crusade News* (November 1956).

[A] party of explorers, crossing this central desert, [once] ran out of food. [Their] leader, Captain King, recommended nardoo as he knew [the] natives ate it. Day after day they fed on it. At first [they] felt satisfied, but soon [their] strength began to fail. Finally, it killed them. They wasted away, lay down, and died of starvation. A solitary survivor was discovered under a tree, and he told the story.

Jesus is [the] Bread of Life![52]

THE THINGS WE LOOK TO FOR MEANING DON'T SATISFY

Themes: Atheism; Contentment; Doubt; Happiness; Money; Pride; Power

1. *Money.* Jay Gould, American millionaire, exclaimed with [his] dying breath: "I'm the most miserable devil in the world."

2. *Ambition.* Alexander the Great, when [the] whole world (known) lay at his feet, wept with chagrin that [his] exploits must cease, there being "no more worlds to conquer" (in Indian tent).

3. *Popularity.* Lord Byron, with laurels of fame on his brow, wrote in despair before he died, "My days are in the yellow leaf / The Fruit, the flower of life is gone / The worm, the canker, and the grief are mine alone."

4. *Unbelief.* Voltaire: "I wish I had never been born."

5. *Pleasure and Self-Indulgence.* Solomon: wisdom, wine, built houses, vineyard garden and parks, slaves, herds and flocks, silver, gold, singers, and concubines.

6. *Position.* (a) Bismarck said [the] only feeling of real happiness he could recall was when, as [a] boy, [he] shot a rabbit! (b) Beaconsfield wrote, "Youth is a mistake, manhood a struggle, old age a regret."[53]

---

52. *Children's Special Service Mission Magazine* (1940).
53. *Portman Review* (September 1948).

SCIENCE

THE BOOK OF GOD'S WORD AND
THE BOOK OF GOD'S WORKS

Themes: Creation; Revelation; Scripture

Francis Bacon (died 1626) wrote, and Charles Darwin quoted as a motto for his *Origin of Species*, the following exhortation: "Let no man think or maintain that he can search too far or be too well studied in the book of God's Word or in the book of God's works … but rather let men endeavour on endless progress and proficiency in both."

THE CHRISTIAN ROOTS OF MODERN SCIENCE

Themes: Creation; Philosophy

The rise of modern science has Christian roots, especially a set of attitudes toward the material world:

1. *Christianity is interested in the material world.* Creation is good.

2. *Nature is orderly,* consistent, rational.

3. *Nature is intelligible.* "A rational God does not create an irrational universe. Johannes Kepler (1571–1630) and Francis Bacon (1561–1626) both stressed a religious motive for doing science," i.e., the vocation to praise God by understanding his works.

4. "The results of our investigations are to be *shared.* Science is above all a communal affair" (p. 26).[54]

---

54. Diogenes Allen, *Christian Belief in a Postmodern World* (Westminster John Knox, 1989), 23–27.

KEY ASTRONOMICAL DISCOVERIES

Themes: Creation

- Thales of Miletus (c. 600 BC) said [the] earth [was] round.

- Pythagoras (c. 400 BC) said [the] earth [was] spherical and moving.

- Aristarchus of Samos (310 BC–230 BC) insisted [the] earth rotates and revolves and is not [the] center.

- Archimedes of Syracuse (died 212 BC): Liquid displacement.

- Hipparchus of Rhodes and Alexandria (c. 150 BC): [The] earth [is] spherical but stationary and orbited by [the] sun, moon, and planets.

- Claudius Ptolemy (c. AD 140): Systemized Hipparchus's theories that [the] universe [is] revolving round [a] stationary earth. [This was] accepted until [the] fifteenth century (problem = no clocks until [the] end of [the] thirteenth century and no Arabic numerals until [the] twelfth century).

- Nicolaus Copernicus of Poland (1473–1543): Proved [the] sun [is the] center, orbited by earth. …

- Tycho Brahe of Denmark (sixteenth century) observatory, though still earth-centered.

- Galileo of Italy (1564–1642) used [the] telescope [in] 1609 [and] confirmed Copernicus, but [the] Inquisition forced him [to] recant and [be] silent.

- Johannes Kepler of Germany and Prague (1571–1680) discovered planetary orbits are elliptical, speeding up when close to [the] sun.

- Isaac Newton (1642–1727): Universal laws of gravitation. *Principia.* Centrifugal versus gravitational. Moon causing tides. Discovered prism and reflector telescope.

- Sir William Herschel, German-born English (1738–1822): Powerful telescopes. Discovered Uranus, etc.

- Albert Einstein (1839–1955): Relativity.

<u>Thales of Miletus</u> (c. 600 BC) said earth round.

<u>Pythagoras</u> (c. 400 BC) said earth spherical & moving.

<u>Aristarchus of Samos</u> (310 - 230 BC) insisted earth rotates & revolves axis not centre.
Archimedes of Syracuse (†212 BC) 'Liquid displacement'.

<u>Hipparchus</u> of Rhodes & Alex: (c. 150 BC)
Earth spherical but stationary & orbited by sun, moon & planet s.

<u>Claudius Ptolemy</u> (c. 140 A.D) systematized Hipparchus' theories that univ: revolving round stationary earth. Accepted till ⑮.

(Problem = no clocks till end ⑬ & no Arabic numerals till c. ⑫).

<u>Nicholas Copernicus</u> of Poland (1473-1543)
proved sun centre, orbited by earth.
Acc. to Luther a fool the Pope Paul III men
Tycho Brahe of Denmark. (⑯) Observatory no Italians

<u>Galileo</u> of Italy (1564 - 1642) used
telescope, 1609 confirmed Copernicus, but inquisition forced him recant & silew

<u>Johannes Kepler</u> of Germany & Prague, (1571 - 1630)
discovered planets orbits = elliptical, speeds up when close to sun.

<u>Isaac Newton</u> (1642-1727) universal law of gravitation. <u>Principia</u>. centrifugal & gravitation
moon causing tides. Discovered prism & reflecting telescope.

(<u>Albert Einstein</u> (1879 - 1955). Relativity

✓ <u>Sir Wm Herschel</u>, german-born Eng. (1738-1822)
& mendrie telescopes. Discovered Uranus etc.

Astronomy

NO SINGLE THEORY IS ABLE TO EXPLAIN DREAMS

Themes: Vision

To Freud [the] essence of dreams was the expression of repressed desires; to Jung [they were] glimpses of collective unconscious; to Charles Rycroft [they were] involuntary poetic activity; to Francis Crick [they were] a necessary means of ridding the brain of parasitic modes of behavior. Dr. Charles Fisher of Mount Sinai Medical Center: "Dreaming permits each of us to be quietly and safely insane every night of our lives." In *Theatre of Sleep* (Picador, 1986), Guido Almansi and Claude Béguin (husband and wife) give a selection of around two hundred dreams from three thousand years of Western literature. They emphasize the anarchic, mysterious, and ultimately inexplicable nature of dreams. No one theory is able to explain them all.[55]

THE RAPID PROGRESS OF SCIENCE

Themes: Creation

More than one million new scientific discoveries are published every year.

It took Columbus two months to cross the Atlantic; fifty years ago it took two weeks; a Concorde will do it in two hours.[56]

THREE DEFINITIONS OF A PRIMROSE

Themes: Creation

Prof. C. A. Coulson chose a primrose to exemplify the principle of complementarity. To the question "What is a primrose?" [there are] three valid answers.

---

55. J. G. Ballard, Review, *Guardian Weekly* (Summer 1986).
56. Prof. C. A. Coulson at Uppsala (1968).

1. [Wordsworth:] "A primrose by the river's brim / A yellow primrose was to him / And it was nothing more."

2. Scientist: "A primrose is a delicately balanced biochemical mechanism, requiring potash, phosphates, nitrogen and water in definite proportions."

3. "A primrose is God's promise of spring."

All three are correct.[57]

SCIENCE AND RELIGION

EXPERIENCES OF GOD

Themes: God; Presence of God; Prayer

In 1969 the zoologist Professor Sir Alister Hardy set up at Manchester College, Oxford, his "Religious Experience Unit" to collect firsthand experiences of "a benevolent non-physical power which appears to be partly or wholly beyond, and far greater than the individual self."

In early 1980 he produced [an] interim report in *The Spiritual Nature of Man* (OUP). He gives a detailed account, under twelve headings (such as visual sensory experiences, auditory sensual experiences, extrasensory perception, etc.) and eighty-eight subdivisions, of some three thousand experiences.

"For the great majority there is a strong feeling of a transcendental reality ... and institutional religion plays little part in most of these accounts." Hardy concludes: "The main characteristics of man's religious and spiritual experiences are shown in his feelings for a transcendental reality which frequently manifest themselves in early childhood; a feeling that 'something other' than the self can actually be sensed: desire to personalize this presence into a deity, and to have a private I-Thou relationship with it, communicating through prayer."[58]

---

57. C. A. Coulson, *Science and Christian Belief* (OUP, 1955), 70.
58. Alister Hardy, *The Spiritual Nature of Man* (OUP, 1980).

MIRACLES ARE SIGNS OF GOD'S FAITHFULNESS

Themes: Creation; God's Faithfulness; Miracles

In his book *The Clockwork Image*, Professor Donald MacKay writes that "from the theistic point of view the question we ought to be asking about God's created world is not 'How could miracles happen?' but 'How come the world is as regular as it is?' 'Why should the pattern of events be as dependable as it is?' The Bible answers this in terms of the personal faithfulness of God."

But miracles express his faithfulness too. "Biblical theism insists that any breaks with scientific precedent that have occurred were but a further expression of the same faithfulness to a coherent over-all purpose which is normally expressed in the day-to-day reliability of nature on which we depend as scientists."

Compare Peter's reference to Christ's resurrection as something not incredible but inevitable, "because it was not possible for death to hold him" (Acts 2:24). "In other words, it would not have made sense for the Creator, when he came unto his own drama, to have been destroyed in any ultimate sense by characters in that drama."[59]

SCIENCE HAS NOT DISPENSED WITH GOD

Themes: Creation; Providence

"The scientist's religious feeling takes the form of a rapturous amazement at the harmony of natural law which reveals an intelligence of such superiority, that compared with it, all the systematic thinking and noting of human beings is an utterly insignificant reflection."

—Albert Einstein

---

59. Donald M. MacKay, *The Clockwork Image: A Christian Perspective on Science* (IVP, 1974), 63–65.

Science has not dispensed with God. *True, scientists have discovered the secrets of many natural processes. But in so doing,* they have been "thinking God's thoughts after him" because they are processes which God himself has established and continues to operate. Scientists are understanding and explaining God's ways; they are not explaining him away.

SEX

A 1971 ARGUMENT FOR SEXUAL PERMISSIVENESS

Themes: Sex; Sexual Immorality

The May 15, 1971 *MGW* had a leader on "the backlash ... against sexual permissiveness": "A backlash implies a return to a different norm. What are we proposing to return to? Is there some more healthy, stable and satisfying morality to which we can return? To the morality of the after war years? To the Edwardians or the Victorians?" No. Partly because "there is no unchangeable moral code that can be summarised in a decalogue." And partly because "Victorian morality was a fraud, sweeping prostitution and pornography into dark corners."

The old taboos were buttressed by the risk of pregnancy, but the pill "has made loving and responsible sexual relationships possible outside marriage. For those who do not acknowledge the religious prohibitions, it seems arbitrary and unnecessary to deny the place of sex in extramarital love. ... What is the harm if this greater openness makes for greater fulfilment and personal happiness? Is it not a positive advance in the human condition?" True, the experts disagree, but at least "there is some virtue in having a rather more easy-going, open-minded and plain-speaking society than we have had in the past."[60]

---

60. *Guardian Weekly* (May 15, 1971).

THE SEPARATION OF SEX FROM LOVE

Themes: Love; Philosophy; Sex

Do you know Woody Allen's film *Love and Death* (the two topics with which he is obsessed)? In it, Boris at last succeeds in getting his cousin into bed with him. But instead of making love, she starts philosophizing about the universe! When he attempts to seduce her, she exclaims, "Oh Boris, sex without love is a meaningless experience." To which he replies: "Yes, but as meaningless experiences go, it's one of the best!" Woody Allen gives the lie to his own claim.

Jack Dominian writes of "that dissociation of sex from love which is the besetting sin of our age" (*Christian Marriage*, p. 4).

YOU CANNOT TEACH THE BIOLOGY OF SEX
APART FROM AN IDEOLOGY OF SEX

Themes: Philosophy; Sex; Sexual Immorality

The British Health Education Authority conducted in 1994 a survey of 1,400 parents on sex education, which revealed that parents want their children taught the biology, not the morality, of reproduction. Facts should be taught (e.g., regarding pregnancy and AIDS) but not values (e.g., the ethics of sexual behavior).

Indeed, asked what subject parents would prefer schools not to teach, "religious and moral values" topped the list. But it's impossible to teach human beings a biology of sex divorced from an ideology of sex, i.e., a religious and moral framework for sexual behavior. If you divorce sex from ethics, human beings are free to treat sex as mice or rabbits do.

SLAVERY

ARISTOTLE ON SLAVERY

Themes: Slavery

In his passage on slavery in the *Politics*, Aristotle writes of "nature's own slave," created intended for bondage. He is "a chattel that lives," "a part of his master; as it were a living, though separated, portion of his body." He has really no existence apart from his master, for he is "not only the slave of the master, but the master's, wholly his."[61]

HARRIET BEECHER STOWE ON SLAVERY

Themes: Slavery

When Uncle Tom and others were waiting to be auctioned in a slave warehouse in New Orleans, Harriet Beecher Stowe soliloquized on the horror of human beings being sold as property: "That soul, immortal, once bought with blood and anguish by the Son of God, when the earth shook, and the rocks rent, and the graves were opened, can be sold, leased, mortgaged, exchanged for groceries or dry goods, to suit the phases of trade, or the fancy of the purchaser."[62]

JOHN WESLEY ON SLAVERY

Themes: Slavery

Early in 1772 John Wesley referred to the slave trade in his journal as "that execrable sum of all the villainies." And two years later, in 1774, [he] published his own booklet, *Thoughts Upon Slavery*.

---

61. Quoted in Handley C. G. Moule, *Thoughts on Christian Sanctity* (Moody, 1920), 55–56.

62. Harriet Beecher Stowe, *Uncle Tom's Cabin* (Bantam, 1981 [1851–1852]), 324–25.

Six days before his death, Wesley described Wilberforce as "Athanasius contra mundum" and slavery again as "that execrable villainy." In a letter to William Wilberforce three days before his death, John Wesley wrote:

My dear Sir,

Unless the Divine power has raised you up to be as Athanasius contra mundum, I see not how you can go through your glorious enterprise, in opposing that execrable villainy which is the scandal of religion, of England, and of human nature. Unless God has raised you up for this very thing, you will be worn out by the opposition of men and devils; but if God be for you who can be against you? Are all of them together stronger than God? Oh be not weary of well doing. Go on in the name of God, and in the power of his might, till even American slavery, the vilest that ever saw the sun, shall vanish away before it. That he who has guided you from your youth up may continue to strengthen you in this and all things, is the prayer of,

Dear Sir,
Your affectionate servant,
JOHN WESLEY
February 24, 1791

THE ROLE OF EVANGELICALS IN THE ABOLITION OF BRITISH SLAVERY

Themes: Freedom; Slavery

Evangelicals were primarily responsible for the abolition of the institution of slavery throughout the British Empire in the year 1833. The slave trade itself had been abolished in 1807; now the institution of slavery itself was abolished by the payment of twenty million pounds by way of compensation.

W. E. H. Lecky, the rationalist historian, in his *History of European Morals*, writes, "The unweary, unostentatious, and inglorious crusade of England against slavery may probably be regarded as among the three or four perfectly virtuous acts comprised in the history of nations."[63]

TRUTH

BENEDICTINE AND FRANCISCAN ATTITUDES TOWARD POSSESSIONS

Themes: Money; Poverty

- *Benedictines* (founded by Benedict of Nursia, d. 547) were not permitted to possess private property—or not without the abbot's specific permission. The Rule of St. Benedict quotes as warrant for this Acts 2:44 and 4:32.

- *Franciscans* (founded by Francis, d. 1226) follow [the] Rule of St. Francis, whose chapter 6 enacts: "The brothers shall possess nothing, neither a house, nor a place, nor anything." Instead, they must seek alms.

CONVERTED ALONG WITH HIS CAR

Themes: Conversion; Wealth

The Rev. Duncan Campbell, leader of [the] Hebrides Revival which began in October 1949, told [the] story of a young man who was converted. He had a fine car. He came to [the] minister and said, "I and my car were used in the service of the devil to damn young men and women. But when I met God; when Jesus Christ came into my life; when I was converted, God almighty converted my car also." Now the minister has a car and a chauffeur!

---

63. W. E. H. Lecky, *History of European Morals from Augustus to Charlemagne*, 3 vols. (Longmans, 1869), 1:161.

THE COVETOUSNESS OF EBENEZER SCROOGE

Themes: Greed; Money; Wealth

English literature knows no more covetous character than Charles Dickens's creation in *A Christmas Carol*, Ebenezer Scrooge. Near the beginning of the book he describes him as "a squeezing, wrenching, grasping, scraping, clutching, covetous old sinner" who moreover, was "hard and sharp as flint, from which no steel had ever struck out generous fire, secret and self-contained, and solitary as an oyster." Then: "The cold within him froze his old features, nipped his pointed nose, shrivelled his cheek, stiffened his gait; made his eyes red, his thin lips blue; and spoke out shrewdly in his grating voice."[64]

"MONEY IS THE OBJECT"

Themes: Greed; Money; Wealth

James Gulliver, who at one time was "Scotland's best known tycoon" and had "an extraordinarily astute business brain," made his first million aged thirty-three. At [the] peak of his business career he was chairman of the Lowndes Queensway Group, which ran a chain of furniture and carpet stores. But at [the] end of 1989 its shares were suspended, while in February 1990 he resigned, and seven months later the receivers were called in. "Wee Jimmy" (as he is known north of [the] border) was [a] multi millionaire, had five homes in different parts of Europe, and had a passion for yachts and exotic cars. In an interview with *You* magazine on September 11, 1988, he said, "I do not believe that money is no object. Money is *the* object."[65]

---

64. Charles Dickens, *A Christmas Carol*.
65. Press cuttings supplied by Jeremy Vine.

THE PERSISTENCE OF RIGHTEOUSNESS AND TRUTH

Themes: Righteousness; Truth

"Truth does not cease because people give up believing it." Nor does righteousness cease because people give up practicing it![66]

THREE KINDS OF TOLERANCE

Themes: Freedom; Neighbors

There are three kinds [of tolerance]:

1. *Legal* tolerance, which defends minority rights and protects people's freedom to 'profess, practise and propagate' religion. Christians should be in the forefront of those demanding this.

2. *Social* tolerance, which encourages mutual respect and good neighborliness. Christians should promote this too; it arises from recognizing every human being is a creature.

3. *Intellectual* tolerance, however, is to cultivate a mind so broad that there's no keeping anything in or out. This is not virtue; it's [a] vice of the feebleminded. It can degenerate into an unprincipled confusion of truth with error and goodness with evil.

WORDS HAVE THEIR OWN INTEGRITY

Themes: Power; Speech; Truth

Remember [Alice's] spirited exchange with Humpty Dumpty [in *Through the Looking Glass*]? "'When I use a word,' Humpty Dumpty said, in a rather scornful tone, 'it means just what I choose it to mean, neither more nor less.' 'The question is,' said Alice, 'whether you *can*

---

66. Edward R. Norman, *Christianity and the World Order* (OUP, 1979), 14.

make words mean different things.' 'The question is,' said Humpty Dumpty, 'which is to be master—that's all.' "

That is, Humpty Dumpty claimed the right to control words, to impose on them the meanings he wanted them to have. But words have their own integrity.

WAR

"ALL WILL BE OBLITERATED"

Themes: Peace; War

On August 27, 1979, Earl Mountbatten of Burma was killed by [an] IRA bomb. Three months previously (May 11, 1979) he gave a speech in Strasbourg, France about nuclear war. Today we have missiles, he said, "a thousand times as horrible" as [the] bomb which destroyed Hiroshima. "A new world war can hardly fail to involve the all-out use of nuclear weapons." So "in the event of a nuclear war there will be no chances, there will be no survivors—all will be obliterated." Therefore, "as a military man who has given half a century of active service, I say in all sincerity that the nuclear arms race has no military purpose. Wars cannot be fought with nuclear weapons. … There are powerful voices around the world who still give credence to the old Roman precept, 'if you desire peace, prepare for war.' This is absolute nuclear nonsense."[67]

---

67. Louis Mountbatten, speech in Strasbourg, May 11, 1979.

AUGUSTINE ON THE PRIORITY OF PEACE

Themes: Peace; War

Augustine denounced Rome's glorification of armed violence (*City of God* 3.14; 12.22). Though conceding that "just wars" were possible, one must "lament" their necessity, not "glorify" in them (ibid., 19.7). "War should be waged only as a necessity." The priority of peace was fundamental to him: "Peace is not sought in order to kindle war, but war is waged in order to obtain peace" (*Epistles* 189.2).

BOUTROS-GHALI'S CALL FOR A GLOBAL POLICE FORCE

Themes: Peace; War

In July 1992, when a UN force had just begun taking nonmilitary supplies into beleaguered Bosnia, an editorial appeared in the *New York Times*: "Wanted: Small, highly mobile army, able to respond overnight to civil disorder. ... Reply UN, NY."

It was an attempt to summarize Secretary General Boutros-Ghali's report to [the] Security Council. If the world is to have peace, he argued, it must have peace officers. He asked nation-members to make available one thousand troops each, ready on a day's notice for peacekeeping operations authorized by the Security Council. In summary, a global police force. It springs straight from [the] UN Charter, Article 43.[68]

---

68. *Guardian Weekly* (July 4, 1992).

CHURCH FATHERS ON NONVIOLENCE

Themes: Conflict; Peace; Persecution; Violence; War

- "We who formerly slew one another not only do not make war against our enemies but, for the sake of not telling lies or deceiving those who examine us, gladly die confessing Christ" (Justin Martyr, AD 120–202).

- "For we no longer take sword against a nation nor do we learn any more to make war, having become sons of peace for the sake of Jesus who is our leader" (Origen, AD 185–254).

- "Is it right to occupy oneself with the sword when the Lord proclaims that he who uses the sword shall perish by the sword? How shall Christians wage war, nay, how shall he even be a soldier in peace time, without the sword which the Lord has taken away?" (Tertullian, AD 160–230).

- "We who with our prayers fight the demons who bring about war are of greater assistance to the rulers than those who go into battle. We fight much better for the Emperor. We do not accompany him into battle, and we would not do so, even if he were to demand it; but we fight for him with our own army, with our prayers to God" (Origen, AD 185–254).

THE CLOSENESS OF WAR AND THE NEED FOR PEACE

Themes: Peace; Violence; War

- It has been said that "since 1945 American and other diplomats have met at least 6,000 times to discuss disarmament or arms control, but not a single warhead has been destroyed as a result of all these meetings."— Sidney Lear, *Progressive* (October 1977), p. 42.

- Several times accidental nuclear explosions have nearly happened. In 1961, a B-52 bomber carrying two 24-megaton bombs crashed near Goldston, North Carolina; and five of the six interlocking safety devices in one bomb were triggered.—Dale Aukerman, *Darkening Valley* (Seabury, 1981), p. 156.

- "Today the choice is no longer between violence and nonviolence. It is either nonviolence or non-existence."—Martin Luther King Jr., *Stride Toward Freedom: The Montgomery Story* (Harper, 1958), p. 224.

A CONFLICT-FILLED PEACE CONFERENCE

Themes: Conflict; Peace

The Ninth World Congress against [the] Atomic and Hydrogen Bomb was due to be held in Hiroshima on August 5, 1963. But it never really took place. Less than an hour before the opening ceremony was due to begin in the Hiroshima Peace Park, leaders of the Japanese Socialist Party and others decided to boycott it, leaving the communists in command of the field. The head of the Chinese delegation delivered a violent attack on the Test Ban Treaty, and the whole Russian delegation rose while he was still speaking and turned their backs on him, snubbing him publicly. Meanwhile there were outbursts of yelling, screaming, drum-beating, and fights in sections of [the] crowd until 1,500 riot police marched into the park to remove the offenders.

Thus did a peace conference held in a peace park break up in violent confusion and conflict.

THE INADEQUACY OF JUST WAR
THEORY FOR THE NUCLEAR AGE

Themes: War

The "just war theory" was gradually developed, beginning with
Augustine, and continuing through Aquinas, Vitoria, and Grotius. It
laid down a series of conditions:

- final resort

- legitimate authorization

- just cause

- right intention

- balance of foreseen consequences

- moderation of means

All [these are] intended to control and contain [the] destruction of
human lives. But nuclear warfare [is]:

- *Uncontainable,* being inherently indiscriminate in its
  effects and incapable of discriminating between com-
  batants and noncombatants (despite targets and control
  of fallout).

- *Uncontrollable:* once "the nuclear Rubicon is crossed,"
  escalation is inevitable.[69]

"THE LAMPS ARE GOING OUT"

Themes: Depression; War

Edward, Viscount Grey of Fallodon (1862–1933), as he stood at the
windows of his room at the Foreign Office, watching the lamplight-
ers turning off the lights in St. James's Park, on August 4, 1914, said:

---

69. John Mahoney, SJ, *The Times* (February 21, 1981).

"The lamps are going out all over Europe; we shall not see them lit again in our lifetime."

A MIDDLE GROUND BETWEEN NONVIOLENCE AND MUTUALLY ASSURED DESTRUCTION

Themes: Violence; War

Andrei Sakharov, who played a primary role in the development of the Soviet hydrogen bomb, and in 1975 was awarded the Nobel Peace Prize for his defense of human rights, reviewed Freeman Dyson's *Disturbing the Universe* (Harper & Row). Dyson is British, working in [the] US, and has contributed to quantum field theory, nuclear physics, rocket technology, and astrophysics. But this is a book of philosophical reflections regarding the ethics of weaponry and disarmament. He recalls his moral doubts when working for RAF Bomber Command. "Somewhere between the gospel of non-violence and the strategy of Mutual Assured Destruction there must be a middle ground on which reasonable people can stand, a ground which allows killing in self-defense but forbids the purposeless massacre of innocents" (in [the] chapter "The Ethics of Defense").

"With all my heart and soul I support this thesis," comments Sakharov, though adding that it's "an inadequate general principle for making decisions under the concrete, contradictory conditions of global confrontation and an inadequate personal position for real influence on world events." In [the] same chapter "Dyson supports George Kennan in his call for the rejection of the principle of 'first strike nuclear weapons' " as amoral.[70]

---

70. Andrei Sakharov, *Guardian Weekly* (October 14, 1979).

"WE CANNOT AFFORD WELFARE AND WARFARE"

Themes: Peace; War

At a special service at Westminster Abbey in June 1982, timed to coincide with the Second UN Special Session on Disarmament, Bishop George Appleton (formerly archbishop in Jerusalem) described what could be achieved if only 5 percent of the world's arms budget of £250,000 million were available for development: enormously reduced hunger and poverty, clean water for all, medical care, longer life, no more shanty towns, improved education, etc.

"We cannot afford welfare and warfare," he said.

WHY TRUMAN DECIDED TO DROP THE BOMB

Themes: Killing; War

Harry Truman had been president for only four months when he authorized the Hiroshima bomb. In his memoirs (1955) he wrote: "In all, it had been estimated that it would require until the late fall of 1946 to bring Japan to her knees," and "General Marshall told me that it might cost half a million American lives to force the enemy's surrender on his home grounds." He believed he'd end the war a year earlier and save many lives by the bomb. Secretary of War Henry Stimson wrote in his 1947 memoirs (in collaboration [with] McGeorge Bundy) that the invasion plans would involve military and naval forces "of the order of five million men" or more, and that the major fighting wouldn't end till [the] end [of] 1946. Stimson called [the] bomb "our least abhorrent choice." Another factor weighing with Truman was the murderous Okinawa Campaign (April 1–June 21), which cost 48,000 American casualties—and in which the Japanese used many "kamikaze," namely, suicide aircraft.[71]

---

71. Chalmers M. Roberts, *Guardian Weekly* (August 11, 1985).

WESTERN CULTURE

THE CHANGING YOUTH OF FRANCE

Themes: Family: Children

In 1968 it seemed like every young person in France was marching for revolution in the streets—a Marxist revolution that seemed to almost topple the government of Charles De Gaulle. Recently the French popular magazine *L'Express* revealed that today's 11.3 million French "young people" are pacifists, nature-lovers, hardworking, and independent. They want a warm family life, a safe job, and a life free of political restraint. They reject the nuclear age and military regimes, and they want to live close to nature.

In 1958 French young people wanted to build cathedrals. In 1968, they wanted to destroy them. Today [in 1979], they simply want to build a cottage with a forest at the bottom of the yard, the weekly said.

THE FOOLISHNESS OF IMPOSING
THE WEST ON THE EAST

Themes: Foolishness; Pride

Rudyard Kipling in a poem described a young Englishman who went to Asia with the arrogant determination to Westernize everything, especially (I think) in terms of Western business methods. But he failed and died in the attempt:

> The end of the fight is a tombstone white with the name of
> the late deceased,
> And the epitaph drear: "A Fool lies here who tried to hustle
> the East."[72]

---

72. Rudyard Kipling, *The Naulahka*.

THE FRUITS OF MORAL DISINTEGRATION

Themes: Health and Healing; Sexual Immorality

1. "Postpone operation until the moral disintegration of the enemy makes the delivery of the mortal blow both possible and easy" (Lenin).

2. Dr. Claude Scott Nicol, director of the venereal disease department of St. Thomas's and St. Bartholomew's hospitals, said on September 5, 1962 at [a] world forum on syphilis in Washington attended by representatives of forty nations that the "alarming increase in sexually transmitted diseases" was due to a breakdown of moral standards. [The] problem [is] not medical but moral. "It is the problem of a change in our moral values which has encouraged sexual promiscuity"—a trend begun early in [the] twentieth century when many turned from religious faith to Freud.

INSCRIPTION ON BROADCASTING HOUSE IN LONDON

Themes: Honesty and Dishonesty; Wisdom

Translated from the Latin: "The first directors dedicate to Almighty God this temple of the arts and muses; praying that good seed may bear a good harvest; that all monstrous things and things hostile to peace may be driven out; and that whatsoever things are honest and of good report, the people inclining their ear to these things may tread the way of righteousness and wisdom."[73]

---

73. Inscription in Broadcasting House, London; home of the BBC.

POLITICAL CORRECTNESS: PROS AND CONS

Themes: Government, Politics and National Identity; Philosophy

Origins: New England colleges regarding "things acceptable to people like us"—unprejudiced, enlightened, and socially sensitive.

Agenda: Political correctness (a) acknowledges unjust discrimination (race, gender, ethnicity, sexuality); (b) analyzes its roots and consequences; and (c) takes "political" action regarding employment, university admission, housing, sexual harassment, etc.

Consequences:

> *Negatives:* Compensating for inequalities by (a) new vocabulary (e.g., "African American"); (b) concerted reformist efforts; (c) forging new social consciousness.

> *Positives:* Celebrating diversity by (a) broadening curriculum (e.g., emphasis on 3/W); (b) recruiting minority faculty and students; (c) fostering tolerance.

Critics of political correctness accuse it of overcompensating in such [a] way as (a) to curb free discussion of issues; (b) to censor unpopular opinions ([a] new ethos of hypersensitivity inhibits people for fear of being labeled racist, sexist, etc.); (c) to create paranoia regarding sexual harassment policies; and (d) to fight for tolerance while being intolerant of alternative views and insensitive to those who hold them.

VIEWING HUMANITY IN THE ABSTRACT

Themes: Creativity; Neighbors; Philosophy

Christopher Booker's TV documentary *City of Towers* showed how the devastation of European/British cities in World War II made possible the fulfillment of the French architect Le Corbusier's dream of an ideal city, which became very attractive to town planners, especially the skyscraper housing blocks, "because human beings could be fitted into them like toys." But the euphoric development boom of the '60s and early '70s ended not only because the quadrupling of oil prices knocked the bottom out of the market, but because there was a growing public reaction in favor of preserving the small and the human environment.

Booker described the alliance of architects, developers, and town planners in the boom decade as "the greatest social disaster" since [the] War, because it referred to "humanity" in the abstract, and lost sight of "people."[74]

WHAT AMERICA STANDS FOR

Themes: Freedom; Government, Politics
and National Identity; Justice

In a BBC interview with Mr. Zbigniew Brzezinski, assistant to President Carter for national security affairs (printed in *The Listener*, June 14, 1979), answering a question "What does America stand for in the world?"—he replied that "most Americans do not share a common past" but rather "a common future which is derived from certain shared philosophical assumptions about the nature of man." He went on to speak of the idea of "self fulfillment, personal dignity, freedom, equality and justice." These give [the] US "a very special role to help translate that idea progressively and gradually into reality." For "the fundamental alternatives for the future of mankind … are either wide cooperation, pointing towards the beginnings of the emergence of something that might be called the genuine global community, or … destructive fragmentalism or chaos."[75]

---

74. Christopher Booker, *City of Towers* (1979).
75. Zbigniew Brzezinski, *The Listener* (June 14, 1979).

In a BBC interview with Mr. Zbigniew Brzezinski asst. to Pres. Carter for national Security affairs (printed in <u>The Listener</u> 14 June 79), answers a q. of 'what does America stand for in the world', — he replied that 'most Americans do not share a common past' but rather 'a common future which is derived from certain shared philosophical assumptions about the nature of man'. He went on to speak of the idea of 'selffulfilment, personal dignity, freedom, equality & justice'. These give u.s. 'a v. special role to help translate that idea progressively & gradually into reality'. For the fundamental

WOMEN AND MEN

GOD AS FEMALE

Themes: Women

Carter Heyward pleads in her *Touching Our Strength* that we replace Christ with Christa, who symbolizes "the erotic as power and the love of God as embodied by erotically powered women." This agenda found full expression in November 1993 in Minneapolis at an ecumenical conference on "Re-imagining God." "This second reformation," claimed Virginia Ramey Mollenkott, "is much more basic and important to the health of humankind" than the first in the sixteenth century. "Sophia" was adopted as their goddess.

A MAN'S GOD

Themes: Sex; Women

Eva Figes in *Patriarchal Attitudes* (Faber, 1970; Panther, 1972), her "case for women to revolt," has a chapter entitled "A Man's God." To her, the whole Judeo-Christian religion is "a religion created by men, for men" (p. 68). She refers to the Old Testament thus: "The male Jehovah is a stern Hebrew patriarch who leaves us in no doubt about the position of women" (p. 41).

But she relies too much on fanciful Jewish midrashes on [the] Old Testament and seems not to know of those passages where God likens [him]self to a mother (Isa 49:13; 66:15). She equally misinterprets [the] Apostle Paul. She writes of Christianity's "basic disapproval of sexuality" (has she ever read Song of Solomon?!) as having "diminished the standing" of women—"there is no hint of the sacred tasks of womanhood in the biting tones of St. Paul: 1 Corinthians 14:34, 35" (pp. 55, 56).

Earlier she writes: "The idea that a woman who does not find total fulfilment in submitting herself utterly to the will of a husband is somehow going against the natural order of things, is still with her" (p. 24).

WHY EVE WAS TAKEN FROM ADAM'S SIDE

Themes: Creation; Women

Commenting on Genesis 2:21, 22 with quaint profundity, Matthew Henry writes that she was "not made out of his head to top him, not out of his feet to be trampled upon by him, but out of his side to be equal with him, under his arm to be protected, and near his heart to be beloved."

Similarly Peter Lombard in [the] twelfth century: "Eve was not taken from the feet of Adam to be his slave, nor from his head to be his lord, but from his side to be his partner."[76]

WORK

WORK AS SERVICE

Themes: Service; Work

A senior official engaged in public-health work wrote to me October 14, 1959: "The work covers a rather comprehensive field of preventive medicine and environmental health control. Perhaps I have misused the word 'work,' because it is a continuous task that I have undertaken more as a service, as indeed it is—a human service. To me there is a tremendous gap between work as such and the spirit of service. To work for one's own ends, the pay packet, the 'perks,' security of

---

76. Peter Lombard, *Book of Sentences*, c. 1157/8 (just before he became bishop of Paris).

tenure and eventual pension is not enough for me. I like to think that I am responsible for a part of the greater human field pattern whereby we all subscribe of our best to the whole effort for human welfare according to our talents, obey the will of our wonderful Creator. With this trend of thought and outlook, I go into action each day happily."[77]

WORK A SOURCE OF DIGNITY

Themes: Image of God; Work

In January 1981 I was shown round Handicrafts Centre in Dacca, Bangladesh, operated by HEED [Health, Education, and Economic Development]. Here young people from refugee camps were being taught a skilled trade (carpet making, tapestry, weaving, straw art). I was tremendously impressed by the degree of their concentration on their work. They hardly noticed us, or looked up, as we walked by. They were absorbed in their craft. Their work had given them dignity, significance, a sense of self-worth.

WORLDVIEWS

THE CHANCE OF LIFE EVOLVING

Themes: Atheism; Creation

[The] *Daily Express* (August 14, 1981) had [the] headline: "Two sceptical scientists put their heads together and reach an amazing conclusion: THERE MUST BE A GOD."

The story was of Sir Fred Hoyle, antitheist mathematician and astronomer, and Chandra Wickramasinghe, professor of applied maths and astronomy, University of Wales, Cardiff—[a] Buddhist atheist. Both calculated independently, based on [the] known minimum

---

77. Letter to JRWS from S. L. Mackie, chief health inspector, Port of London.

requirements for a living cell, that [the] probability of life evolving on earth in 5 billion years was 1 out of 1,040,000, that is to say, zero.

Their second calculation concerned [the] probability of life evolving anywhere in [the] universe. Assuming it contains 100 billion galaxies, each of 100 billion stars, each having one planet and universe 20 billion years old, then [the] probability is nil.

Hoyle said the probability of an evolutionary origin of life equals [the] probability of [a] tornado sweeping through [a] junkyard and assembling [a] Boeing 747. They both now believe in supernatural creation.[78]

CHARACTERISTICS OF THE "NEW LEFT"

Themes: Philosophy

The "New Left" differs from the old orthodox communism in three major respects:

1. New Left follows Marx the sociologist and philosopher of alienation, rather than the later Marx, the economist, the author of *Das Kapital*. "Though Marx is discredited as an economist, the New Left gives him new life in the role of a philosopher" (p. 8).

2. New Left despises today's industrial workers as a new bourgeoisie, and sees the modern proletariat as peasants, the ghetto negroes, the colonial oppressed and the dropouts. (NB: [This is] a myth because Che, Castro, and Debray are middle class.)

3. New Left glorifies violence. To Marx it was inevitable but regrettable. To orthodox communists violence is used but veiled ("Communist theory proclaims minimal force," p. 9). But to Sartre, Fanon, etc., violence became itself "a changing force" (Fanon).[79]

---

78. Fred Hoyle and N. C. Wickramasinghe, *Evolution from Space* (Dent, 1981), 24, 94, 147.

79. Maurice Cranston, ed., *The New Left* (Bodley Head, 1970).

CLOSE ENCOUNTERS OF THE THIRD KIND

Themes: Idolatry; Revelation; Worship

Steven Spielberg's science fiction motion picture *Close Encounters of the Third Kind* seems to offer a secular alternative to an experience of God. A summary of its message:

1. "We are not alone" in the universe or condemned to "cosmic loneliness" (Russell). There are other and superior beings in space.

2. They are friendly. Awe-inspiring in their power, but friendly, even taking the initiative to make contact with us (= grace).

3. Bourgeois suburbanites are excluded from the Transcendent of their incredulity. They dismiss believers as mad.

4. And the establishment (symbolized by the army) not only disbelieve themselves, but do their best to stop other people believing.

5. But little children (like four-year-old Barry) respond to the call of the Transcendent with joy and eagerness and have no fear.

6. And simple believers like Roy Neary cannot be put off. He feels self "invited," even "compelled" toward the rendezvous, the mountain.

7. Scientists also discover truth by openminded investigation and fall to knees in wonder, almost in worship.

8. In the end, the close encounter with this Other Reality is overwhelming. It brings rapture, a kind of beatific vision on [the] last page. "Nearly walked forward … leading the way deep into the fiery heart of the mystery." Then down "the great phantom starship began to lift off through layer after layer of clouds. Until this great city in the sky became the brightest of the brightest stars." Jillian took [a] picture. Last words—"The Indisputable Proof."

FEAR OF DISCOMFORT

Themes: Comfort; Doubt; Fear; Pride

Stuart Manson FRCS wrote [to me on] May 18, 1955, re: Billy Graham Wembley Crusade: "I haven't been able to persuade the men concerned (doctors, etc.) to come. They fear the same as I did—false emotion, public display, and above all they fear, as I now know what is really the basic trouble, the possibility that they will be made desperately uncomfortable by the challenge at the end (which, thanks to the newspapers, everyone now knows about). But who am I to talk? Last year I wouldn't come with you to Harringay for the same reasons, and now I hope I would go anywhere at any time for Him."

H. L. MENCKEN ON THE CONSCIENCE

Themes: Atheism; Government, Politics and National Identity; Guilt

H. L. Mencken, "the sage of Baltimore," was a social commentator, literary critic, and lexicographer. To him both democracy and religion were absurdities—democracy because it was based on the fiction that "inferiority by some strange magic becomes a sort of superiority," and religion because it was not subject to empirical or rational analysis and hence "violated every intellectual decency." He wrote: "Conscience is a mother-in-law whose visit never ends."[80]

---

80. Charles A. Fecher, *Mencken: A Study of His Thought* (Knopf, 1978).

Stuart Mawson FRCS wrote 18 May 55 re. Billy Graham Wembley crusade:

"I haven't been able to persuade the men concerned (doctors etc.) to come. They fear the same as I did – false emotion, public display & above all they fear, as I now know what is really the basic trouble, the possibility that they will be made desperately uncomfortable by the challenge at the end (which thanks to the newspapers everyone now knows about). But who am I to talk? Last year I wouldn't come with you to Haringay for the same reasons, and now I hope I would go anywhere at any time for Him."

agnosticism

HOW WORLDVIEWS ARE ADOPTED

Themes: Philosophy; Truth

Dr. Michael Ramsden (director, Zacharias Trust) at Zurich in April 1998 summarized the ways in which a worldview comes to be adopted:

1. by knowing (epistemology) truths to be mastered
2. by feeling (existentialism) states to be experienced
3. by doing (pragmatism) actions to be followed
4. by being (ontology) new birth leading to new character

"I HAVE NO NEED OF THAT HYPOTHESIS"

Themes: Atheism; Creation

In 1799 Pierre-Simon, Marquis de Laplace, mathematician, presented Napoleon with a copy of his newly published *Celestial Mechanics*. After looking through it, Napoleon commented: "You have written this huge work on the heavens without once mentioning the Author of the universe?" Laplace replied: "Sir, I have no need of that hypothesis."

IMPOSSIBILITY OF AGNOSTICISM

Themes: Atheism; Doubt; Philosophy; Revelation

[Agnosticism is an] impossible, illogical position to hold.

Agnosticism = not atheism. [The term was] first used by Professor Huxley in [the] 1860s [as a way to speak of an] "unknown god." Atheism denies his existence; agnosticism rejects atheism and declares that he exists but cannot be known.

[Is] this position untenable? On the contrary, [the] assertion of agnosticism that [God] cannot be known is [a] most reasonable, logical, and indeed essential position to adopt. Failure to adopt it has occasioned many errors.

Man cannot know God by himself. Man's mind cannot unaided reach or fathom [the] mind of God. [The human] mind [is] finite; [there is a] great gulf [we] can't climb up into. [We are] capable of remarkable achievements, yet in religion ([which addresses the] infinite realm), [we are] out of [our] depth and element.

Man [is] obliged [to] remain agnostic. God [is] always [a] great unknown, unless he makes [the] first move.

LOGICAL POSITIVISM FAILS ITS OWN TESTS

Themes: Atheism; Philosophy; Truth

In *Taking Leave of God* (1980) Don Cupitt declared that God is not a reality, this idea having been demolished by both science and logical positivism. In its place he elaborated "Christian Buddhism."

"Cupittism is the end-point in the evolution of post-Protestant liberal theology" (Clifford Longley in *Times* Jan ?, 1983). The old orthodoxy he mocks as a religion of "walking corpses and empty tombs."

Then in 1982 Keith Ward published his riposte *Holding Fast to God*. He says he recognizes in Cupitt precisely the philosophical atheism he'd abandoned ten years previously! Of course the god of whom Cupitt takes leave and the God to whom Keith Ward holds fast are not precisely the same god, and Ward accuses Cupitt of a caricature. The fundamental difference between them is philosophical. Cupitt as a logical positivist argues there's no verifiable evidence for god. Ward replies that to limit truth to what can be verified experimentally or according to the mathematical laws of logic is to make a statement about the nature of truth which is itself neither demonstrable nor logical. Thus logical positivism fails to pass its own tests.[81]

---

81. Clifford Longley's summary.

MARXISM VS. CHRISTIANITY

Themes: Philosophy

Contrast Marxism and Christian views of:

1. History (inevitable progress or return of Christ)

2. Man (divine image and therefore of intrinsic worth; or animal and therefore pawn)

3. Sin (private ownership or meanness)

"MOST IGNORANCE IS INVINCIBLE IGNORANCE"

Themes: Atheism; Doubt; Foolishness; Revelation; Wisdom

Aldous Huxley, who used with great brilliance to advocate [the] view that life had no meaning, later revised his opinion: "Is the universe possessed of value and meaning? I took it for granted that there was no meaning. I had motives for not wanting the world to have meaning. Most ignorance is invincible ignorance—we don't know because we don't want to know. Those who detect no meaning in the universe generally do so because it suits their book that the world should be meaningless.

"The manifestly poisonous nature of the fruits forced me to reconsider the philosophical tree on which they are grown" (interview in 1941).[82]

SIGNS OF WESTERN MATERIALISM

Themes: Atheism; Creation; Philosophy

There can be no doubt that [the] contemporary Western world is extremely secular or materialistic. Already in [the] nineteenth century, when French astronomer Pierre-Simon Laplace presented his work to

---

82. A. G. Reekie, *How to Endure Illness* (J. Clarke, 1943), 92.

Napoleon and Napoleon asked, "Why [was] God never mentioned?" [Laplace responded,] "Sir, I had no need of that hypothesis."

Some years ago I knew a professor of biology in [the] University of London, Joseph Henry Woodger (b. 1894), [who was] so wise that friends called him "Socrates." His special interests were language or logic, despite his chair. He worked in Middlesex Hospital, where [he] found himself surrounded by materialists: "I work in an atmosphere so materialistic that [the] word 'spirit' is never mentioned, unless prefaced by [the] adjective 'methylated' "!

THE TENETS OF HUMANISM

Themes: Atheism; Philosophy

1. According to H. J. Blackham (director of the British Humanist Association) in *Humanism* (Penguin, 1968), the four basic tenets of humanism are:

   a. "man is on his own"

   b. "this life is all"

   c. "an assumption of responsibility for one's own life"

   d. "and for the life of mankind" (p. 13)

2. "Humanism is the human case and the human cause, an age-old conviction about the human case … which will induce men and women … to espouse the human cause with head and heart and with two hands" (p. 9). cf. BHA ad "Humanists put humanity first."

3. "The fundamental thing is respect for the human being in every person … this is the fundamental humanism: man as an end" (p. 16).

4. Dr. Harry Stopes-Roe, V/C of BHA in *CT* (August 12, 1977), defined humanism as "our aspiration to man's fulfilment (i.e., happiness) by human effort alone."

5. In a 1970 TV dialogue between Bishop Trevor Huddleston and Lord Ritchie Calder, the bishop after stating his personal belief in Christ asked Ritchie Calder to state his belief in humanism briefly. "I believe in me" was the reply.[83]

"THE TRUTH IS THAT THERE IS NO TRUTH"

Themes: Depression; Humility; Pride; Truth

Jean-François Lyotard's *La condition postmoderne* (1979)—best seen as [a] reaction against modernism, that is, [the] Enlightenment's "assertion of the omnicompetence of human reason" (p. 163), "objective science, universal morality and law, and autonomous art" (p. 165). However, [the] Enlightenment's "universals" turned out to be ethnocentric (p. 166), and now there's widespread disillusion with, and colleges of confidence in the Enlightenment project (p. 166).

Os Guinness: "Where modernization was a manifesto of human self-confidence is self-congratulation, postmodernism is a confession of modesty, if not despair. There is no truth; only truths. There is no grand reason; only reasons. ... There is no grand narrative of human progress; only countless stories of where people and their culture are now."

To sum up, "the truth is that there is no truth."[84]

---

83. H. J. Blackham, *Humanism* (Penguin, 1968).

84. Alister E. McGrath, *A Passion for Truth: Intellectual Coherence of Evangelicalism* (IVP, 1996).

4

PRAYERS

A BLESSING

Themes: Blessing

> *Go out into the world in peace.*
> Be of good courage;
> Hold fast to what is good;
> Never return evil for evil, but overcome evil with good.
> Strengthen the timid.
> Support the weak.
> Help the needy.
> Honor everybody.
> Love, serve, and witness to the Lord Jesus,
> rejoicing in the power of the Holy Spirit.
>
> And may the blessing of Almighty God,
>   Father, Son, and Holy Spirit,
> rest on you and remain with you forever.

COLLECT FOR WHITSUNDAY

Themes: Holy Spirit; Joy; Wisdom

Almighty God, you taught the hearts of your believing people by sending them the light of your Holy Spirit. Grant that through the same Spirit we may have a balanced judgment in all things and may always rejoice in the strength he gives us; through [the] merits of Jesus Christ our Savior, who lives and reigns with you, in [the] unity of [the] same Spirit, one God, [forever and ever. Amen.]

PRAYER TO BENEFIT FROM LUKE

Themes: Health and Healing; Scripture

Almighty God, you called Luke the physician, who is honored in Scripture, to be one of the Gospel writers and a physician of the soul. Grant that by the health-giving medicines of the doctrine he has passed on to us, all the diseases of the souls may be healed, through the merits of your Son Jesus Christ our Lord.

PRAYER FOR CHRISTIAN ASSURANCE
OF LIFE AFTER DEATH/FUNERAL

Themes: Assurance; Death and Dying

We worship you, Lord Jesus Christ,
because *by your death and resurrection* you have broken [the]
    power of death
and through *your gospel* have revealed life and immortality.

We pray that you will be our *life* in this world
and our *resurrection* in the world to come;
so that we may not fear death for ourselves or others
but rather rejoice in your great salvation;

For you are the Resurrection and the Life,
the First and the Last,
and are alive for evermore.

PRAYER FOR THE CHURCH AS THE TEMPLE OF THE SPIRIT

Themes: Church Fellowship and Unity;
Nature of the Church; Holy Spirit

Lord Jesus Christ, we thank you that you have given your Spirit to live in your people as his temple; receive our prayers for your worldwide church. May its study be diligent, its worship joyful, its fellowship loving, its behavior righteous, its service humble, and its witness continuous. Fill us all with the same Spirit today, that we may be clothed with power for our witness and ministry, and that your name (with Father and Holy Spirit) may be forever glorified.

PRAYER FOR THE CHURCH TO BE SALT AND LIGHT

Themes: Nature of the Church; Mission;
Reconciliation; Righteousness; Service

Lord Jesus, you have set your church in the world as *salt* to hinder its decay, and *light* to illumine its darkness. Forgive us for our failures to be the new society you intend, and renew us by your Holy Spirit. Grant that in a world of alienation your people may offer reconciliation; in a world of oppression, righteousness; and in a world of competition and greed—the freedom of unselfish service. Help us to bring friendship to the lonely, support to the weak, deliverance to the slaves of passion and fear; and to all those despised and rejected by men the steadfast love of God.

For then the people who walk in darkness will see a great light, even yourself, Lord Jesus, the light of this dark world, for your name's sake.

PRAYER FOR THE ECONOMIC NEEDS OF THE NATION

*Themes: Economics; Government, Politics
and National Identity; Justice*

Righteous Lord God, you love justice and hate oppression and self-ishness. You care for the needy and downtrodden and topple the power-hungry from their thrones.

Have mercy on our country in its present economic plight. Give to those who negotiate (for government, management, and labor) the wisdom of righteousness and peace, that they may restrain not inflation only but also human greed; and that they may secure for all a good job and a fair wage, and the relief of those in want, through Jesus Christ our Lord.

PRAYER FOR EVANGELISM: ONE

*Themes: Evangelism; Friendship; Humility; Birth
of Jesus; Jesus: Death; Love; Mission*

Lord Jesus Christ, in your great love for us in our alienation, you entered our world, assumed our nature, lived our life, bore our sins, and died our death. Now you send us into the same world in the same way that you were sent. Give us your mind of humility and your heart of love. Teach us truly to enter into other people's worlds in friendship, that we may serve them as you did and share with them your gospel, and enable us to do so with such gentleness and understanding that they recognize it for the good news it is, for your Name's sake.

PRAYER FOR EVANGELISM: TWO

Themes: Nature of the Church; Evangelism; Service

We worship you, Lord God, that you have exalted your son Jesus Christ above all other beings, that every knee shall bow to him and every tongue confess him Lord. We thank you that your church is the most international society on earth. Yet we confess to you with shame how small is your church in comparison with your world, and how introverted *we* your people often are. Turn your church inside out, we pray O Lord, that during the rest of this century we may together give ourselves to the service and the evangelization of the world.

Through Jesus Christ who gave himself as a ransom for all.

PRAYER FOR FREEDOM: ONE

Themes: Freedom; Responsibility; Thankfulness

Almighty God, we thank you for the liberties which this country enjoys, and for those who have worked and fought to secure them; for freedom from war and want; for freedom of thought, conscience, and speech; and for freedom of worship.

Give us grace to defend these liberties and to use them responsibly in your service, through Jesus Christ our Lord.

PRAYER FOR FREEDOM: TWO

Themes: Freedom; Poverty; Sickness

Our Holy Father, we commend to your mercy those for whom life does not spell liberty—

> prisoners of conscience;
> the hungry, the homeless and the handicapped;
> the sick in body or mind;
> the elderly who are confined to home or hospital;

those who are enslaved by their passions
and those who are addicted to drugs.

Grant that, whatever their outward circumstances,
they may find inward freedom,
through him who proclaimed release to captives,
even Jesus Christ our liberator.

PRAYER FOR FREEDOM FROM FEAR

Themes: Fear; Forgiveness; Freedom; Guilt

Lord Jesus Christ, you came to set at liberty those who are oppressed;
and *we* are oppressed by the tyranny of our guilt and of our fears.

Hear our cry. Forgive our sins. Deliver us from evil.

Teach us to find our freedom in your service, until at last we are
free from bondage to decay and enjoy the liberty of the glory of God's
children in heaven, for your name's sake.

PRAYER FOR A GENERAL/PRESIDENTIAL ELECTION

Themes: Government, Politics and National Identity

Almighty God, we commit to you the _____ election campaign.
Restrain the candidates and their aides from all falsehood. Enlighten
the minds of those who vote, that they may exercise their choice
responsibly in your sight; that the best possible administration may
be given to the country, which will promote unity and stability for the
nation, social justice for the people, liberty for the church, and wise
and generous service to the world, and glory to your name.

PRAYER FOR THE GIFTS OF THE SPIRIT

Themes: Church Fellowship and Unity; Holy Spirit: Gifts; Service

Heavenly Father, we thank you that as one human body is a single whole with many different organs, so too there are both unity and variety in Christ's Body, the church. We rejoice together in the rich diversity of your gifts. We also pray that we may neither be proud of our own gifts nor be jealous of the gifts of others, but may faithfully use the gifts you have given us in the service of others, for the good of your church, and for the glory of your Name, through Jesus Christ our Lord.

PRAYER FOR HOMES

Themes: Family; Family: Husbands; Family: Wives;
Family: Children; Family: Parents; Marriage

Our Heavenly Father, all human fatherhood is but a reflection of yours, and all our love is derived from your love. So bless every home of our parish and congregation. Grant that husbands may love and keep their wives, and wives may love and submit to their husbands; their children may love and obey their parents, and their parents may love and care for their children, not provoking them to anger, but bringing them up in the discipline and instruction of the Lord Jesus, for his Name's sake.

PRAYER FOR INDUSTRY

Themes: Justice; Peace; Work

O God, the King of righteousness, we pray that you lead us in ways of justice and peace. Inspire us to break down all tyranny and oppression; to gain for every man his due reward, and from every man his due service; that each may live for all, and all may care for each, in the name of Jesus Christ our Lord.[1]

PRAYER FOR LOVE AND MARRIAGE

Themes: Family; Family: Children; Family: Parents;
Love; Marriage; Sex; Sexual Immorality

Almighty God, you created man male and female; you have said that a man and a woman should leave their parents, cleave to one another and become one flesh; and you have taught us that what you joined together we are not to separate. Deliver our nation at this time from all corrupting influences. Let your judgment fall on those who degrade and exploit sex for their own profit. May marriage be held in honor among us all, and sex be acknowledged as a sacred trust from you. Grant to both young and old the grace of self-control. Beautify our homes with your presence, that husband and wife, parents and children, may love one another as you have loved us, through Jesus Christ our Lord.

PRAYER FOR MISSION

Themes: Discipleship; Evangelism; Mission

Risen Lord Christ, all authority is yours; you have commissioned your people to go into all the world to preach the gospel, make disciples, baptize them into the church, and teach them all your truth; and you have promised to be with them always wherever they go.

Give your blessing to those who are seeking to witness to you and help those who've heard and obeyed your call to go to another land for you. Help them to master its language, understand its culture, and serve its people with humility and love.

---

1. William Temple, slightly modernized.

Grant that throughout the whole world your gospel may spread, your church grow, and your name be honored and glorified, for your great and unique Name's sake.

PRAYER FOR NATIONAL UNITY (1974)

Themes: Conflict; Government, Politics and National Identity; Prejudice; Reconciliation

Almighty God, you are one Lord and you have made us one humanity. We worship you for your unity, and we thank you for ours. So look in pity on our present national disunity. Forgive the selfishness and prejudice which divide us from one another. Deliver us from suspicion and greed. Enable us to welcome our rich cultural diversity as a gift from you; to work for mutual understanding and respect and to secure equal opportunities for all.

We pray through him who came to reconcile us to you and to each other, Jesus Christ our Lord.

PRAYER FOR THE NEEDY

Themes: Grief; Poverty; Sickness

Lord Jesus, you demonstrated on earth your compassion for all human beings in need. Continue your gracious ministry toward them through us, today. Befriend the outcast, heal the sick, feed the hungry, comfort the sad, raise the fallen, and to humble penitent sinners speak your word of peace—that your kingdom may spread and your Name be honored and glorified.

PRAYER FOR PEACE

Themes: Conflict; Evil; Justice; Kingdom of God;
Peace; Reconciliation; Violence; War

Almighty God, you are the Lord of History and the Ruler of Nations, and you can turn even the anger of human beings into praise. Have mercy on our restless world, torn by hatred, fear and violence. Hold back the greed and cruelty of evil men. Have pity on the victims of oppression and terrorism. Increase in us the hatred of war and the love of peace, and deliver all people from racial and sectarian bitterness. Raise up peacemakers in every community with a sense of justice and the spirit of wisdom. Let your people throughout the world be free to serve you in quietness, to order their lives according to your will, until that day when kingdoms of this world will become your kingdom and [the] kingdom of your Christ.

PRAYER FOR PEACE (EARLY IN THE FALKLANDS WAR)

Themes: Peace; War

Almighty God, the only ruler of nations, we commit to you the grave situation in the South Atlantic. You have taught us in your Word and in your Son that you love justice and peace, and that the use of force is never better in your sight than a painful necessity.

Grant to the leaders of Britain and Argentina, of [the] United States and United Nations, wisdom and restraint; grant courage to those whose duty it is to go into action, and to their relatives at home; give special grace to [the] islanders and please grant a solution by negotiation rather than by an escalation of war, for the honor and glory of your Name, through Christ our Lord.

PRAYER FOR THE POOR (1980)

Themes: Giving; Mercy; Poverty

Lord Jesus, although you were rich, you voluntarily became poor for us. Kindle in us your own compassion for [the] poor and deprived peoples of the world. Give the rich nations of [the] North Atlantic the courage to implement the proposals of the Brandt Commission Report, to transfer resources for development and to grant more favorable trade terms. Give us as individuals the courage to develop a more simple lifestyle and to give more generously to world need. So grant that men, women, and children throughout the world who bear your image may be delivered from the burdens of illiteracy, hunger, poverty, and disease, and be free to live and die with dignity, for [the] glory of your Name.

PRAYER FOR THE POOR AND HOMELESS

Themes: Poverty; Service

> Lord Jesus, you left your heavenly home for us
> and were yourself homeless on earth
>> born in a stable
>> a refugee baby in Egypt
>> during your ministry [with] nowhere to lay your head
>> after death buried in a borrowed tomb.
>
> Have mercy
>> on millions of refugees throughout [the] world
>> on thousands of homeless people in our country.
>
> Move the government to make more adequate provision for
>> [the] homeless.
> Prosper the voluntary organizations like Shelter.
> Bless the work of ASLAN (All Souls Local Action Network)
>> and their ministry to [the] destitute.

And grant that
    in housing [the] homeless
    feeding the hungry
    clothing the naked
    caring for [the] uncared-for
We may find ourselves privileged to be ministering to you.

PRAYER FOR THE SICK: ONE

Themes: Death and Dying; Depression;
Health and Healing; Sickness

Lord Jesus Christ, in the days of your earthly ministry the sick were brought to you for healing. Hear us now as we bring to you in our prayers those suffering from any illness of mind or body, and those afflicted by pain, fear, bitterness, depression, incapacity, old age, or the approach of death. May the reality of your presence shine light into their darkness! And whether by restoration in this life or by resurrection in the next, make them perfectly whole, for the glory of your saving name.

PRAYER FOR THE SICK: TWO

Themes: Addiction; Mercy; Sex; Sexual Immorality; Sickness; Suffering

Lord Jesus, you never failed to show compassion toward those in any kind of need, especially [the] sick in mind or body. Teach us to care as you cared, and as you care still. We bring to you now (in [the] arms of our faith and love)

    those who suffer from any kind of sexual weakness or deviation,
    all those addicted to narcotics or pornography,
    the victims of sexual assault,
    the children of broken homes,
    and young people swept off [their] feet by [a] floodtide of
        permissiveness.

Have mercy on them, we pray, and give them comfort and strength according to their need. Bless FOL [Festival of Light], and especially its care committee, as it seeks to minister to them, and enable it to extend and deepen its care.

Show us what we can do to encourage the weak, deliver the captives, raise the fallen, and bind up the brokenhearted—for [the] glory of your Name.

PRAYER FOR SOCIAL JUSTICE

Themes: Conflict; Education; Health and
Healing; Justice; Sanctity of Life; Work

Righteous Lord God, you love justice and hate evil, and you care for the weak, vulnerable, needy, and the oppressed. Bless our country and its leaders with the wisdom of righteousness and peace. May they secure the right of protection for the unborn, equality of educational opportunities for the young, work for the unemployed, health care for the sick, and food for the hungry. Help management and labor to cooperate for the common good, giving honest work and receiving a fair wage. Deliver our land from all tribal, social, and religious strife, and make our national life more pleasing in your holy sight, through Jesus Christ our Lord.

A Prayer for Social Justice.

Righteous LG., you love justice and hate evil and you care for the weak, vulnerable, /needy & the oppressed.

Bless our country & its leaders with the wisdom of righteousness and peace. May they secure the right of protection for the unborn, equality of educational opport^y for the young, work for the unemployed, health-care for the sick, & food for the hungry. Help management & labour to ~~work~~ ~~together~~ cooperate for the common good, giving honest work & receiving a fair wage. Deliver our land from all tribal, social and religious strife, & make our national life more pleasing in your holy sight, thr' Js. our L.

Country!

PRAYER FOR THE SUFFERING

Themes: Death and Dying; Depression;
Disability; Poverty; Sickness; Suffering

Lord Jesus, your compassion was always aroused by the sight of human suffering. So we bring to you the suffering world today—

> The sick in mind and body
> The bereaved and the dying
> The victims of war and violence, tornado and cyclone
> The casualties of economic recession
> The poor, hungry, and neglected
> Those who struggle with handicaps (blind, deaf, crippled, dumb)
> People imprisoned and tortured for their convictions
> Those in the deep darkness of depression or despair
>
> Let your light shine into their darkness,
> Raise up good Samaritans to come to [their] aid,
> Reveal yourself to them that they may put their trust in you.
> And then give them confidence that,
> As you entered your glory through suffering,
> So their sufferings will be eclipsed by the glory which is one day to be revealed.

PRAYER FOR THOSE WHO DOUBT

Themes: Doubt; Evangelism; Laziness and Apathy; Mission

Lord Jesus Christ, we thank you for your sympathetic understanding toward those who have doubts and difficulties. We pray for them today.

Stir into serious concern those who are paralyzed by apathy. Shine into the minds of those who doubt your truth and love. Arrest those who are determined to live their own life in [their] own way, and break into their self-centeredness with your liberating power. Give to all of us the courage to lay aside our pride, prejudice, and fear, and to seek you with our whole heart.

Then Lord Jesus, we humbly pray, fulfill your promises that "he who seeks finds," and that "to him who knocks the door will be opened."

PRAYER FOR UNITY

Themes: Church Fellowship and Unity; Courage; Love; Wisdom

May God give us:

> the *discernment* to distinguish between essentials and nonessentials;
> the *courage* to hold fast to essentials;
> the *generosity of spirit* to give everyone liberty in nonessentials;
> the *love* for all human beings (whatever their beliefs)
>> which is patient and kind,
>> which neither envies nor boasts,
>> which is neither rude nor proud,
>> which rejoices in the truth,
>> which never fails.

PRAYER FOR A WEDDING

Themes: Marriage

Almighty God, look mercifully on _____ and _____ in the new life which they have begun together. Unite them evermore in your love. Keep them faithful to their promises. Strengthen them with every good gift. And let your peace be always with them, through Jesus Christ ...

PRAYER FOR WORK: ONE

Themes: Church Fellowship and Unity; Worship; Work

It's such a pleasure, Heavenly Father, on this your day to enjoy the opportunities you have given us to worship you, to listen to your Word, and to have fellowship with each other.

But tomorrow morning we'll be back at our job—for many of us among people who neither know nor honor you.

Give us grace to be the same people at work on weekdays as we are at worship on Sundays.

Help us to remember your presence, to be:

> Conscientious in the tasks entrusted to us
> Honest in our use of time/money, and
> Unselfish in our service of others—

That we may witness to your Son Jesus Christ

> Not merely by the words we speak
> But by [the] quality of our life and love.

May our light (which is Christ's light) so shine before others that [they might give him the glory].

PRAYER FOR WORK: TWO

Themes: Creation; Image of God; Service; Work

Almighty God, we worship you that you are yourself a worker, creating the world in six stages and resting on [the] seventh, and that you have made us in your image that we may be workers too; we commit to you our week for work. Enable us to use our gifts in the service of others. Deliver us from laziness, boredom, and dishonesty. Have mercy also on the unemployed, and help us to build a society in which no one is redundant. Grant that whatever we do, we may do it heartily, not primarily for any earthly employer or supervisor, but for Jesus Christ our Lord.

Amen.

PRAYER FOR THE WORLD

Themes: Justice; Kingdom of God; Love; Peace

Our Heavenly Father, we look out from the comfort, warmth, and security of this building to the world of tragedy and pain. We remember before you the victims of famine and flood, and of man's inhumanity to man. We cry to you to restrain human passions, to establish peace in place of violence, justice in place of oppression, and love in place of greed; and to make your people throughout the world a much more powerful influence for good, until that great day when Christ returns in glory, and the kingdoms of the world become your kingdom, and you reign in perfect justice and peace, as King of kings and Lord of lords, forever.

Amen.

TRINITARIAN MORNING PRAYER

Themes: Discipleship; God's Mercy; Presence of God; Trinity; Holy Spirit: Fruit

Good morning, Heavenly Father,
  good morning, Lord Jesus,
  good morning, Holy Spirit.

Heavenly Father, I worship you as the creator and sustainer of the universe.
  Lord Jesus, I worship you, Savior and Lord of the world.
  Holy Spirit, I worship you, sanctifier of the people of God.
  Glory to the Father, and to the Son, and to the Holy Spirit.

Heavenly Father, I pray that I may live this day in your presence and please you more and more.
  Lord Jesus, I pray that this day I may take up my cross and follow you.
  Holy Spirit, I pray that this day you will fill me with yourself and cause your fruit to ripen in my life: love, joy, peace,

patience, kindness, goodness, faithfulness, gentleness, and self-control.

Holy, blessed, and glorious Trinity, three persons in one God, have mercy upon me.

Amen.

SUBJECT INDEX

NAME INDEX

SCRIPTURE INDEX

Old Testament

New Testament